MARC REKLAU

The Change Your Habits, Change Your Life Series

Change Your Habits, Change Your Life Box Set 1

MARC REKLAU

www.goodhabitsacademy.com

Good Habits Box-Set Copyright © 2018 by Marc Reklau

All rights reserved.

Without limiting the rights under copyright reserved above no part of this book may be reproduced in any form or by any electronic or mechanical means including information storage and retrieval systems, without permission in writing from the author. The only exception is by a reviewer, who may quote short excerpts in a review.

Disclaimer

This book is designed to provide information and motivation to our readers. It is sold with the understanding that the publisher is not engaged to render any type of psychological, legal, or any other kind of professional advice. The instructions and advice in this book are not intended as a substitute for counseling. The content of each chapter is the sole expression and opinion of its author. No warranties or guarantees are expressed or implied by the author's and publisher's choice to include any of the content in this volume. Neither the publisher nor the individual author shall be liable for any physical, psychological, emotional, financial, or commercial damages, including, but not limited to, special, incidental, consequential or other damages. Our views and rights are the same:

You must test everything for yourself according to your own situation talents and aspirations

You are responsible for your own decisions, choices, actions, and results.

Marc Reklau

Visit my website at www.marcreklau.com

Your free gift

As a way of saying thank you for your purchase I want to gift you these free coaching worksheets that are exclusive to my readers, subscribers and coaching clients.

These worksheets include the exact life-changing exercises that transformed my life and took me
from jobless to International Bestselling author.

Get your free coaching worksheets here

Welcome to the Good Habits Box Set

Little did I know five years ago when I started changing a couple of small habits, that my whole life would change so amazingly. Then again that's exactly how change happens: doing small things differently every day can lead to enormous changes over time. As they say: "First we make our habits, then our habits makes us."

When I was preparing the file for this book bundle I read through a lot of the chapters and I had to admit to myself that there's really nothing new in my books. I didn't reveal any huge new secrets. Everything has been written before. You might know most of the things we will be talking about in these books because many of them are even common sense. But then again common sense is known to be the least common of all senses and the problem is that the huge majority of people never applies the things they know or read.

These habits work you find in this box set work - I'm living proof of that fact - but only a small percentage of people actually do them.

So my goal in writing this books was to take make the information you dear reader as simple and easily digestible as I can and lead you as quickly as possible to the life-changing exercises at the end of each chapter and get you to do them, because doing them over a period of time *will* change your life.

You don't even have to do all the habits in the books. If you take some of the habits I'm going to show you and put them in to practice every day for the next 4 to 6 weeks your life will never be the same! (says the guy who went from Jobless to International Bestselling author with more than 200,000 readers thanks to these exact habits)

These exercises work but you have to work, too. Remember: It's what you do <u>every day</u> that will change your life - not what you do every now and then.

This Box set includes three books including my international #1 Bestseller 30 DAYS:

30 Days - Change your habits, change your life
The book contains the best strategies to help you to create the life you want. The book is based on science, neuroscience, positive psychology, and real-life examples, and contains the best exercises to quickly create momentum towards a happier, healthier, and wealthier life. Thirty days can really make a difference if you do things consistently and develop new habits!
More than 180,000 combined sales and downloads since March 2015, translated in to 10+ languages including German, Russian, Japanese, Korean, Chinese and many others

The Productivity Revolution
The Productivity Revolution shows the best strategies to double productivity. You'll learn how to dramatically increase your productivity, how to gain an extra hour a day to do the things you love, and how to finally stop feeling overworked and overwhelmed.

Destination Happiness
Destination Happiness shows you **scientifically proven exercises and habits** that help you to achieve a successful, meaningful and happy life. Happiness and Optimism can be learned and science can now prove it as a fact that happiness leads to success in every field of your life. Find out how huge the impact of happiness and optimism is at your job as well as in your life and don't be fooled by the simplicity of some of the exercises.

So let's dive right in and have some fun!

30 DAYS

CHANGE YOUR HABITS
CHANGE YOUR LIFE

A couple of simple steps every day to
create the life you want

MARC REKLAU

"The beginning is the most important part of the work."

Plato

CONTENTS

Introduction……………………………………...…….……13
1 REWRITE YOUR STORY………………...…..………..17
2 SELF-DISCIPLINE AND COMMITMENT…………..……19
3 TAKE FULL RESPONSIBILITY OF YOUR LIFE!………..21
4 CHOICES AND DECISIONS……………………...………25
5 CHOOSE YOUR THOUGHTS………………...……..…..27
6 WHAT DO YOU BELIEVE?……………………………..29
7 THE IMPORTANCE OF YOUR ATTITUDE …..…….…33
8 PERSPECTIVE IS EVERYTHING………………...………35
9 HAVE PATIENCE AND NEVER GIVE UP! …..…….…37
10 LEARN THE "EDISON MENTALITY" ……….....………39
11 GET COMFORTABLE WITH CHANGE AND CHAOS!..42
12 FOCUS ON WHAT YOU WANT…………………………43
13 WATCH YOUR WORDS……………………………..…44
14 NEW HABITS, NEW LIFE!………………………………47
15 KNOW YOURSELF…………………………...…..…..…49
16 KNOW YOUR TOP 4 VALUES…………………………..53
17 KNOW YOUR STRENGTHS……………………………..55
18 HONOR YOUR PAST ACHIEVEMENTS………………..57
19 WRITE DOWN YOUR GOALS AND ACHIEVE THEM..59
20 NEXT!………………………………………………………62
21 AVOID ENERGY ROBBERS……………………………..64
22 MANAGE YOUR TIME…………………………………..65
23 START TO GET ORGANIZED! …………………………69
24 SAY "NO" TO THEM AND "YES" TO YOURSELF…….71
25 GET UP EARLY! SLEEP LESS…………………………..73
26 AVOID THE MASS MEDIA………………………………75
27 DO YOU "HAVE TO" OR DO YOU "CHOOSE TO"…..77
28 FACE YOUR FEARS!………………………………………79
29 ELIMINATE EVERYTHING THAT ANNOYS YOU…….81
30 CLEAN OUT YOUR CUPBOARD……………………….83
31 UNCLUTTERING AND TOLERATIONS………………..84
32 THE MOST IMPORTANT HOUR………………………..85
33 FIND YOUR PURPOSE AND DO WHAT YOU LOVE. ..87
34 TAKE A WALK EVERY DAY……………………………89
35 WHAT ARE YOUR STANDARDS?………………………91
36 ADAPT AN ATTITUDE OF GRATITUDE!……………..93
37 THE MAGIC OF VISUALIZATION……………………94

38 WHAT IF?...97
39 LET GO OFF THE PAST..99
40 CELEBRATE YOUR WINS..................................100
41 BE HAPPY NOW!..101
42 MULTITASKING IS A LIE!..................................103
43 SIMPLIFY YOUR LIFE..105
44 SMILE MORE!...107
45 START POWER NAPPING..................................109
46 READ HALF AN HOUR EVERY DAY....................110
47 START SAVING...111
48 FORGIVE EVERYBODY......................................113
49 ARRIVE 10 MINUTES EARLY..............................115
50 SPEAK LESS, LISTEN MORE!.............................116
51 BE THE CHANGE YOU WANT TO SEE................117
52 STOP TRYING AND START DOING.....................119
53 THE POWER OF AFFIRMATIONS........................121
54 WRITE IT DOWN 25 TIMES A DAY......................123
55 STOP MAKING EXCUSES...................................124
56 KEEP EXPECTATIONS LOW AND THEN SHINE...125
57 DESIGN YOUR IDEAL DAY..................................126
58 ACCEPT YOUR EMOTIONS................................127
59 DO IT NOW!..129
60 FAKE IT TILL YOU MAKE IT...............................131
61 CHANGE YOUR POSTURE.................................133
62 ASK FOR WHAT YOU REALLY WANT..................135
63 LISTEN TO YOUR INNER VOICE........................137
64 WRITE INTO YOUR JOURNAL............................139
65 STOP WHINING!...141
66 BECOME A RECEIVER.......................................143
67 STOP SPENDING TIME WITH THE WRONG PEOPLE
....145
68 LIVE YOUR OWN LIFE....................................... 147
69 WHO IS NUMBER ONE?....................................149
70 YOUR BEST INVESTMENT................................151
71 STOP BEING SO HARD ON YOURSELF.............153
72 BE YOUR AUTHENTIC SELF..............................155
73 PAMPER YOURSELF...157
74 TREAT YOUR BODY LIKE THE TEMPLE IT IS.........158
75 EXERCISE AT LEAST 3 TIME A WEEK................159
76 TAKE ACTION. MAKE THINGS HAPPEN!...........161
77 ENJOY MORE..163

78 STOP JUDGING…………………………………..…..…..164
79 A RANDOM ACT OF KINDNESS EVERY DAY………165
80 SOLVE YOUR PROBLEMS, ALL OF THEM……….…166
81 THE POWER OF MEDITATION………………………167
82 LISTEN TO GREAT MUSIC – DAILY!…………………169
83 NO WORRIES……………………………………..……171
84 USE YOUR TRAVEL TIME WISELY………………..…173
85 SPEND MORE TIME WITH YOUR FAMILY…………..174
86 DON'T BE A SLAVE OF YOUR PHONE………………175
87 HOW TO DEAL WITH PROBLEMS……………………176
88 TAKE TIME OFF……………………………..……..…177
89 HAVE A HIGHLIGHT EVERY DAY..………..…..……179
90 STEP OUT OF YOUR "COMFORT ZONE"…..……….181
91 WHAT PRICE ARE YOU PAYING……………….……..183
92 THINGS ARE ONLY TEMPORARY……..…..……..…185
93 GET A COACH!.…………………………………….…187
94 LIVE YOUR LIFE FULLY. DO IT NOW!………..………189

The Productivity Revolution…………………………….…..191

Destination Happiness…………………………………….…..301

ACKNOWLEDGMENTS

Thanks to my father (R.I.P.), who in his very own way helped me become the person I am today. My mother Heidi for handing me the book that changed my life about 25 years ago, teaching me values and letting me go without any emotional blackmailing when I had to follow my heart for the first time and every time thereafter. My granny - for being one of my best buddies and providing retreat when I needed it. My cousin Alexander Reklau, who - when we were 16 years old - spoke very wise words which became part of my life story and probably saved me: "My father did with his life what he wanted; I will do with my life what I want!" I picked these words up two years later after burying my father and decided to live by them ever since.

My friends Pol and Inma for letting me stay at their house on the beautiful Island of Ibiza. A wonderful place to get the creative juices flowing. My editor Gisela who helped me fine-tune the book. My friend and mentor Stefan Ludwig, who provided me with his advice for over ten years now. My friend Claudio – always there. Sabrina Kraus, Mari Arveheim, and Marc Serrano Ossul for their feedback during the writing process. My own coach Josep Anguera, who with his skills helped me to get unstuck after 5 years of stagnation. Talane Miedaner, whose book "Coach yourself to success" was my first contact with coaching and applying some of the tips she suggested changed my life dramatically.

Thank you to all of my clients for trusting me, letting me be a part of your enormous growth, and allowing me the opportunity to grow with you all.

Last but not least, thanks to everybody I met along the way. You were either a friend or a teacher, or both!

INTRODUCTION

"If you think you can you're right, if you think you can't you're right"
Henry Ford

Look around you. What do you see? Look at your surroundings, the atmosphere, and the people around you. Think of your current life conditions: work, health, friends, people surrounding you. What do they look like? Are you happy with what you see? Now look inside of you. How do you feel RIGHT NOW in this moment? Are you satisfied with your life? Are you longing for more? Do you believe that you can be happy and successful? What is missing from your life that you need to call your life happy and/or successful? Why do some people seem to have everything and other people nothing? Most people have no idea how they get what they get. Some of us just blame it on fate and chance. I'm sorry that I have to be the one to tell you: "Sorry friend! You have created the life you have! Everything that happens to you is created by YOU - either consciously by design or unconsciously by default; it's not a result of fate or circumstances.

I decided to write this book because I'm seeing so many people that are dreaming of improving their life, being happier, becoming wealthier yet according to them, the only way that could happen would be due to some kind of miracle: winning the lottery, marrying rich, or some other stroke of luck. They are looking for outside influences to happen by chance and change everything. They think life happens to them. Most of them have no idea that they can be in total control of their life each and every moment and every day of their lives. So they continue daydreaming, doing those things that they've always done, and waiting for some miraculous outcome. Sometimes they actually don't even know what they want! The following is a conversation I actually had:

Q:"What would you do if you had enough time and money?"
A:"Man! That would be great! I would be happy!"
Q:"And what would 'being happy' look like to you?"

A:"I would do everything I want to do!"
Q:"And what is 'everything you want to do'?"
A:"Oh! Now you got me. I don't even know!"

The true tragedy is that if they would only stop for one moment, ask themselves what **they really want in life**, write down their goals and start working towards them, they could actually make those miracles happen. I see it day in and day out with my coaching clients: people that come to me because they want to change something in their lives, and instead of sitting around and waiting and dreaming of a better life, they actually take matters in their own hands and start taking action! And the results are fabulous!

Remember: You are leading the life that you have chosen! How? This is because we create our life every moment through our thoughts, beliefs, and expectations and our mind is so powerful that it will give us what we ask for. The good thing is that you can train your mind to give you only the things you want, and not the things that you don't want! And it gets even better: you can learn how to deal with things that you can't control in a more efficient and less painful manner.

I've been studying the principles of success and how to achieve happiness for nearly 25 years now. What I always subconsciously knew became a structured method using the tools and exercises of coaching. More than ever, I'm convinced that success can be planned and created. For the skeptics who think that all this is metaphysical nonsense, just look at the enormous progress science has made and how it can now prove many things which only 25 years ago could
only be believed without being proven.

The most important message in this little book is: **Your happiness depends of YOU, and nobody else!** In this book, I want to introduce you to some proven tips, tricks and exercises that can improve your life beyond your imagination **if you practice them constantly and persistently**. More good news: You don't need to win the lottery to be happy! You can start by doing little things in your life differently in a constant and consistent manner, and over time results will show. This is how my coaching clients achieve incredible results: creating new habits and working towards their goals consistently, and doing things that bring them closer to their goals every single day. It is possible! You can do it! You deserve it!

Simply reading the book won't help you a lot, though. You have to take ACTION! That's the most important part – (and it is also the part that I struggled with the most for many, many years). **You have to start doing and practicing the exercises and introducing new habits into your life.**

If you are very curious - read the whole book once with a pen or pencil and a notebook in hand to make notes if you like. Then read the book a second time – this is when the rubber meets the road – and now start doing some of the exercises and introducing new habits into your life. If you do the exercises in this book regularly and consistently, your life will change for the better! Experts in the field of success teachings, coaching and Neuro-linguistic Programming agree that it takes 21 to 30 days to implement a new habit. 30 days that can make a difference in your life. 30 days of working consistently on yourself and your habits can turn it all around – or at least put you in a better position. At least try it out! Stay with some of the exercises for at least 30 days. Do the ones that come easy to you. If it doesn't work out for you, write me an email with your complaint to marc@marcreklau.com.

I have also provided a couple of WORK SHEETS on www.marcreklau.com
Download them and **HAVE FUN!**

1
REWRITE YOUR STORY

"Change the way you look at things and the things you look at change"
Wayne W. Dyer

The first time I came in contact with this idea was nearly 25 years ago while reading Jane Robert's book "Seth speaks". Seth says you are the writer, director and main actor of your story. So if you don't like how the story is playing out…change it! At that time I thought it's kind of a comforting idea, gave it a try, and have lived by it ever since - in good times and bad times. It doesn't matter what happened in your past. Your future is a clean sheet! You can reinvent yourself! Every day brings with it the opportunity to start a new life! You get to choose your identity at each and every moment! So who are you going to be? It's up to you to decide who you are going to be from this day on. What are you going to do?

If you DO some of the things suggested in this book, create new habits, and do just some of the many exercises that you will find here, things will start to shift. It's not going to be easy and you will need discipline, patience, and persistence. But the results will come.

In 2008, when FC Barcelona's coach Josep "Pep" Guardiola took charge of the team that was in a desolate state, he told the 73000 people in attendance in the stadium and the millions of viewers on Catalonian television, in his inauguration speech: "We can't promise you titles, what we can promise you is effort and that we will persist, persist, persist until the end. Fasten your seatbelts - we are going to have fun". This speech started the most successful period in the 115 years history of the club and few people think it can ever be repeated. The team went on to win 3 national championships, 2 national cups, 3 Spanish Supercups, 2 European Supercups, 2 Champions Leagues, and 2 World Club Championships in their 4 years of domination of World football.

If you don't follow soccer: This is like a mediocre NFL team winning 4 Superbowls in a row.

They rewrote their story.

Now it's your turn. Make some effort and persist, persist, persist! Don't give up! Fasten your seatbelts and have some fun!

2
SELF-DISCIPLINE AND COMMITMENT

"It was character that got us out of bed, commitment that moved us into action and discipline that enabled us to follow through."
Zig Ziglar

"If you cannot do great things, do small things in a great way."
Napoleon Hill

This is one of the first chapters, because it will be the foundation of your future success! Your way to success and happiness is deeply connected to your willpower and commitment. These character traits will decide whether you do what you said you would do and go through with it. These will keep you going towards your goals even when everything seems to go against you. Self-discipline is doing the things you need to do, even if you are not in the mood for it. If you train to be self-disciplined and have the will to succeed, you can do great things in your life. But even if you don't have the slightest bit of self-discipline within you right now - don't worry. You can start training your self-discipline and willpower from this moment on! Self-discipline is like a muscle. The more you train it, the better you get. If your self-discipline is weak right now, start training it by setting yourself small, reachable goals.

Write down the success you have and keep in mind that you don't have limits - only the ones you set for yourself. Visualize the benefits you will have at the end of the road: For example if you want to go running at 6 a.m. in the morning and you just don't seem to make it out of bed - imagine how good you will feel when you are at the fitness level that you want to be at and how great you will look. Then jump out of bed, put on your running clothes, and go! Remember: This book will only work if you have the will and the discipline to make it work!

What is your word worth? Take your commitments seriously! Because not keeping your commitments has a terrible consequence: you lose energy, you lose clarity, you get confused along the way to your goals, and even worse you lose self-confidence, and your self-esteem takes a hit! To avoid this, you have to become aware of what is really important to you and act in line with your values.

A commitment is a choice! Only make commitments that you really want. That can mean fewer commitments and more "NOs". If you commit - keep your commitment whatever it takes. Give them the importance and value that they deserve and be aware of the consequences of not keeping them.

Time to take action! Ask yourself the following questions:

In what areas are you lacking self-discipline at the moment? Be completely honest.

What benefits will you obtain if you had more self-discipline?

What will be your first step towards reaching your goal?

Write down your plan of action in small steps. Give yourself deadlines.

How will you know you've reached your goal of having more self-
discipline in _____?

3
TAKE FULL RESPONSIBILITY FOR YOUR LIFE!

"Peak performance begins with your taking complete responsibility for your life and everything that happens to you."

Brian Tracy

"Most people do not really want freedom, because freedom involves responsibility, and most people are frightened of responsibility."

Sigmund Freud

There is only one person that's responsible for your life and that is YOU! Not your boss, not your spouse, not your parents, not your friends, not your clients, not the economy, not the weather. YOU! The day we stop blaming others for everything that happens in our life, everything changes! Taking responsibility for your life is taking charge of your life and becoming the protagonist of it. Instead of being a victim of circumstances, you obtain the power to create your own circumstances or at least the power to decide how you are going to act in the face of circumstances that life presents to you. It doesn't matter what happens to you in your life; it matters what attitude you adopt. And the attitude you adopt is your choice!

If you blame your life situation on others, what has to happen to make your life better? All of the others have to change! And that my friend I tell you, is not going to happen. If you are the protagonist, YOU have the power to change the things that you don't like in your life! You are in control of your thoughts, actions, and feelings. You are in control of your words, the series you watch on TV, and the people you spend your time with. If you don't like your results, change your input - your thoughts, emotions, and expectations. Stop reacting to others and start responding. Reaction is automatic. Responding is consciously choosing your response.

"You take your life in your own hands, and what happens? A terrible thing: no one to blame" - Erica Jong

	Reactive Responsibility (Victim)	Proactive Responsibility (Protagonist)
Internal and external dialogue	I depend on external factors. I can't change anything. Life happens to me.	I initiate change. Life happens, but I choose my behavior
Focus	Outside of me. Focuses on excuses (Crisis, age, "it's not a good time")	Inside of me. Options and power of choice. Success only depends on me. (e.g. change jobs)
Problems	Focusing on problems. Everybody else is wrong. I'm right. Searching for causes.	Focusing on solutions. I act where I have control and accept where I don't have control
Luck vs. Influence	Life is not fair. You can't influence it. It's just a matter of luck.	Luck doesn't exist. Focus on opportunities, create them if necessary. It depends on the work you put into it.

The victim says: Every bad thing in my life is others' fault, but if you are not part of the problem, then you also can't be a part of the solution or - in other words - if the problem is caused by the outside, the solution is also on the outside. If you're coming in late to work because of "traffic", what has to happen so that you can get to work on time? Traffic has to disappear magically! Because as long as there is traffic - you will always be late. Or you can act like a protagonist and leave home on time. Then it depends on you.

So once again: even if you don't have control over the stimuli that environment sends you continuously, you have the liberty do choose your behavior in facing the situation.

The person with a "victim mentality" only reacts, is always innocent, and constantly blames others for his or her life situation, while using the past as justification and putting their hopes on a future which will miraculously bring solutions to problems or a change in others who are causing the troubles.

The protagonist knows that he or she is responsible, chooses adequate behavior and holds himself accountable. He uses the past as a valuable experience from which to learn, lives in the present where he sees constant opportunities for change, and decides and goes after his future goals. The most important question is: "Who will you choose to be – by your actions – when life presents you with these circumstances?"

Gandhi said it very nicely: "They can't take away our self-respect if we don't give it to them."

Ask yourself the following questions:

- Who are you blaming for your life situation right now? (Your partner? Your boss? Your parents? Your friends?)
- What would happen if you stopped blaming the others for what happens to you in your life?
- What would happen if you would stop being a victim of the circumstances?
- Is it comfortable for you being the victim?
- What benefits does it have for you to be a victim?
- What would happen if you stopped suffering in your life and took the decision to change it?
- What would you change?
- Where could you start?
- How would you start?

Action Step:
Write down five things that you can do in the coming week to start changing the course and start taking charge of your life.

4
CHOICES AND DECISIONS

"Once you make a decision, the universe conspires to make it happen."
Ralph Waldo Emerson

Maybe you have heard that your life is the result of the decisions you made. How do you feel about that? Is this true for you? It's important that from now on, you are aware of the power you have over your life by making decisions!

Every decision, every choice has an important influence on your life. In fact, your life is a direct result of the choices and decisions you made in the past and every choice carries a consequence! Start making better choices. **Remember that you choose your thoughts and even your feelings.**

The most important thing is to make decisions. Whether the decision is right or wrong is secondary. You will soon receive feedback that will help you to progress. Once you have made a decision, go with it and take the consequences. If it was wrong, learn from it and forgive yourself knowing that at that point in time and with the knowledge you had, it was the best and the right decision to take.

YOUR ATTITUDE + YOUR DECISIONS = YOUR LIFE

Victor Frankl was a Jewish psychologist imprisoned in Germany's concentration camps during the Second World War. He lost his entire family except his sister. Under these terrible circumstances, he became aware of what he named "the ultimate human freedom", which not even the Nazi prison wards could take away from him: they could control his external circumstances, **but in the last instance it was him who CHOSE HOW these circumstances were going to affect him!**

He found out that between STIMULUS and RESPONSE there was a small space in time in which he had the freedom to

CHOOSE his RESPONSE! This means that even if you may not be able to control the circumstances that life presents to you, you can always **choose** your response in facing those circumstances, and by doing so have a huge impact on your life.

In other words, what hurts us is not what happens to us, but our response to what happens to us. The most important thing is how we RESPOND to what happens to us in our lives. And that is a CHOICE!

Do you want to be healthier? Make better choices about food and exercise. Do you want to be more successful? Make better decisions about who you surround yourself with, what you read, and what you watch. There are no excuses!

Forgive me if I make the assumption that your life situation is not worse than Victor Frankl's when he made this discovery: for me being a Jew in a German concentration camp in WW2 is as bad as it gets.

Questions to ask yourself:

What decisions could you make today to start change?

Will you choose to be more flexible? More positive? Healthier? Happier?

Action Steps:
1) Write down at least three changes that you want do make today:
   1 _____
   2 _____
   3 _____

2) Read Viktor Frankl's book "Man in search of meaning".

5
CHOOSE YOUR THOUGHTS

"The universe is change; our life is what our thoughts make it."
Marcus Aurelius

"You are today where your thoughts have brought you; you will be tomorrow where your thoughts take you."
James Allen

If you want to improve your life, the first thing you have to do is improve your thoughts. Your thoughts create your reality so you better have them under control! By controlling your thoughts, ultimately you control your life and your destiny. So observe your thoughts every now and then. Peace Pilgrim's quote "If you realized how powerful your thoughts are, you would never think a negative thought." says it all: don't get stuck in negative thoughts. Replace them with positive thoughts such as "everything is going to be all right" every single time they come up.

Think positive! A positively thinking person is not a dreamer, who thinks there are no problems in life. Instead he or she recognizes that problems are opportunities to grow, and knows that they only have the meaning that they are given. **Positive thinking is to see reality as it is, accept it, and make the best of it.**

Don't let your thoughts dominate you, instead dominate your thoughts and control their quality. Train your mind to concentrate only on positive, creative, and inspiring thoughts. If you train your mind like this for a while you will see that the circumstances of your life change too. You are the creator of your thoughts, but you are not your thoughts. Your thoughts are energy and the energy follows the thought. Thoughts create emotions, which create behavior, which create actions, and those actions have consequences in your daily life.

THOUGHT → EMOTION → BEHAVIOR → ACTION

Your thoughts depend on your beliefs about life. If you don't like what you are receiving then have a look at what you are sending! Everything that is in your life has been created by your thoughts, expectations, and beliefs. So analyze them! If you change your beliefs, you will get new results!

Practice a thought often enough so that it becomes a belief, and your behavior and actions will follow its lead. For instance, if you constantly worry about not having enough money, you'll create behaviors based on fear. You'll play smaller. You'll try to hang on to the money you have versus playing to win.

Action Step:

Try to have no negative thoughts for 48 hours. Block them from the first moment and substitute them with positive thoughts of love, peace, and compassion. Even if it seems difficult at the beginning, hang in there. It gets easier. Then try this for 5 days, and finally a week. What has changed in your life since you started thinking positively?

6
WHAT DO YOU BELIEVE?

"These then are my last words to you. Be not afraid of life. Believe that life is worth living and your belief will help create the fact."
William James

"The outer conditions of a person's life will always be found to reflect their inner beliefs"
James Allen

What do you believe? This is extremely important, because ultimately your beliefs create your reality! You create what you believe and your world is only your interpretation of the reality. In other words, we don't see the world how it is, but how we were conditioned to see it. Our perception is only an approximation of reality. Our maps of reality determine the way we act more than reality itself. Each **one of us sees the world through the lenses of their own beliefs.**

Does this sound like hocus-pocus to you? It did to me too until I studied two semesters of Psychology at my High School and learned about the **Placebo Effect, The Pygmalion Effect, and Self-Fulfilling prophecies.** Studies on these subjects out there show how powerful our thoughts and beliefs really are! But what is a belief? It's the conscious and unconscious information that we accept as true. Robert Dilts defines beliefs as judgments and assessments about ourselves, others, and the world around us. A belief is a habitual thought pattern. Once a person believes something is true (whether it's true or not) he or she acts as if it were - collecting facts to prove the belief even if it's false.

Beliefs are like a self-fulfilling prophecy. They work like this: **your beliefs influence your emotions, your emotions influence your actions and your actions influence your RESULTS!**

Depending on your belief-system you live your life one way or another.

I want you to realize that life doesn't just happen to you! It's a reflection of your beliefs, thoughts, and expectations. If you want to change your life you have to first change your patterns of thinking. Even if beliefs come from early childhood programming for most of us, we are able to change them. **Nobody can impose your beliefs on you.** It's always you who in the last instance can permit a belief to be true for you or not!

Believing in yourself is an attitude. It's a choice! Remember what Henry Ford said! If you think that you won't make it, if you think that it's impossible, then you will not achieve it even if your effort is huge. For many decades it was thought impossible that man could run a mile under four minutes. There were even scientific papers and studies on the subject. These studies could all be shredded on May 6th 1954, when Roger Bannister proved everybody wrong at a race in Oxford. From then on over a 1000 people have done it.

I highly recommend that you let go of limiting beliefs such as:

- One can't be totally happy as there is always something that goes wrong.
- Life is tough.
- Showing emotions is for weak people.
- Opportunity only knocks once.
- I'm helpless and have no control over my life.
- I don't deserve it.
- Nobody loves me.
- I can't.
- It's impossible.
- ….

And pick up some empowering beliefs such as:
- I create my destiny.
- Nobody can hurt me if I don't allow it.
- Life is great!
- Everything happens for a reason.

- Everything is going to be all right.
- I can do it!

Ask yourself the following questions:

- What do I believe to be true about myself?
- What are my beliefs concerning money?
- What are my beliefs concerning my relationships?
- What are my beliefs about my body?

To change a belief follow this exercise and say to yourself:

1) This is only my belief about reality. That doesn't mean that it is the reality.
2) Although I believe this, it's not necessarily true.
3) Create emotions which are opposite to the belief.
4) Imagine the opposite.
5) Be aware that the belief is only an idea that you have about reality and not reality itself.
6) For just 10 minutes a day ignore what seems to be real and act as if your wish has come true. (See yourself spending money, being healthy, more successful, etc.)

Alternative exercise:

1) Write down the limiting belief.
2) Remember the sequence: belief – emotion – action – result.
3) To get a different result – in what way do you need to act?
4) How do you need to feel in order to act differently and get a different result?
5) What do you need to believe in order to feel differently, act differently, and get a different result?

7
THE IMPORTANCE OF YOUR ATTITUDE

*"Everything can be taken from a man but one thing:
the last of human freedoms –
to choose one's attitude in any given set of circumstances"*
Victor Frankl

Your Attitude is crucial for your happiness! It can change your way of seeing things dramatically and also your way of facing them. You will suffer less in life if you accept the rules of the game. Life is made up of laughter and tears, light and shadow. You have to accept the bad moments by changing your way of looking at them. Everything that happens to you is a challenge and an opportunity at the same time.

Look at the positive side of things in life even in the worst situations. There is something good hidden in every bad – although sometimes it might take some time to discover it. I'll tell you again: it's not what happens in your life that's important; it's how you respond to what happens to you that makes your life!

Life is a chain of moments – some happy, some sad - and it depends on you to make the best of each and every one of those moments. Did your wife leave you? So will you be unhappy forever or will you go out and meet new people? Losing your job might open new doors.

Many years ago all of the success teachers and positive thinkers described it this way: "If life gives you a lemon, add sugar to it, and make lemonade out of it". Younger readers might say that "If life gives you a lemon, ask for some salt and Tequila". You get the point, don't you?

For example, some healthy attitudes are:
- Allow yourself to make mistakes and learn from them.
- Admit that there are things you don't know.

- Dare asking for help and let other people help you.
- Differentiate between what you have done in your life until now and what you want to do or better still, will do from now on!

Action Step:
Think of a negative situation and turn it around.

8
PERSPECTIVE IS EVERYTHING

"The optimist sees the donut, the pessimist sees the hole."
Oscar Wilde

"A pessimist is somebody who complains about the noise when opportunity knocks."
Oscar Wilde

William Shakespeare said "There is nothing either good or bad, but thinking makes it so". Put things into perspective! The closer you are to the problem and the more in front of it, the less you see. Step back and get a more global view of it. Understand how you feel faced with the problem and evaluate the real importance of it. Even seeing the problem as a challenge will be helpful!

Every negative experience in your life has something good in it - search for it! If you get into the habit of always searching for the good in every situation you will change the quality of your life drastically. Experiences themselves are neutral until we start to give them meaning. Your vision of the world and your perspective "decide" if something is "good" or "bad".

What may be a great tragedy to you could be a wakeup call for me to take my life into my hands and thrive. In coaching we use what is called "Reframing" to change the perspective that a client has of an event. One of my favorites is changing "Failure" to "Feedback" or "Learning experience".

How do you feel if you say **"I failed terribly in my last relationship"?** Now try saying **"I learned so much from my last relationship, I'm sure I will not make the same mistakes again!"** Can you feel the difference?

Here are some more examples of reframing:

I'm jobless	I have time to figure out what I really want to do for a living
I'm sick	Cleansing, Giving my body a break
That's the way I am	I can look for another perspective
I can't	Let's see which options I have
Impossible	Possible
Problem	Challenge / Opportunity to grow
Failure	Learning experience
I have to / I should	I choose to / I will
I try	I do
Always	Until now
Never	Sometimes

Action Step:

Write down at least five situations in your life that you thought were negative, however with time you clearly saw that you got something good out of it.

9
HAVE PATIENCE AND NEVER EVER GIVE UP!

"Our greatest weakness lies in giving up. The most certain way to succeed is always to try just one more time"
Thomas Alva Edison

"Success is not final, failure is not fatal: it is the courage to continue that counts."
Winston Churchill

Perseverance is more important than talent, intelligence, and strategy. There is great virtue in never giving up. When life doesn't go according to plan, keep moving forward, no matter how small your steps are. The top two habits that will decide between success and failure, between real change and staying in the same place are patience and perseverance.

It's highly possible that before success comes, there may be some obstacles in your path. If your plans don't work out see it as a temporary defeat, and not as a permanent failure. Come up with a new plan and try again. If the new plan doesn't work out either, change it, adapt it until it works.

This is the point at which most people give up: They lack patience and persistence in working out new plans! But watch out. Don't confuse this with persistently pursuing a plan that doesn't work! If something doesn't work…change it! Persistence means persistence toward achieving your goal.

When you encounter obstacles - have patience. When you experience setback - have patience. When things are not happening - have patience. Don't throw your goal away at the first sign of misfortune or opposition. Think of Thomas Edison and his ten thousand attempts to make the light bulb. Fail towards success like he did! Persistence is a state of mind. Cultivate it. If you fall down, get up, shake off the dust, and keep on moving towards your goal.

The habit of persistence is built as follows:

1. Have a clear goal and the burning desire to achieve it.
2. Make a clear plan and act on it with daily action steps.
3. Be immune to all negative and discouraging influences.
4. Have a support system of one or more people who will encourage you to follow through with your actions and to pursue your goals.

10
LEARN THE "EDISON MENTALITY"

"I failed myself to success"
Thomas Alva Edison

"It is hard to fail, but it is worse never to have tried to succeed."
Theodore Roosevelt

Let's talk about failure! This subject is so important and yet so misunderstood! Paulo Coelho hits the spot when he says **"There is only one thing that makes a dream impossible to achieve: the fear of failure."** The fear of failure is the number one dream killer, but why? Why are we so afraid of failure?

Why can't we see it like Napoleon Hill who indicated that "Every adversity, every failure, every heartache carries with it the seed of an equal or greater benefit." Or in other words, how would our life change if we could see failure exactly like Napoleon Hill did?

Why not see it as a learning experience that is necessary for growth and which provides us with information and motivation? What would happen if you could fully embrace the idea that in reality failure is a sign that points towards progress?

Learn the "Edison Mentality". Edison himself said things like "I failed myself to success" or "I have not failed. I've just found 10,000 ways that won't work." This is what enabled him to bring many of his inventions to us. The man just didn't give up!

Accept your mistakes as feedback and learn from them! Luckily, as kids we didn't have the mentality which many of us have adapted as adults – because if we did then many of us wouldn't know how to walk! How did you learn walking? By falling many times and always getting up again. Unfortunately, somewhere along the road you picked up the idea that failure is something terrible. And as a result of this nowadays we fail once and then stop doing things simply because it didn't work out the first time, because we got rejected, because our business venture didn't work out right away.

NOW is the time to change your mentality towards failure! Why don't you look at it in this way from now on: **Every failure is a great moment in our life, because it allows us to learn and grow from it!**

Even more and more companies nowadays are shifting to a new mentality by allowing their employees to make mistakes, because they noticed that if people are afraid to make mistakes, creativity and innovation die and the company's progress slows down. At the end of the day it comes down to this:

Success is the result of right decisions. Right decisions are the result of experience, and experience is the result of wrong decisions.

Here is a story of a famous "failure" that literally failed his way to success:
- Lost job, 1832
- Defeated for legislature, 1832
- Failed in business, 1833
- Elected to legislature, 1834
- Sweetheart (Ann Rutledge) died, 1835
- Had nervous breakdown, 1836
- Defeated for Speaker, 1838
- Defeated for nomination for Congress, 1843
- Lost re-nomination, 1848
- Rejected for Land Officer, 1849
- Defeated for Senate, 1854
- Defeated for nomination for Vice-President, 1856
- Again defeated for Senate, 1858
- Elected President, 1860

This is the story of **Abraham Lincoln**, a man we would not exactly characterize as a failure, would we?

And here are some other famous failures:

Michael Jordan:
cut from his high school basketball team.
Steven Spielberg:
rejected from film school three times.
Walt Disney:
fired by the editor of a newspaper for lacking ideas and imagination.
Albert Einstein:
He learned to speak at a late age and performed poorly in school.
John Grisham:
first novel was rejected by sixteen agents and twelve publishing houses.
J.K. Rowling:
was a divorced, single mother on welfare while writing Harry Potter.
Stephen King:
his first book "Carrie" was rejected 30 times. He threw it in the trash. His wife retrieved it from the trash and encouraged him to try again.
Oprah Winfrey:
fired from her television reporting job as "not suitable for television."
The Beatles:
told by a record company that they have "no future in show business".

Answer the following questions:

Have you had any failures in the last years?

What did you learn from it?

What was the positive you got out of it?

11
GET COMFORTABLE WITH CHANGE AND CHAOS!

"Be willing to be uncomfortable. Be comfortable being uncomfortable. It may get tough, but it's a small price to pay for living a dream."
Peter McWilliams

The way to success goes through change and chaos. For personal growth you have to be in a constant state of feeling slightly uncomfortable. **Get into the habit of doing things that others don't want to do.** You have to choose to do what needs to be done regardless of the inconvenience!

That means: to forgive instead of holding a grudge, to go the extra mile instead of saying it can't be done; to take 100% of the responsibility for your behavior instead of blaming others.

Most of us think that to change our lives we have to make huge changes, and then we get overwhelmed by the hugeness of the task and end up not doing anything, and get stuck with our old habits. The answer is: baby steps! Start changing small things which don't require a big effort and those small changes will eventually lead to bigger changes. Start changing your way to get to work, the restaurant you're having lunch at, or meet new people.

Action Steps:

1) Do something that makes you feel slightly uncomfortable every day.
2) What will you change tomorrow? Your daily routine? Exercise? Eat healthier?

12
FOCUS ON WHAT YOU WANT, NOT ON WHAT YOU LACK!

*"It is during our darkest moments that
we must focus to see the light."*
Aristotle Onassis

The number one reason why people are not getting what they want is because they don't even know what they want. The number two reason is that **while they are telling themselves what they want, they are concentrating on what they don't want, and what you are concentrating on...Expands! Remember to focus on what you want from now on!**

Where is your focus? On the positive or the negative? On the past or the present? Do you focus on problems or solutions? This is crucial! Here is where the law of attraction goes wrong for most people and they give up! They say "I'm attracting money", "I'm prosperous", but at the same time they focus most of their time on the bills they have to pay, on the money that goes out, on the fact that they are not earning too much. So what happens? They attract more of the things they don't want!

You will attract more of what you focus on! Your energy will flow into the direction of your focus and your focus determines your overall perception of the world. Focus on opportunities and you will see more opportunities! Focus on success and success will come to you.

Use the following questions to change your focus:
How can I improve this situation?
What can I be thankful for?
What is great in my life right now?
What could I be happy about right now if I wanted to?
Is this still important in ten years?
What is great about this challenge? How can I use this to learn from it?
What can I do to make things better?

13
WATCH YOUR WORDS

"But if thought corrupts language, language can also corrupt thought."
George Orwell, 1984

"The only thing that's keeping you from getting what you want is the story you keep telling yourself."
Tony Robbins

Watch your words! Don't underestimate them! They are very powerful! **The words that we use to describe our experiences become our experiences!** You probably encountered a situation or two in your life, when spoken words did a lot of damage. And this is true not only in talking to others, **but also talking to yourself**. Yes, this little voice in your head - the one that just asked "Voice, what voice?"

You are what you tell yourself the whole day! Your inner dialogue is like the repeated suggestion of a hypnotist. Are you complaining a lot? What story are you telling yourself? If you say that you are bad, weak, and powerless then that's what your world will look like! On the other hand, if you say you are healthy, feeling great, and unstoppable you will also reflect that. Your inner dialogue has a huge impact on your self-esteem.

So be careful with how you describe yourself: such as "I'm lazy", "I'm a disaster", "I'll never be able to do that", or my personal favorite "I'm tired" because of course the more you tell yourself that you are tired, the more tired you will get! Watching your inner dialogue is very important!

The way you communicate with yourself changes the way you think about yourself, which changes the way you feel about yourself, which changes the way you act and this ultimately influences your results and the perception that others have of you.

Keep the conversation with yourself positive such as "I want to achieve success", "I want to be slim", "God, I am good", because your subconscious mind doesn't understand the little word "NO". It sees your words as IMAGES.

Don't think of a pink elephant! See - I bet you just imagined a pink elephant.

And - I will repeat myself – please focus on what you want. Keep in mind that your words and especially the questions you ask yourself have a huge influence on your reality.

I tell my coaching clients to never tell me or themselves that they can't do something, but instead always ask **"How can it be done?"** If you ask yourself "how", your brain will search for an answer and come up with it. The good thing is that you can really change your life by changing your language, talking to yourself in a positive way, and starting to ask yourself different questions.

Why wait? Start asking yourself different questions now!

14
NEW HABITS, NEW LIFE!

"We are what we repeatedly do. Excellence, then, is not an act, but a habit."
Aristotle

It takes about 21 days to implement a new habit. About 2500 years ago, the Greek philosopher Aristotle said that you change your life by changing your habits. The coaching process is, in its essence a process of changing the client's habits over time by introducing new ways of doing things and substituting old behaviors.

The most important step in the process of changing your habits is to become aware of them! Did you hear the saying that If you keep doing what you are doing you will keep getting the results you are getting? Einstein himself defined the purest form of insanity as "doing the same things over and over, expecting a different result".

Is this you? Don't worry and go on reading! If you want different results in your life then you have to start doing things differently. You can change this and it's relatively easy if you put in some work and discipline. Develop habits that steer you towards your goals. If you do that- success in your live is guaranteed.

Here are some examples of "bad" habits that might be good to get rid of: being constantly late, working late, eating junk food, procrastinating, interrupting while somebody else is talking, being a slave to your phone, etc.

Our goal in this chapter is to introduce 10 new healthy daily habits into your life within the next three months. I don't want you to be overwhelmed, so why not introduce three habits each month? With time these habits will improve your life considerably and they will substitute ineffective habits which until now have drained your energy.

Action Step:

What 10 habits are you going to introduce?
It's not necessary to introduce BIG changes. The usual habits my clients introduce are:

- Exercise 3 times a week.
- Focus on the positive.
- Work on your goals.
- Walk by the beach or in the woods.
- Spend more time with your family.
- Eat more vegetables.
- Meet with friends.
- Read 30 minutes a day.
- Spend 15 minutes on "alone time" a day , etc.

It helps to have a visual display! And don't forget to reward yourself for your successes!

Start RIGHT NOW by making a list of 10 daily habits you will introduce into your life from today.

15
KNOW YOURSELF

The first step before changing your life is becoming aware of where you are and what's missing. **Please take some time to answer the following questions.**

What are your dreams in life?
_____
_____
_____

At the end of your life, what do you think you would most regret not having done for yourself?
_____
_____
_____

If time and money were not factors, what would you like to do, be, or have?
_____
_____
_____

What motivates you in life?
_____
_____
_____

What limits you in life?
_____
_____
_____

What have been your biggest wins in the last 12 months?
_____
_____
_____

What have been your biggest frustrations in the last 12 months?
_____
_____
_____

What do you do to please others?
_____
_____
_____

What do you do to please yourself?
_____
_____
_____

What do you pretend not to know?
_____
_____
_____

What has been the best work that you have done in your life until today?
_____
_____
_____

How exactly do you know that this was your best work?
_____
_____
_____

How do you see the work you do today in comparison to what you did 5 years ago? What's the relationship between the work you do now and the work you did then?
_____
_____
_____

What part of your work do you enjoy the most?

What part of your work do you enjoy the least?

What activity or thing do you usually postpone?

What are you really proud of?

How would you describe yourself?

What aspects of your behavior do you think you should improve?

At this moment in time, how would you describe your commitment level to making your life a success?

At this moment in time, how would you describe your general state of well-being, energy, and self-care?

_____
_____
_____

At this moment in time, how would you describe how much fun or pleasure you are experiencing in your life?

_____
_____
_____

If you could put one fear behind you once and for all, what would it be?

_____
_____
_____

In what area of your life do you most want to have a true breakthrough?

_____
_____
_____

16
KNOW YOUR TOP 4 VALUES!

"Efforts and courage are not enough without purpose and direction."

John F. Kennedy

Let's talk about values. Not in a moral or ethical way, but looking at what fuels you and what motivates you. Being clear about and knowing your values is one of the most important steps to getting to know yourself better.

By knowing your values, you will be able to attract more of what you want in your life. If there is a big difference between the life you are living and your values, this might create suffering and tension. Once you find out what your values are, you will be able to understand yourself and your actions a lot better. **When your goals are aligned with your values you will notice that you achieve them much quicker and hit a lot less resistance.**

Everything changed for me around two years ago when I gained a clear knowledge of my values. I finally knew where the tension and stress at my work and in my life came from (not one of my core values was being applied!) and I could understand my reactions in various situations a lot better. So what is **really** important to you?

Find out what your most important values are that bring you joy, peace, and fulfillment. From the list of values **(you can download it on my webpage for free)** choose 10. You may find that you can group values. **Then narrow them down to your top four values.**

Also answer the following questions:
What is very important in your life?
What gives purpose to your life?
What are you usually doing when you experience that feeling of inner peace?

What are you doing that is so much fun that you usually lose track of time?
Think of some people that you admire. Why do you admire them? What kind of qualities do you admire in them?
What activities do you enjoy the most? What kind of moments bring you joy and fulfillment?
What can't you put up with?

Visualization:

Take some time. Close your eyes and relax.
Imagine that it is your 75th birthday. You're strolling around in your house. All your friends and family are present. What would you like the most important person in your life, your best friend, and a family member say to you? Write it down.

1) The most important person in your life says....

2) Your best friend says....

3) Your (family member) says…

17
KNOW YOUR STRENGTHS

"A winner is someone who recognizes his God-given talents, works his tail off to develop them into skills, and uses his skills to accomplish his goals."
Larry Bird

You don't have to be good at everything. Focus on your strengths. Remember that what you focus on tends to expand. What are you good at? Time to find out – isn't it? So let's get started:

List your TOP FIVE Personal Qualities and Professional Strengths below:
(What are your unique strengths? What are you most proud of? What do you do best?)
_____
_____
_____

List your Most Significant Personal and Professional Accomplishments:
(What are you most pleased about and proud of having accomplished?)
_____
_____
_____

List your Personal and Professional Assets:
(Who do you know? What do you know? What gifts do you have? What makes you unique and powerful?)
_____
_____
_____

Once you know your strengths it's time to strengthen them. Practice them and concentrate on them - the ones you have and the ones you want (see also chapter 60: Fake it till you make it).

Action Step:

If you are up for it, send an email to 5 friends and/or colleagues and ask them what they consider your greatest strengths! This can be quite inspiring and a true self confidence booster!

18
HONOR YOUR PAST ACHIEVEMENTS

"The more you praise and celebrate your life, the more there is in life to celebrate"

Oprah Winfrey

This is a very important chapter. It's one of my favorite exercises to boost my clients' self-confidence (and my own). Its purpose is to empower you and make you aware of what you have already achieved in your life! We are always so centered in the things that don't work so well or what we haven't achieved that we forget what we have already achieved.

I'm sure that you have fantastic achievements in your life and in this chapter you will become aware of those past successes and use them as rocket fuel to achieve your goals and future successes! So the big question is: **What great things have you achieved in your life so far?**

You put yourself through college, traveled the world, have a great career, have lots of great friends. Maybe you lived abroad for a while all on your own. Or maybe you have overcome a tough childhood and major personal setbacks. Maybe you raised fantastic children. Whatever challenges you've overcome or successes you have achieved—now is the time to look back and celebrate them.

Remember the chapter about focus? In this case, it means that the more you remember and acknowledge your past successes, the more confident you'll become. And because you are concentrating on successes you will see more opportunities for success!

Make your list! Remind yourself of your past successes! Give yourself a pat on the shoulder and say to yourself "Well done!"

The important thing is the experience of success! Get into the same state that you were in, see the success once again in your mind, feel again how it felt then!

Action Step:

1) Write down a list of the biggest successes you've achieved in your life!

2) Read them out loud and allow yourself to feel fantastic for what you have accomplished!

19
WRITE DOWN YOUR GOALS AND ACHIEVE THEM!

"People with clear, written goals accomplish far more in a shorter period of time than people without them can ever imagine."
Brian Tracy

"A goal is a dream with a deadline."
Napoleon Hill

The huge majority of us don't have even the slightest idea of where to start to make our dreams come true. **Most people over-estimate what they can do in a month and under-estimate what they can do in a year.**

If you go one step at a time and remain flexible, then over time you can achieve things that you couldn't even imagine before. And the funny thing is: It's not even about reaching the end goals; **it's about the person you become in the process.**

The journey is more important than the destination – and also in goal setting! So why write down your goals? **Because they will drive you to take action!** Having clearly defined goals in your life is crucial to your way towards success and happiness.

They are like a GPS system leading the way. But to be led, first of all you have to know where you want to go! This is so important that entire books are written on the subject of goal setting! I will make it as short as possible.

The first step to achieving your dream goals is to put them in writing. I was very skeptical about this until I started writing down my goals and then I wish I had started two decades ago. I became so much more productive and focused that I could hardly believe it. As I said before, for many years I didn't care about goal setting.

To be honest, I think it made me feel uncomfortable because committing to goals and writing them down suddenly meant that I could measure what I had achieved and what I did not achieve, and I didn't have the courage to do that.

It's important to write down your goals for various reasons:

1) When you write them down, you declare to your mind, that out of the 50000 to 60000 thoughts you have a day, THIS ONE written down is the most important.

2) You start concentrating and focusing on the activities that bring you closer to your goal. You also start taking better decisions, while you are focused on where you want to go, always keeping in mind whether what you are doing in this moment is really the best use of your time.

3) Having a look at your written goals everyday forces you to act and helps you to prioritize your actions for the day by asking yourself questions such as "In this moment, is doing what I'm doing bringing me closer to my goals?"

Before starting the change process, you have to be clear about your goals. Then break them down in small achievable action steps and make a list of all the steps that you will take to get there. Calculate how long it will take you.

Don't forget to set a deadline for each action step and goal. Don't worry if you don't reach the goal by the exact date you set; it's just a way of focusing on the goal and creating a sense of urgency. One of my favorite quotes from my coaching training is **"If you put a date on a dream it becomes a goal."** So it's GO time for you now:

In the following exercise I want you to write down what you want your life to look like in 10 years. When you write it down, I want you to **write down what you want, not what you think is possible.** So **GO BIG!** There are no limits to your imagination. The answers you write here are the direction in which your life is headed.

Create a clear vision of your goals in your mind. See yourself as already having achieved the goal: How does it feel? How does it look? How does it sound? How does it smell?

The goals have to be yours, specific, stated positively, and you have to commit to them. Another important point: **When pursuing your goals, reward yourself for the effort put in, and not just for the results.** Self-punishment is not allowed! Keep in mind that you are much further than you were a week or a month ago.

Other useful tips that enhance your goal setting journey:

• Put a little card with your goals written on it in your wallet and reconnect 4-5 times daily.
• It's very beneficial to have a to-do list. Put your action steps on it, as well as the time it takes to do the task as and put the deadlines for each task.
• Balance your goals (physical, economic, social, professional, family, spiritual).

Exercise:

1) What do you want your life to look like in 10 years? There are no limits! Go big!
2) What do you have to have achieved in 5 years to get closer to your goal in 10 years?
3) What do you have to have achieved in 1 year to get closer to your goal in 5 years?
4) What do you have to have achieved in 3 months to get closer to your 1-year-goal?
5) What are the things that can you do NOW to reach your 3 month goal?

Action Step:
Write down at least three things and TAKE ACTION!

20
NEXT!

I take rejection as someone blowing a bugle in my ear to wake me up and get going, rather than retreat.
Sylvester Stallone

Another one of the biggest fears that we have is the fear of rejection! We don't ask the girl for a dance because we fear rejection, we don't send the CV because we fear rejection, we don't even ask for the upgrade to business class or the best table in the restaurant because we fear rejection!

To reach your goals in life, you will have to learn how to handle rejection. It's a part of life and to overcome it you have to become aware that - same as failure - it's only a concept in your mind! The most successful people are not much different from you. **They are just better at handling rejection!** Now that's something, isn't it? On your way to your goals, you will probably have to face rejection many times. Just don't give up. And above all **don't take rejection personally!**

Think about it. If you ask someone out and he or she doesn't want to go out with you, actually nothing has changed. He or she was not going out with you before and she is not going out with you now. Your situation is the same. **Rejection is not the problem; it's the inner dialogue you start after being rejected that is the problem:** "I knew I can't do it. I know I'm not good enough. Father was right. I will never achieve anything in life". The important thing is to go on! The most successful salesmen's goal is to hear 100 "No's" a day, because they know that if they hear 100 "No's", there will also be some "Yes's". **It's a numbers game!**

The most successful "Don Juans" of my friends are the ones who dealt with the "No's" the best. They knew that if they talk to 25 girls a night, eventually there will be someone who will have a drink with them. Others gave up after hearing two or three "No's".

Just be prepared to get rejected many times on your way to success. The secret is to not give up!

When somebody tells you "No, thanks" you think **"NEXT"**. Did you know that Sylvester Stallone's script for the movie "Rocky" was rejected over 70 times? Jack Canfield's and Mark Victor Hansen's "Chicken Soup for the Soul" was rejected a 130 times and that Canfield was actually laughed at when he said that he wanted to sell 1 million books. His editor told him he'd be lucky to sell 20,000. Well, the first book "Chicken Soup for the Soul" sold 8 million copies, the whole series about 500 million! Even J.K. Rowlings' "Harry Potter" was rejected 12 times!

Answer the following questions:

What are you taking away from this chapter?

How will you deal with rejection from now on?

21
AVOID ENERGY ROBBERS

"Energy and persistence conquer all things."
Benjamin Franklin

"The energy of the mind is the essence of life."
Aristotle

Your energy is crucial for boosting you towards your goals and happiness. There are some things in your life that drain your energy and then there are things that add energy. Don't underestimate the importance of energy and keep it up! In my coaching processes, we put a lot of emphasis on activities that bring energy and cut loose things that drain energy out of my clients' lives.

When you operate on low energy you don't feel good, you are not happy, you send out low vibes, and chances are that you will attract what you are sending! Stop doing or exposing yourself to things that drain your energy like unhealthy eating habits, alcohol, drugs, caffeine, sugar, tobacco, lack of exercise, negativity, sarcasm, unfocused goals, the news, and tabloid newspapers among others. All these things drain your energy. And beware of the "energy vampires" amongst your colleagues, friends, and even family. Why would you spend time with people that only drain you?

Become very selfish on how you manage your energy:
- Eliminate all distractions.
- Finish your unfinished business.
- Work on your tolerations. (See Chapter 29)
- Say good bye to all energy robbing people and relationships.

Questions:
What are the energy robbers in your life?

What will you do about it?

22
MANAGE YOUR TIME

"There is nothing so useless as doing efficiently that which should not be done at all."
Peter F. Drucker

Do you work lots of overtime and still don't have time for everything you need to do? Are you one of those people that would love to have 28 hours in a day? Well, unfortunately you also have only 24 hours like everybody else on this planet.

Oh and I'm sorry, I forgot: There is no such thing as time management! You can't manage time. What you can do is use your time wisely and manage your priorities. **Everyone who comes to me and most of my friends say "I don't have time to_____ (fill in the blank)."** The fastest way to gain time is to watch one hour less of TV every day. That's 365 hours a year, which equals 28 hours a month! What would you do with seven extra hours a week? Another trick to gain more time is getting up earlier (see Chapter 25).

Set priorities and choose what activities to invest your time in. **Set clear rules about when you are available and when you are not available and don't let other people steal your time.** The funny thing is, the more you value your time, the more you will have of it, because people will also value your time.

If you allow people to interrupt you all the time, you're essentially showing them that your time is not very valuable in which case you will not be able to work effectively, no matter how many hours you work. Recent studies have found out that each 5 minute interruption at work costs you 12 minutes, because your brain needs 7 minutes to refocus!

How many interruptions do you have per day? 10? 12? Imagine how much time you can gain back when you decrease the number of interruptions. Every 3 minute interruption costs you 10 minutes. Let's say you get interrupted 12 times in one working day: 2 hours gone! In a month that's like having an extra week!

Don't let employees, friends, or clients interrupt you. Set those clear rules NOW.

Another big time robber is social media and e-mail. **Setting fixed times for your social media activity and checking emails is another means to gain a lot of time.**

I started gaining a lot of time at work when I learnt to say "NO". (See Chapter 24). My personal number one time saving technique is taking 30 to 60 minutes on Sundays to plan my week ahead. I put my personal and professional goals for every week in my excel sheet.

And don't forget to schedule in some free time, relaxation time, like power naps, reading, meditation, etc. and some buffer time for emergencies too. I also take 15 minutes every day to plan my next day. In this way, I give my subconscious mind a chance to work on it already while I sleep. This works! When I start the next day I don't have to think much: I just go to work.

Some more time saving tips:
- Make a to-do list with date and the time the task takes.
- Limit your phone calls to 5 minutes per call.
- Be aware of the result you want for each call that you make.
- Work against time and you'll get your work done faster (set an alarm clock and work against it).
- Write 5 things you want for the next day each evening and list them in order of priority.
- Create blocks of time (90 minutes blocks).
- Track your time. Take a look at how you are currently using your time by tracking your daily activities.
- Do the unpleasant things first.
- Stop being busy and go for results.

Be careful with the following time robbers:
- Lack of information for completing a task.
- You do everything yourself (Is delegating an option?).
- You get distracted easily (Focus and set boundaries!).
- Your phone calls are too long (Put a 5 minutes limit).
- You spend a lot of time in searching for files (Get organized!)

- You keep doing things the same way and don't realize that there could be a more efficient way of doing it.
- You think you have to be reachable all the time and every where (Really?).

So what are you going to do next? **Will you insist on the excuse that you have no time** or will you start making time with one little thing at a time and experience the change for yourself? What are you going to do? Remember it's all about decisions and habits!

Action Step:

Write down 5 things you will start doing NOW!

_____
_____
_____
_____
_____
_____

23
START TO GET ORGANIZED!

"Organizing is what you do before you do something, so that when you do it, it is not all mixed up."
A.A.Milne

"For every minute spent organizing, an hour is earned."
Anonymous

Are you too busy to get organized? You are surrounded by mountains of paper and have post-its all over your table. And you feel you are really busy but you just can't breathe and you just can't handle your work even if you do extra time? **THEN READ CLOSELY NOW, because I'm especially talking to YOU!**

It's not that you are too busy to get organized, it's because you are not organized that you are so busy! And to make it worse: **Being busy doesn't mean that you are effective! Just because you have the messiest table in the office, doesn't mean you are the one who works hardest.** There are studies that today's executives spend between 30% and 50% of their time searching for paperwork! Can you believe that?

So, my overwhelmed worker, go on reading and TRY OUT these little tips, as they can change your life! I have been there and I turned it around using the little tips below:

- Spend the first 15 minutes of your working day prioritizing what to do.
- Spend one hour a week for organizing and filing papers.
- Spend 15 minutes a day throwing away papers and clearing away your desk
- Spend the last 15 minutes of your working day to go through your tasks for tomorrow. What's important? What's urgent?
- Use your e-mail inbox as a to-do list. Tasks solved get archived and tasks unsolved stay in the inbox.

- If there are any e-mails and tasks that you can do in less than 5 minutes, always do them right away! ALWAYS!
- Don't accept any new tasks until you are in control.
- Do the job right the first time, so that it doesn't come back to haunt you and cost you more time later.

Do you remember that typical colleague who always completed his work fast, but not thoroughly and then during every step of the process you had to go back to him for more information? Instead of doing it well one time with all of the correct documentation which takes 15 minutes, he rushed it in 5 minutes, and later you had to go back to him three more times thus losing another 30 minutes. So instead of 15 minutes he actually took 35 minutes to complete the task. Do it right the first time!

Like everything else in this book, saying "That won't work for me" doesn't count as an excuse! Try it for at least two weeks and if it still doesn't work for you write me an email and complain to me!

Action Step:

Which of the tips will you try first?

24
SAY "NO" TO THEM AND "YES" TO YOURSELF

"I don't know the key to success, but the key to failure is trying to please everybody."
Bill Cosby

Here is another one of these small exercises that improved my life a lot: When I stopped wanting to please others and started being myself, a lot of it came with the word "No". Every time you say "No" when you mean "No", you are actually saying "Yes" to yourself!

Before learning to say "No", I often went out with my friends although I didn't want to or went to events I didn't enjoy. The result was I was there physically but mentally I was in another place and honestly I was not the best company. When I decided that a "Yes" is a "Yes" and a "No" is a "No", I felt much better. I went out less with my friends and telling them "NO" was hard at the beginning, but the result was that when I was with my friends I was fully there.

In my work life, the impact was even bigger. When I started working in Spain I wanted to be a good colleague and said yes to every favor I was asked for. Guess what happened? I ended up being totally overwhelmed at work, because I was asked for a lot of favors – usually work nobody else wanted to do.

It took me a while to put my foot down, but finally I said "Enough!". From then on my first answer to all questions for favors was "NO! Sorry. Can't do it. Very busy at the moment!" By starting to say "No" often, I improved my work life a lot and actually freed up a lot of time.

But make sure you say "NO" without feeling guilty! You can explain to the person in question that it's not anything personal against them, but for your own wellbeing. I could still do my colleagues a favor, but only if I had enough time and decided to.

Suddenly I was in the driver's seat. If I was up for it I would mention to the colleague in question that I'm only doing a favor and in no case do I want to end up doing the job. Selfish? Yes! But keep in mind who the most important person in your life is. That's right! YOU are the most important person in your life! You have to be well! Only if you are well yourself, can you be well towards others and from this level you can contribute to others, but first be well yourself.

You can always buy some time and say "maybe" at first, until you come to a definite decision. Life gets a lot easier if you start saying "No"!

Ask yourself the following questions:

Whose life are you living? Are you living your own life or trying to please and fulfill the expectations of others?

Who and what are you going to say NO to starting NOW?

Action Step:

Make a list of things that you will stop doing!

25
GET UP EARLY! SLEEP LESS!

"It is well to be up before daybreak, for such habits contribute to health, wealth, and wisdom."
Aristotle

The first benefit of getting up an hour earlier is that you gain around 365 hours per year. 365! Who said "I don't have time!"? When clients come to me telling me that they don't have time, the first thing I ask them is how many hours of TV are they watching. This usually provides them with the time they need. To those who stopped watching TV and still don't have enough time I ask them to get up one hour earlier.

There is a very special energy in the morning hours before sunrise. Ever since I started getting up around 5.30 or 6 o'clock, my life changed completely. I'm much more calm and relaxed and don't start the day already running around stressed. I usually go running half an hour before the sun rises so that on my way back I see the sun rising "out of" the Mediterranean Sea. This is absolutely mind boggling and already puts me in a state of absolute happiness.

And for those of you who don't live next to the sea: A sunrise "out of" fields, forests, or even a big city is just as exciting. Just go watch it and let me know! Starting your day like this is very beneficial for your happiness and peace of mind. Another great advantage of getting up earlier is that it reinforces self-discipline and you'll gain self-respect. Many successful leaders were and still are members of the early birds club, for example, Nelson Mandela, Mahatma Gandhi, Barrack Obama, and many more.

It's scientifically proven that 6 hours should be enough sleep per night paired with a 30 to 60 minutes power nap in the afternoon. Your freshness depends on the quality of your sleep, not on the quantity. You have to try and figure out for yourself how many hours of sleep you need to feel refreshed.

But you should definitively give it a try. It will improve your quality of life a lot. Don't forget that getting up early is a new habit, so give it some time and don't give up after the first week if you still feel tired after getting up earlier. The habit needs at least 3 to 4 weeks to kick in. If you absolutely can't get up one hour earlier, try half an hour.

And don't forget that your attitude, thoughts, and beliefs about getting up an hour earlier play a big role, too. To me it was always intriguing how it was so difficult for me to get up at 6.45ish to go to work after 7 or 8 hours of sleep, but before every vacation I usually slept 4 hours and woke up before the alarm clock went off and I was totally refreshed and energized. In the end, getting up or hitting the snooze button is a decision you make. It's up to you. How important is a better lifestyle and more time for you?

26
AVOID THE MASS MEDIA

"A democratic civilization will save itself only if it makes the language of the image into a stimulus for critical reflection — not an invitation for hypnosis."
Umberto Eco

"The news is glorified gossip."
Mokokoma Mokhoana

You want to make fast progress, don't you? Here is one tip that will set free a lot of energy and time! How many hours do you spend in front of the "box" every day? The average American spends 4 to 5 hours a day in front of the TV, and same goes for Europeans. That's between 28 and 35 hours a week! Boom! That's a lot of time you can gain right there!

Apart from gaining time there is an even more beneficial side effect! TV is one of the biggest energy drainers, if not the number one! Do you ever feel renewed or reenergized after watching TV? **Stop watching the news, or better still turn off your television!**

Why would you expose yourself to so much negativity? Don't expose yourself to too much of the garbage that out there is on TV. Substitute your habit of watching TV for a healthier habit like taking a walk, spending more time with your family, or reading a good book.

I stopped watching the news many years ago when I became aware that while on the train to work I got upset over things heard and seen on the morning news and I thought to myself, "I can't go to my stressful workplace being already stressed, simply because of what politician A said or banker B did or because there is a war in C. Just one week after stopping watching the news I felt a lot better! Don't believe me? Just try it for yourself! **Don't watch the news for a week and see how you feel.**

I'm not telling you to become ignorant – even though here in Spain they say **"the ignorant is the happiest person in the village"**. You can still read the newspapers. I would recommend the headlines only. You will still be up to date with the important stuff, because your family, friends, and colleagues will keep you updated. Just choose and be selective how much garbage you expose your mind to.

If you need more reasons to stop watching television read one of the great books that are out there about how the media manipulates us and how nearly everything is fake! Control the information that you are exposed to. Make sure it adds to your life. Instead of watching trash TV, watch a documentary or a comedy. Instead of listening to the news in your car listen to an audio-book or motivational CDs.

27
DO YOU "HAVE TO" OR DO YOU "CHOOSE TO"?

"It's choice – not chance – that determines your destiny."
Jean Nidetch

Do you have many things in your life that you "should" or "have to" do, but never do? How many "shoulds" do you have in your life? Should you exercise more, go to the gym more, stop smoking, eat healthier, and spend more time with your family?

Those "shoulds" don't help you to get anywhere; they only imply that you are not good enough and just drain your energy, because they come with a bad conscience and self-torture.

"Why am I not going to the gym? I'm so bad! I will never lose weight" and so on and so forth. **Make a list of all your "shoulds" and then forget it!**

What? Forget it? Yes! I'm not kidding, forget it! If you have had a goal since last year and haven't done anything about it, then you are better off forgetting about it. If your goal is going to the gym and you didn't go for a year, let it go.

With the goal you also let go off the bad con-science and the self-punishment for not accomplishing it. Throw out all your "shoulds" and set some new goals!

Stop doing things that you "have to" do and instead **choose your goals** and - very important- substitute "I should" and "I have to" with "I choose to", "I decide to", "I will" and "I prefer to".

I choose to exercise more, I will eat healthier, I choose to read more. How does that feel? It's important that you enjoy your activities – if not, don't do them. Try out this little exercise:

I have to _____A_____.
If I don't do _____A_____, then _____B_____ will happen.
And if _____B_____ then _____C_____ and then _____D_____ and _____E_____ and then ___Z_____.

I prefer _____A_____ to _____Z_____ That's why I choose _____A_____

Action Step:

Make your list of "shoulds" and let go of them or rephrase them to "I choose to" or "I decide to".

28
FACE YOUR FEARS!

"The fear of suffering is worse than the suffering itself."
Paolo Coelho

"You gain strength, courage, and confidence by every experience in which you really stop to look fear in the face. You must do the thing which you think you cannot do."
Eleanor Roosevelt

Don't let your fears frustrate you, limit you, or paralyze you! David Joseph Schwartz puts it this way: "Do what you fear and your fear disappears" and Mark Twain already knew over a hundred years ago that **"20 years from now you will be more disappointed with the things you didn't do than with the ones that you did."** Or as one of my favorite sayings goes: "Never regret the things you did; only those you never tried!"

So face these fears! Ninety percent of them are pure imagination anyway. Illusions! Incredible stories of drama and disaster that will probably never happen and are made up by your mind - "the world's greatest director of soap operas", as T. Harv Eker says - to keep you in your comfort zone. The only problem is that great things like development, growth and success happen outside of the comfort zone.

Fears are a survival mechanism of your mind. Your mind wants to keep you safe and anything that your mind doesn't know, scares it. I had many fears in my life and still do but I learned to overcome them and behind my fears great opportunities waited for me. So I made it a habit to use my fear as a springboard. Just ask yourself, **"What's the worst thing that can happen to me if I do this?"** Then evaluate if the risk is worth taking or not.

Be careful! There is also a price for not taking a risk or stepping out of your comfort zone. Ask yourself **"What price am I paying for staying the same or not doing this?"**

Is it an even higher one than the price of taking the risk? This also includes intangible things like inner peace, happiness, health etc. **Change your relationship with fear. Let it warn you and consult you, but don't let it paralyze you!** For example, I used to be totally paralyzed by fear, and stayed stuck in my job for five years because of fear of change or the unknown. Nowadays when I'm invaded by fears and doubts I think to myself, "Hm, if there are so many doubts and fears I must be on a good track. I better take action."

Try new things and attempt the seemingly impossible! Ironically it's the things that you most fear that will be the most positive for your development and growth once you overcome them. Do the things you fear: make that call you don't want to make, send that email you don't want to send, ask that person you're afraid to ask and see what happens. When you notice fear have a look at it, observe it, analyze it, but don't believe it. Instead ask it, **"Fear, my old friend! What are you doing here again? Do you want to warn me or do you want to paralyze me? What's your game?"**

What are you afraid of? Failure? Success? Making mistakes? Taking the wrong decisions? Do as Susan Jeffers says: "Feel the fear and do it anyway"! If you want to reach new territories you have to take some risks and continuously do things that you are afraid of. Mistakes don't matter as long as you learn from them and don't make the same mistakes over and over again. The same goes for decisions – by the way not taking a decision or procrastinating is also a decision!

Answer the following questions in your workbook or journal:

1) What is stopping you from living the life you want to live?
2) What excuses are you making for justifying staying where you are?
3) What's the worst thing that can happen if you do what you are afraid of doing?

29
ELIMINATE EVERYTHING THAT ANNOYS YOU

"Great things are done by a series of small things brought together"
Vincent van Gogh

"It isn't the mountains ahead that wear you out. It's the grain of sand in your shoe."
Robert Service

This is usually one of the first exercises I do with my coaching clients. **Everything that annoys you drains your energy.** In coaching, we call it tolerations. For example, a missing button on your favorite shirt, the dirty shower curtain, a kitchen cupboard that doesn't close, your boss micromanaging you, money owed to you, a disorganized guest room, broken tools, a messy and disorganized desk, clothes that don't fit any more etc. are tolerations. For as long as you don't fix them they keep draining your energy. As soon as you eliminate them you will have more energy to concentrate on the things that move you forward.

So your exercise will be to make a list of all the things that annoy you: **in your private life, your job, your house, your friends, yourself, etc.**

Don't get scared if you write down 50 to 100 things. It's normal. Once you write them all down group them. Which ones are easy to handle? Which ones can YOU handle? For now, leave the ones that don't depend on you.

Have a look at them after two or three weeks. The funny thing I've seen with my clients is that some of the tolerations that don't depend on you disappear on their own once you take care of the ones that you can handle.

For example, my client Martina had huge problems with a colleague at work. He really drained her energy.

She worked on the tolerations she could handle and the list got emptier. Three months later her colleague suddenly changed jobs and left the company! Now was that just a coincidence or was it a consequence of her working on her tolerations? I'll leave the choice to you. Fact is that she is a lot happier at work now! Try it out for yourself and keep me posted!

Action Step:

Make a list of all the things that annoy you. In your private life, your job, your house, your friends, yourself, etc.

Start working on it as described above!

30
CLEAN OUT YOUR CUPBOARD

"Bottom line is, if you do not use it or need it, it's clutter, and it needs to go."
Charisse Ward

Do you want something new to come into your life? Do you ever notice that as soon as you get rid of some stuff and create space the universe doesn't take long to fill this space again? It's all about energy. If you have too much stuff that you don't use in your house, it drains your energy!

Coaching is about improving your whole environment and that includes uncluttering. Start with your cupboard. Here are some tips:
- If you haven't worn it for a year, you probably won't wear it any more.
- When you think "This will be useful one day" or "This re minds me of good times" - out it goes.

When I unclutter I usually give stuff away for free. It just makes me feel better and somehow I think life/God/the universe will reward me for it. Once you are done with the cupboard take on the whole bedroom. Later move on to the living room, clean out your garage and end up cleaning up your entire home & office.

Get rid of everything that you don't use any more: clothes, journals, books, CDs, even furniture, and so on. One of my clients uncluttered his whole apartment in one weekend. He felt so much better and lighter and got an energy boost that helped him to finish a whole bunch of his short term goals. He never looked back. **When will you start uncluttering?**

   Action Step:
Schedule a weekend and get rid of everything you don't need any more! **SCHEDULE THE WEEKEND NOW!**

31
UNCLUTTERING AND TOLERATIONS GO HAND IN HAND – A REAL LIFE EXAMPLE

"Clutter is nothing more than postponed decisions."
Barbara Hemphill

Uncluttering and Tolerations go hand in hand. I have here a real life example of my client Lawrence, who describes what happened during the process:

"When I went through the process of uncluttering my life, it was like I was creating a new sense of freedom for myself. Before I understood what cluttering is, I had been going through life picking up so many bad habits and discouraging thoughts along the way... They weren't the type of habits like a vice, for example, smoking or drinking. They were more like small tolerations that were seemingly insignificant to begin with, but as I gained more and more of them in my life and just accepted them as something I couldn't change, they grew heavier until I was very weighed down. These tolerations made me feel like I was moving like a sloth. Things like procrastination, lack of sleep, not gaining fulfillment from my work, getting used to take-out food too often, beating myself up for not achieving more success...Somewhere along the way I lost sight of my goals in life and I just allowed these tolerations to clutter things up to the point that I felt stuck.

When my coach Marc introduced the idea of uncluttering to me, it was truly a revelation. I understood what it meant immediately, but I just didn't know why I was this way or how to fix it and climb out of the hole. With the tools that Marc helped to equip me with, I can now recognize my tolerations and work on unloading them. I've identified the ones that I could quickly fix and have gotten rid of them: fixing the window sill that wouldn't open, hanging up the paintings that I left in storage when I moved, replacing my old mattress that was not so comfortable. I also recognize the tolerations that will take more time to resolve, and I work on them all the time, like challenging myself more at work and getting gratification from that productivity. I've written down all of them to keep track of and to hold myself accountable, and I write down new tolerations as I identify them along the way.

Uncluttering the tolerations in my life, that were jumbled together in my mind and slowing me down, has made me feel like I am 10x lighter now. I have more energy, more spirit, and more enthusiasm. And as I uncluttered the tolerations, I found that my physical surroundings became uncluttered as well. My apartment is cleaner and more open, so I feel like I'm in a clutter-free environment at home."

32
THE MOST IMPORTANT HOUR...

"Write it on your heart that every day is the best day in the year."
Ralph Waldo Emerson

The most important hour of your day is composed of the thirty minutes after you wake up and the thirty minutes before you fall asleep. This is when your subconscious is very receptive so it's of big importance what you do in this time.

The way you start your day will have a huge impact on how the rest of your day develops. I'm sure you have had days which have started off on the wrong foot and from then on it got worse and worse – or the opposite where you woke up with that feeling that everything will go your way and then it did. That's why it's very important to begin your day well. Most of us just get into a rush from minute one after waking up and that's how our days unfold. No wonder most people run around stressed nowadays. What would getting up half an hour or an hour earlier every morning do for you?

What if instead of hurrying and swallowing down your breakfast or even having it on the way to work, you get up and take half an hour for yourself? Maybe you even create a little morning ritual with a 10 or 15-minute meditation. Do you see what this could do for your life if you made it a habit? Here are some activities for the morning ritual. Give it a shot!

- Think positive: Today is going to be a great day!
- Remember for 5 minutes what you are grateful for.
- 15 minutes of quiet time.
- Imagine the day that is about to start going very well.
- Watch a sunrise.
- Go running or take a walk.
- Write in your journal.

The last half an hour of your day has the same importance! The things you do in the last half an hour before sleeping will remain in your subconscious during your sleep. So then it's time to do the following:
- Write into your journal again.
- Now is the time for reflecting on your day. What did you do great? What could you have done even better?
- Plan your day ahead. What are the most important things you want to get done tomorrow?
- Make a to do list for the next day.
- Visualize your ideal day.
- Read some inspirational blogs, articles, or chapters of a book.
- Listen to music that inspires you.

I highly recommend that you NOT WATCH THE NEWS or MOVIES that agitate you before you are about to go to sleep. This is because when you are falling asleep you are highly receptive to suggestions. That's why it's a lot more beneficial to listen or watch positive material. The planning ahead of your day and the list of things to do can bring you immense advantages and time saving. The things you have to do will already be in your subconscious plus you will get to work very focused the next day if you already know what your priorities are.

Questions:

How will your mornings and evenings look from now on?

Will you get up 30 minutes earlier and develop a little ritual?

What will your last activities be before you go to sleep?

33
FIND YOUR PURPOSE AND DO WHAT YOU LOVE

"The purpose of life is not to be happy. It is to be useful, to be honorable, to be compassionate, to have it make some difference that you have lived and lived well."
Ralph Waldo Emerson

"The two most important days in your life are the day you are born and the day you find out why."
Mark Twain

One of the most important things along your life's journey is the discovery of your purpose. So what exactly does that mean? It means doing what you love to do. Your answers to the questions **"What would you do if success was guaranteed?"** or **"What would you do if you had ten million dollars, seven houses, and have traveled to all of your favorite destinations?"** will lead you to your purpose.

You spend more time at your job than with your loved ones, so you better enjoy what you are doing! The 2013 Gallup "The state of the American Workplace report" states that up to 70% of people are not happy at their work! 50% are not engaged, not inspired, and just kind of present and around 20% have resigned internally and are actively disengaged! I was part of the 50% for five years and it was horrible. The worst thing was that I didn't even notice it! We all have great ideas or dreams about what we could be, have, and do. What happened to your dreams? This is where the value exercise from Chapter 16 comes into the picture.

The ideal picture is to build your goals around those values and have a job which allows you to live according to your values. You don't have to rush into something new, but you can start doing more of the things you love. It sounds like jargon, but when you have found your purpose, things will start to fall into place. You will start to attract people, opportunities, and resources naturally and incredible things will start to happen!

Nothing attracts success more than somebody who is doing what they love to do! My friend Yvonne followed her hunch, dropped out of Law School, and started selling shoes at a big department store. She loves to help people and she loves shoes so for her the choice was obvious. She went with her gut even though people made fun of her. She was even called the "female Al Bundy". Not a great compliment. But she didn't care about the jokes and went on to become the number one Sales Woman in the department store, selling hundreds of thousands of dollars' worth of shoes each year, taking home Employee of the Year awards one year after another and earning a decent salary. In fact she does so well that the VIP clients only want to be served by her. She enjoys every minute of her work.

If you feel like you are driving without a roadmap or a GPS and don't really know where to go or if you never quite know what you are doing here and why, and you feel kind of lost and empty, then that's a sign that you have not found your purpose. But don't worry, that can be fixed in no time. You can find clues to your purpose by examining your values, skills, passions, and ambitions and by taking a look at what you are good at. Here are some more questions that should help you. Have the courage to answer them to yourself and write them down. Nobody else but you can see the answers. **(Don't skip them, like I did for 15 years! When I finally answered them, everything changed!)**

Answer yourself the following questions:
Who am I? Why am I here? Why do I exist?
What do I really want to do with my life?
When do I feel fully alive?
What were the highlights of my life?
What am I doing when time flies by? What inspires me?
What are my greatest strengths?
What would I do if success was guaranteed?
What would I do if I had ten million Dollars, seven houses, and had traveled all around the world?

Action Step:
Watch the video "What if money was no object?" (3:04) on YouTube.

34
TAKE A WALK EVERY DAY

"An early-morning walk is a blessing for the whole day."
Henry David Thoreau

Whenever possible, go out and spend time around nature. Take a walk and connect with it. Watch a sunset or a sunrise. If you are going for a run or a walk in the mornings you'll surely say that Henry David Thoreau is right!

Our rhythm of life has become so fast and so stressful that taking some time and walking through the woods can bring you down to earth and provide you with deep relaxation. Listen to the silence and enjoy it. Taking a walk is a great way to reenergize your body and your mind.

A new Stanford study that just came out concludes that walking improves your creative thinking. When a friend's wife had a hard time at work and was on the edge of burning out she started taking long walks for an hour and a half each day. That helped her to disconnect from her stressful workday, forget her anger of the day, and talk about and analyze her emotions. Due to this activity she also fell asleep easier and had a better and more refreshing sleep at night. After only a week she felt a lot better! Another advantage of the long walks what that she got tired, lowered her guard, and even started listening to what her husband had to say …

When will you start walking one hour per day? Do it for 30 days and let me know how it feels!

35
WHAT ARE YOUR STANDARDS?

"I teach people how to treat me by what I will allow."

Stephen Covey

Expect and demand more from yourself and from those around you. If you really want to make a change in your life you have to raise your standards. Have a zero tolerance policy for mediocrity, procrastination, and behavior that impedes your best performance!

Your standards could be, for example, to always tell the truth, to always be punctual, to really listen to people until they are finished, and so on. Hold yourself to high standards and - what is of the same or even more importance - set boundaries for those around you!

Boundaries are things that people simply can't do to you like yelling at you, make stupid jokes around you, or disrespect you. Communicate clearly and make it a habit to address anything that bothers you on the spot. Remember what the proverb says: "In the right tone you can say everything, in the wrong tone nothing, the art is to find the right tone". Practice saying things in a neutral tone of voice like you'd say "the sun is shining".

If somebody is overstepping your boundaries **inform** them: "I didn't like that comment" or "I don't like you talking to me in that tone". If they go on, **request** them to stop: "I ask you to stop talking to me like this". By now most people should get it, but there are always one or two that continue. If that happens - **insist**: "I insist that you stop talking to me in that way." If all three steps don't help – **leave!** Walk away neutrally stating "I can't have this conversation, while you are _____. Let's talk later."

Action Steps:
Write down the following things:
1. Things you will no longer accept in your life.
2. All the behaviors you will no longer tolerate from others.
3. All the things you want to become.

36
ADAPT AN ATTITUDE OF GRATITUDE!

"Be thankful for what you have; you'll end up having more. If you concentrate on what you don't have, you will never, ever have enough."

Oprah Winfrey

Listen to Oprah! Be grateful for what you have every day and you will attract more things to be grateful for. Gratitude recharges you with energy and boosts your self-worth. It's directly linked to physical and mental well-being.

The "attitude of gratitude" leads you directly to happiness and is the best antidote to anger, envy, and resentment! Let it become part of your nature! **Be grateful for what you have, for all the small things around you, and even for the things you don't have yet!**

Don't say: **"I'll be grateful when…"** like I did for many years. Take the shortcut: Be grateful NOW - no matter what - and make gratitude a daily habit: Start the day by saying thank you for what you have (instead of complaining about what you don't have). This will have an immediate effect on your life. Focus on the good things that you can find every day. The following exercises are part of every one of my coaching processes. Do them and observe what happens.

Action Steps:
1) Make a list of everything you have in your life that you are grateful for. Write down everything you can think of. (This should be a long list)

2) For 21 days every day write 3 to 5 things that you are grateful for, that day in your journal. Before going to sleep relive the moments. Relive the happiness.

37
THE MAGIC OF VISUALIZATION

"The best way to predict the future is to create it."

Peter Drucker

Visualization is a fundamental resource in building experiences. The subconscious part of your brain cannot distinguish between a well done visualization and reality. This means that if you visualize your goals with a lot of emotion and in great detail, your subconscious mind will be convinced that it's really happening. You will then be provided with motivation, opportunities, and ideas that will help you to transform your life into that desired state. What am I saying? Can you practice sports by pure visualization?

Well actually you can. There are various studies that confirm the power of visualization. As early as in the 80's, Tony Robbins worked with the U.S. Army and used visualization techniques to dramatically increase pistol shooting performance. There have also been other studies done for improving free throw shooting percentages of Basketball players using the same techniques. The results were amazing! If you look closely at athletes they all visualize their races and matches.

Look at how skiers, formula 1 drivers, golfers, tennis players, and even soccer players visualize in-game situations, days and hours before the actual match. Jack Nicklaus, Wayne Gretzky, and Greg Louganis - to name a few - are known to have achieved their goals with visualization.

In coaching we use visualization techniques with goals. See yourself as already having achieved the goal. See it through your own eyes and put all your senses in it: smell it, hear it, feel it, taste it. The more emotions you put into it, the more of an impact it will have. If you do this for 15 minutes every day over time you will see enormous results. Make time for you daily visualization either in your morning ritual or in the evening before going to bed.

It can be helpful to make a collage of images that represent your goal on a A3 sheet of cardboard and put it up in your bedroom or somewhere where you can see it. Buy some journals and cut out the photos that represent your goals. You could also create a screensaver of various photos on your computer or desktop.

If your goal is wealth, put a photo of you dream house, a photo of dollar bills, or whatever wealth means to you. If you search for "vision board" on Google, you will surely find lots of examples. Look at your collage every day 5 minutes after getting up and 5 minutes before going to bed and imagine yourself vividly with your goal already accomplished.

38
WHAT IF?

"Our expectancies not only affect how we see reality but also affect the reality itself."

Dr. Edward E. Jones

Always expect the best! Life doesn't always give you what you want, but it sure gives you what you expect! Do you expect success? Or do you spend most of your time worrying about failure? Our expectations about ourselves and others come from our subconscious beliefs and they have an enormous impact on our achievements. Your expectations influence your attitude and your attitude has a lot to do with your success.

Your expectations also affect your willingness to take action and all your interactions with others. Many of us know all this and yet most of us expect negative outcomes when asking one of the favorite questions of the mind: the question "What if". By asking it, we are often focused on what doesn't work: "What if it doesn't work out?", "What if she doesn't go out with me?", "What if I don't get the job?", "What if I don't get the raise?", "What if I lose my job?" However neither does that feel good, nor is it good to focus on what we fear.

Why not turn this around and ask yourself for every limiting or negative thought, "What if the opposite is true"?, "What if it worked out great?", "What if she says yes?", "What if I get a raise?", "What if I become a millionaire with this idea?", "What if I found resources?", "What if I can make it happen?", "What if now is the time?", "What if this little book helps me change my life for real?"

The single adjustment in how you ask a question transforms you, your energy, and the answer you get. It changes your thinking and your inner dialogue. Suddenly you start asking what if up questions in your head, rather than what if down questions.

The benefits of shifting your thinking will be:
- Less stress, fear, and anxiety.
- You will feel more peaceful.
- Your energy level will go up.
- It allows you to be the inventor of your own experience.

Try it out! How did you feel just now reading it? Write a list of all your fears and negative "What ifs" and then turn it around.

39
LET GO OF THE PAST

"We must be willing to let go of the life we've planned, so as to have the life that is waiting for us."

Joseph Campbell

"When I let go of what I am, I become what I might be. When I let go of what I have, I receive what I need."

Tao Te Ching

Every moment you spend in your past is a moment you steal from your present and future. Stop reliving your drama– Don't hang onto it. **LET GO OF IT!** Only if you have the courage to let go of the old, can you be open to new things entering your life.

Don't waste your time thinking of things that could or should have happened or that didn't work out as you wanted in the past. It doesn't make sense! You can't change it! Remember **to focus on what you want, not what you don't want.** If you focus on situations that didn't work out in the past, you might attract more of these situations. **Learn from your past experiences and move on.** That's all you have to do from now on. Easy, isn't it? Concentrate on what you want to do well in the future and not what went wrong in the past. You need to let go of the past so that you are free and new things can come into your life! Let go of old baggage, finish unfinished business, and get closure with people. Deepak Chopra is right when he says **"I use memories, but I will not allow memories to use me."** Complete the past so that you can be free to enjoy the present.

From now on, adopt the mindset that you will always finish your business. Don't leave anything incomplete in your relationships, work, and all other areas. Keep moving forward.

Action Step:

What is incomplete in your life? Make a list and work on it!

40
CELEBRATE YOUR WINS!

"Celebrate what you want to see more of."

Thomas Peters

On your way forward to changing your life and reaching your goals it's also important to be aware of your progress! Stop every now and then and celebrate your wins! **Celebrate that you are better than you were last week! Don't let your small victories go unnoticed!**

During the work with my clients, one of their consistent tasks is to celebrate their small wins. Every action step completed is worth celebrating. **For every exercise in this book that you complete, reward yourself:** buy yourself something you always wanted, go to the movies, do whatever feels good for you.

If you learnt new habits and see great improvement, go on a short trip! You earned it! What will you reward yourself with for your progress so far? Will you have a spa day or a nice dinner? Will you go for a walk?

1._____
2._____
3._____
4._____
5._____

41
BE HAPPY NOW!

"Happiness is the meaning and purpose of life"
Aristotle

Happiness is a journey, not a destination! Happiness is also a choice! It is an inner state, not an external state. Happiness is a habit, a state of mind. Happiness is so many things!

But the decisive and most important thing is: What is happiness to YOU? You can be happy right now! You don't believe me? Okay. Close your eyes for a moment. Think of a situation that made you really, really happy. Relive this situation in your mind. Feel it, smell it, hear it! Remember the excitement and joy! And? How did it feel? Did it work? How are you feeling now? Happiness doesn't depend on your car, your house, or anything in the outside world. You can be happy right here, right now!

Don't miss out on the small pleasures of life, while you go after the big ones. Enjoy the beauty around you! Enjoy the small things! Don't postpone life until you win the lottery or retire. Do the fun things now with what you have. Live each day fully as if it were your last! Start by being happy now. Smile as much as you can - even if you are not in the mood, because by smiling you're sending positive signals to your brain. Fun and humor are essential for a good, long life, job satisfaction, personal fulfillment, personal relationships, and life balance. So laugh lots and have lots of fun! Which of these reasons do YOU have right now for being happy?

- You have a great job.
- You love your work.
- You have great kids.
- You have a great partner.
- You have great parents.
- You are free.
- ...

Questions

What is happiness for you? (Be specific.)

How many smiles have you gifted last week?

How many smiles have you received?

Action Steps:

Remember the moments that made you the most happy in your life. Write down at least five moments that made you feel exceptionally great:
1._____
2._____
3._____
4._____
5._____

Re-live these moments with all their emotions and happiness. How does it feel?

42
MULTITASKING IS A LIE!

"Most of the time multitasking is an illusion. You think you are multitasking, but in -reality you're actually wasting time switching from one task to another."
Bosco Tjan

DO one thing at a time! The newest studies show that multitasking is actually less productive than doing one thing at a time with a concentrated effort.
Some studies even imply that it makes you slower and - careful now -dumber!

Even if you think you are multitasking you are actually doing one thing at a time, aren't you? You might have five tasks on your hands, but I'm sure you don't do all five things at the same time. You are writing an e-mail. You stop writing it and take a phone call. You hang up and continue writing the e-mail. A colleague comes to you with a question. You stop writing your e-mail and answer the question and so on. So forget about multitasking. **Focus on doing one thing at a time and do it with concentration!**

43
SIMPLIFY YOUR LIFE

"Life is really simple, but we insist on making it complicated."
Confucius

"The key is not to prioritize what's on your schedule, but to schedule your priorities."
Stephen Covey

If you started applying some of the things that you have learnt until now in this book your life should already be a little simpler. Did you unclutter? Clean out your cupboard? Get rid of some toleration? Did you get rid of some of the people that drag you down? It was Stephen Covey who said that "most of us spend too much time on what is urgent and not enough time on what is important."

Do you know your priorities or are you just floating around handling whatever comes up, extinguishing fires all the time? Maybe it's time to make some time for the really important stuff in your life. **A huge step towards simplifying your life is to concentrate on the important, on the activities that make sense for you, and find a way to eliminate or downsize the other activities.** This can be done by automating, delegating, eliminating, or hiring help. **If you want to do everything, in the end you'll get nothing done.**

Is your schedule too busy? Do you have too many commitments? Simplifying is about downsizing your life and learning to live with less. What **can you downsize?** Do you own too many clothes and items? Are you spending too much time cooking? Why not get help or just prepare simpler meals? Which of the family can support you?

Can you simplify your financial life by online banking? Why not pay everything in cash and buy only things you really need? What about you online life? Do you spend too much time on social media or instant messaging?

Then it might be time to get a little bit more disciplined. Set fixed times for when you are online and stick to them! Put a timer if necessary. Unclutter the desktop on your PC and your e-mail inbox.

My client Marc did this and virtual uncluttering had the same effect on him as physical uncluttering. He let go of a big weight that he was carrying around and hence got a lot more energy. Check your e-mails only at certain times during the day and turn off the tone of e-mail and text delivery so that you are not distracted all the time. Now is also a good time to unsubscribe from journals that are just piling up and that you never read, and to ask yourself if you really need to read three different newspapers every day. Are you commuting to work? Maybe you can ask your boss to work from home once or twice a week. Are you working too many hours?

See if the chapters on time management and getting organized in this book can help you to reduce your working time and find more time to do the things you love. And do yourself a favor: Don't bring your work home -not physically and not even mentally. If you didn't get it done at work, examine your working habits and change them if possible. This is extremely important. **Stop thinking about work when you are home. Worrying about something that can't be changed at the moment is wasted energy.** Think about what you can do about it tomorrow at work and forget about it for now.

Questions:
1) Where do you see the excess in your life?
2) Do you have too many things you don't need or use?
3) Is your schedule always booked?
4) Do you have time in your schedule for yourself and the things you enjoy doing?
5) What are the most important tasks in your day-to-day life (home and/or work)?
6) Which of the these tasks can be easily delegated, automated, or eliminated?

44
SMILE MORE!

"Sometimes your joy is the source of your smile, but sometimes your smile can be the source of your joy."
Thích Nhât Hanh

Smile! Even if you don't feel like it! Smiling improves the quality of your life, health, and relationships. If you don't do it already, start to smile consciously today. Although I can't confirm the study that is cited in many self-help books and blogs that 4 to 6-years old children laugh 300-400 times a day and adults only 15, it might well be true. Just take our personal experiences with kids and honestly it fits very well with the results of the study.

What is confirmed is that laughing and smiling is extremely good for your health! Science has demonstrated that laughing or smiling a lot daily improves your mental state and your creativity. So laugh more!! Make it a point to watch at least 1 hour of comedy or fun stuff a day and laugh until tears roll down your cheeks. You'll feel a lot better and full of energy once you starte this habit!

A study by Tara Kraft and Sarah Pressman at the University of Kansas demonstrated that smiling can alter your stress response in difficult situations. The study showed that it can slow your heart rate down and decrease stress levels – even if you are not feeling happy. Smiling sends a signal to your brain that things are all right. See also Chapter 60 "Fake it till you make it" and Chapter 61 "Change your Posture". Just try it next time you feel stressed or overwhelmed, and let me know if it works. If you think you have no reason at all to smile, hold a pen or a chopstick with your teeth. It simulates a smile and might produce the same effects. If you need even more incentives for smiling, search for the study by Wayne University on smiling which has found a link between smiling and longevity!

When you smile your entire body sends out the message "Life is great" to the world. Studies show that smiling people are perceived as more confident and more likely to be trusted.

People just feel good around them. Further benefits of smiling are:
- Releases serotonin (makes us feel good).
- Releases endorphins (lowers pain).
- Lowers blood pressure.
- Increases clarity.
- Boosts the functioning of your immune system.
- Provides a more positive outlook on life (Try being a pessimist while you smile…).

Exercise:

For the next seven days stand in front of a mirror and smile to yourself for one minute. Do this at least three times a day and observe how you feel.

45
START POWER NAPPING

"When you can't figure out what to do, it's time for a nap."
Mason Cooley

One of my absolute favorites. And at the same time, it's scientifically proven that a power nap at midday reenergizes, refreshes, and increases productivity. For me it was an absolute eye opener.

During my most stressful period at work - when I was close to burning out, because the stress, and client threats and complaints were getting unbearable (sometimes I thought we were doing emergency surgery, yet we were just producing books.) - I started taking a power nap and the change was extraordinary. I was far less stressed and a lot calmer while hearing complaints and finding solutions. For a while, I slept for 25 to 30 minutes on a bench in a park close by, and later I just put two chairs together in the office and slept there.

It felt as if my working day suddenly had two halves and midday was halftime. I started the "second half" always fresh and I also performed a lot more productively because the typical tiredness after lunch between 2 and 5 p.m. was gone. **Are you going to try power napping? When will you start?**

46
READ FOR HALF AN HOUR EACH DAY

"The man who doesn't read has no advantage over the man that can't read."
Mark Twain

"The man who doesn't read has no advantage over the man that can't read" says Mark Twain. If you read for half an hour a day that's three and a half hours a week and 182 hours a year! That's a lot of knowledge at your disposal. One of my first written goals during my coaching training was "to read more"(not very specific, but it worked). That was at a time that I hadn't read a book for years.

Now I'm devouring an average of two books a week. I studied more in the last 6 months that in the whole 15 years before - including my International Business studies. So always **have a book with you.** If you substitute the habit of watching TV - or even worse - the news by reading a good book just before going to bed, you will derive the additional benefit of peace of mind.

Another side effect is that you increase your creativity. So what are you waiting for? Make a list of 6 books that you will read in the next three months! If you don't know what to read check out my webpage for recommendations. **But make that list NOW!**

47
START SAVING

"Personally, I tend to worry about what I save, not what I spend."
Paul Clitheroe

This one is taught by all the wealth gurus. I read it the first time many years ago while reading Talane Miedaner's book "Coach yourself to success". This single advice changed really everything for me and was the basis for leaving my job and following my dream many years later.

Once you have saved enough living expenses for nine months to one year, things start changing. This is a huge advantage. For example, you stop depending of your boss's mood. You can stand up for yourself and say: "If you have problems with my work just tell me". If at your current job people are not respecting your boundaries or even harassing you, in the worst case you can even quit your job and find another one.

Or take a sabbatical. Furthermore you are not desperate when you're going to job interviews because you don't need the new job that badly. As a coach, for me it was and still is important to always have a reserve, so that I have the freedom to work only with my ideal clients and can afford to say "No" to clients that aren't a fit (which a coach should do anyway, because coaching only works if the "chemistry" is right).

Working out of a need for money surely wouldn't bring as good results. Having a reserve of 9, 12, or even 18 months salaries (the more the better!) saved up just takes a lot of stress off and makes you feel a lot more secure and gives you peace of mind. To start saving you have to spend less or earn more. Most of the time it's easier to cut down your spending and take a look at where your money is going.

The best way is to automatically deduct the sum from your account at the beginning of the month and put it into a savings account.

Questions:

Will you give it a shot?
What's your excuse not to start saving?
When will you start saving?

48
FORGIVE EVERYBODY WHO HAS WRONGED YOU (…AND MOST OF ALL YOURSELF)

"The weak can never forgive. Forgiveness is the attribute of the strong."
Mahatma Gandhi

"People can be more forgiving than you can imagine. But you have to forgive yourself. Let go of what's bitter and move on."
Bill Cosby

Forgiveness is crucial along your way towards success, fulfillment and happiness! Personally I needed a long, long time to learn this! Why forgive someone if the person did me wrong and it's only their fault? **The short answer: It's a selfish act!** You're doing it for yourself, not for the other person! This is not about being right or wrong!

This is about you being well and not losing a lot of energy! Anger and resentment and - even worse - reliving hate over and over again are huge energy drains! Who has sleepless nights? Who is full of anger and doesn't enjoy the present moment? You or the person you're not forgiving? Do yourself a favor and let go!

When a journalist asked the Dalai Lama whether he is angry at the Chinese for occupying his country, he answered: "Not at all. I send them love and forgiveness. It's of no benefit at all to be angry at them. It will not change them, but I could get an ulcer from my anger and that would actually benefit THEM." Adapt the attitude of the Dalai Lama toward the people who have done you wrong and see what happens. Let go, forgive the people that hurt you, forget them and move on.

But be careful. **If you say "I forgive them, but I don't forget" you are not forgiving!**

This doesn't mean you can't put limits on others' behavior or call them out on the spot. But afterwards understand the consequences and let go. Call up people that you have wronged or hurt, and apologize, and if that's too uncomfortable write them a letter.

Above all: forgive yourself! When you learn to forgive yourself it will be easier to forgive others. Just do it! The changes you will see when you manage to forgive others and above all yourself are amazing!

Action Steps:

1. Make a list of everybody that you haven't forgiven.
2. Make a list of everything that you haven't forgiven yourself for.
3. Work on the list.

Questions:

What would your life be like if you accepted yourself just as you are without self-criticism?
What would your life be like if you forgave yourself and others?

49
ARRIVE TEN MINUTES EARLY

"The while we keep a man waiting, he reflects on our shortcomings."
French Proverb

Punctuality is a sign of discipline and respect for others. Without it, you might come across as slightly offensive, even if you are the nicest person in the world. Of course there are cultural differences. For example, while in Mexico and Spain people are very relaxed about punctuality, in Germany not being punctual is seen as highly unprofessional and might ruin your chances in any endeavor.

Here is another great tip from Talane Miedaner's book, "Coach yourself to success" which I have made into a habit: being 10 minutes early to every appointment - not to be especially polite, but instead for myself. This is because when I started being punctual I noticed that those ten minutes made me feel a lot better and gave me a lot of peace of mind.

When I arrived at a place, it wasn't in a rush and I actually had ten minutes to compose my thoughts and get used to the environment, and instead of feeling rushed I felt very relaxed. I also feel very comfortable, professional, and polite when I arrive 10 minutes early. In fact I now feel uncomfortable when I arrive just on time. **Try it and see for yourself if it adds to your life or not!**

50
SPEAK LESS, LISTEN MORE!

"When people talk, listen completely. Most people never listen."
Ernest Hemingway

One of the most important tools of a coach and also one of the most important lesson from my coaching training is the ability and skill of "active listening" or listening profoundly.

Listening profoundly means to listen to the person in front of you while giving your full attention. It means to quiet down the little voice in your head that comes up with advice and a solution thirty seconds after the person starts speaking.

Many people are not listening to understand, but to answer! They are just waiting for their counterpart to pause so that they can begin to speak. **If you are rehearsing what you are going to say next you are not listening!** Don't interrupt. Listen until the person is finished. If you want to give advice, ask for permission. Most of the time the person who is speaking will come up with the solution - if you let her or him finish.

Try it out! You might take your conversations and relationships to a completely new level when, people feel that they are listened to by you. Be a good listener!

51
BE THE CHANGE YOU WANT TO SEE IN THE WORLD!

"Be the change you want to see in the world"
Mahatma Gandhi

Are you trying to change other people? I've got news for you: You can stop right NOW. It's impossible! You can't help people who don't want to get help and you just can't change other people. So stop wasting precious energy and start concentrating on what you can do. And that is being an example!

Be the change you want to see in the world! Have you heard about the idea that other people are like mirrors of us? That means that things we don't like about them, are often things we have to work on ourselves and/or balance them out. When I was "stuck" I always got mad at the lack of manners in young people who didn't offer their seats to elderly people on the train.

Whenever I observed this, I used to start a negative inner dialogue about "where the world is going, this can't be, young people have no manners, why should I get up, I'm 40 years old, blah blah." Until one day I stopped complaining about the young people and offered my seat. Man, that felt good!

I'm not responsible for other people's behavior. I'm only responsible for my own behavior. So by being an example I win twice: Once by not having this inner nagging dialogue and secondly, because I feel like I did something right and that feels so good! And maybe I even served as an example to somebody else to offer his or her seat the next time.

One of the greatest insights that my clients have is when they shift from "others have to change" to "what if I change, maybe then the other also changes". You can literally see the light bulb going on over their heads. You cannot change others. The only thing you can to do is accept them as they are and be the best example and person that you can be.

Are you complaining about your partner, colleagues, or spouse? Be the best colleague or spouse possible!

Are you complaining about your employees? Be the best boss possible! Do you want to be loved just as you are? Start with loving other people just the way they are.

Questions:

What do you want to change?
Why not start with yourself?
What will you do differently?

52
STOP TRYING AND START DOING!

"Try not. Do or do not. There is no try."
Master Yoda, Star Wars

You can do yourself a huge favor if you stop using the word "try". Throw it out of your vocabulary! **Trying implies failure.** What would you rather have a person say to you if you put them in charge of a task: "I'll try to get it done" or "I'll get right on it"? **Do or do not!**

When I was at the beginning of my coaching career I found out quick that those of my clients, who tried to do their homework, usually didn't do it. Those who tried to find more time, didn't find it. Those who tried to exercise three times a week didn't do it.

From then on when someone said to me "I'll try", I asked them "Will you do it or won't you?" **There is no try!** It's as Nike says, "Just do it!" If you do it and it works…great! Well done! If you do it and it doesn't work. Ok. Let's have a look at it. What went wrong? Did you learn something from the experience? What can you change to get the result you want? Go again!

Just trying doesn't take you anywhere. I'm in line with Master Yoda: Do or do not!

53
THE POWER OF AFFIRMATIONS

"Here is a most significant fact—the subconscious mind takes any orders given it in a spirit of absolute FAITH, and acts upon those orders, although the orders often have to be presented over and over again, through repetition, before they are interpreted by the subconscious mind."

Napoleon Hill, Think and Grow Rich

We already talked about the importance of positive self-talk. One very good technique is using Affirmations. By repeating positive statements many times a day you convince your subconscious mind to believe them. And once your subconscious mind is convinced, you start acting accordingly and "attract" circumstances into your life and see opportunities everywhere. It's important to state them positively and in the present so that your subconscious mind can't differentiate between if it's already true or "only" imagined.

Affirmations do have to be personal, positively stated, specific, emotionally charged, and in the present tense. Here are some examples:

- Money comes to me easily and effortlessly.
- Opportunities come into my life right now.
- Speaking in front of a large audience is easy for me.
- I am successful in my business.
- I am healthy and fit.

Use affirmations to attract the things you want in your life. The more you practice, the better you get. The first time you say, "Money comes to me easily and effortlessly", your inner voice will still say, "Yeah right! No way!". However after repeating it 200 times every day for a week you should have silenced your inner critical voice. Make your affirmations your permanent company.

Repeat them as often as you like and have a look at what happens in your life. Nevertheless, there are some studies that claim that affirmations actually have negative effects, when your inner critic just doesn't get convinced. If you can see no benefit at all, try other techniques like subliminal tapes or ask yourself other questions such as, "Why am I so happy? Why is everything working out?"

Noah St. John has written a whole book on the power of asking yourself the right questions. His "Book of Affirmations" might be able to help you!

54
WRITE IT DOWN 25 TIMES A DAY

"It's the repetition of affirmations that lead to belief. And once that belief becomes a deep conviction, things begin to happen."

Muhammad Ali

The purpose of this exercise is to help you to "hammer" your desires into your subconscious mind until you actually believe it's true! Remember how your subconscious mind works. To create a new belief in your belief-system you have to repeat over and over again. Even if this exercise gets boring, go on writing! So how does it work?

1) Pick your statement.
2) Make it personal, start with "I am".
3) Make the statement positive.
4) Use present tense. For example, "I am earning X thousand Euros/Dollars a year."
5) Do this exercise first thing in the morning.

It's good to get a small booklet for it. You can enhance your results by doing the exercise twice a day: in the morning and just before going to sleep.

55
STOP MAKING EXCUSES.

"The only thing standing between you and your goal is the bullshit story you keep telling yourself as to why you can't achieve it."
Jordan Belfort

What happens when you start stepping out of your comfort zone? Due to fears and doubts, your mind comes up with the greatest excuses: "it's not the right moment", "I'm too young", "I'm too old", "it's impossible", "I can't", and my favorite one, "I have no money". Guess what people with money say: "I have no time".

"Yes, but my case is different", you might say. No, it's not! Believe me. The right moment never comes, so you might as well start here and now or wait forever. A crisis is always an opportunity. You're neither too young nor too old. Do a search on the Internet. It's full of stories of people who fulfill their dreams at an older age or start an enterprise at a young age.

No money? Or just spending it in the wrong places by buying a new TV or video game console instead of investing it in your training? The funny thing is people who work with a serious financial advisor or financial coach suddenly find money! In the same way as all of my clients who thought they didn't have time found time. "Yes, but my case is different!" Well, you can keep telling that to yourself for some more time or you get rid of the excuses once and for all and start taking action, because one thing is for sure: If you keep doing what you are doing you will keep getting what you are getting! So what is it going to be?

Questions:

What are you going to choose from now on? Excuses or focused action?

What are the excuses you are using to not change and stay in the same place?

56
KEEP EXPECTATIONS LOW AND THEN SHINE

"Always deliver more than expected."
Larry Page

This is another biggie and probably the best time management trick I ever learnt. It changed my professional and private life in an extraordinary manner and reduced stress at work to virtually zero! Most of my stress at work came from deadlines and I - or we as an enterprise were always struggling, which made days when our products were shipped to the clients - which was every day in high season - horrible and very stressful.

We were always just in time or sometimes maybe a couple of hours late and I had to calm down angry and sometimes hysterical clients…until I started to under-promise: I figured out that over 90% of our late deliveries were just a question of a couple of hours, so I got the permission of my boss and started my own delivery schedule that only I received access to. If production gave me a delivery date of April 5th, I told the client April 10th. So if we delivered on April 7th, instead of an angry client threatening to fine or sue us, I suddenly had extremely grateful clients that thanked me for delivering three days early.

Within a short time we reduced late deliveries from nearly 50% to virtually 0% over the next three years. As it worked out so well I started applying it to my whole life. When my boss gave me a project that took me 3 days, I told her I was going to need 5 days. If I had it completed after four days I looked great and if I took a little longer I
was still on time – and without weekends at the office. If I knew I had to stay at work longer I told my partner I'll be home at 9 p.m. Coming home at 8:30 p.m. I looked like a hero.

57
DESIGN YOUR IDEAL DAY

"I'll see it when I believe it!"
Dr. Wayne W. Dyer

This is the favorite exercise of many coaches and the starting point for many coaching processes. **Design your ideal day!** What **would you like your ideal life to be? What would you do if you had all the time and money in the world? Where would you live? Would you have a house or an apartment? What's your job? Who are you with? What are you doing?** It's time to dream big again! Don't limit yourself. Imagine your ideal life vividly! How does it feel?

Write it down in detail! By now you have learnt about the power of writing things down! **Write down exactly how you would like your ideal life to be.** Have a special notebook or scrapbook for your ideal day/life creation. Many people even make a collage with photos that represent their dreams or ideals and put it up somewhere where they can see it daily. Very important: Make it FUN! It's very important to create this vision and have it in mind. So let's start:

1) No distractions. Sit down for an hour. Turn off everything. No cell phone, no radio, no TV.
2) Make it come alive! Describe everything. What time do you wake up? What kind of home do you live in? How's your health? Who is surrounding you? What's your job? Remember there are NO LIMITS!
3) Once a week, read your ideal day out with enthusiasm. Put a lot of emotion in it!

Optional:
You can also tape record yourself reading out your ideal day with emotion and listen to it every night before going to bed.

Are you ready? Start writing out your ideal day right now!

58
ACCEPT YOUR EMOTIONS

"Your intellect may be confused, but your emotions will never lie to you."
Roger Ebert

Who is responsible of how you feel? YOU! Do you remember what we said about responsibility and choices? Do you remember that you are in control of your thoughts? Well, your emotions come from your thoughts. How? An emotion is energy in motion, a physical reaction to a thought. If you can control your thoughts, you are also capable of controlling your emotions. Don't be scared by them! Your emotions are part of you but they are not YOU. Accept them.

Every emotion has its function. Fear protects you. Anger allows you to defend yourself, put limits on, and show others what bothers you. Sadness allows you to mourn and identify a lack. Happiness allows you to feel great, etc. It's very important to be connected to your emotions and know how to express them and not to neglect them. **Don't fool yourself and say "I'm happy" if you're not.** Instead analyze where the emotion comes from. Don't identify yourself with the emotion. I repeat, you are not your emotions!

Become an observer and watch where your emotions lead you. Observe them and watch them pass by like the clouds on a blue sky. Accept them like you accept rainy days. When you look out of the window and it rains you don't think that it will rain all the time now, do you? You accept the rain as part of the meteorological climate – that doesn't mean that it rains all the time.

You can do the same thing with anger, sadness, fear, etc. Just because they show up at one moment in time doesn't mean that they will be there forever. **It helps to know that emotions are not bad or good. They just are.** If you want to write something to get them out of your system – do it. They will pass.

Emotions are messengers that we feel in our body. Listen to them! If you are hooked to an emotion, you are hooked to the past and you are losing the present moment. What is it you really need? Stop searching outside and start searching inside of you.

MANAGING EMOTIONS
It's the skill to perceive, use, understand, and manage emotions. You can use this on yourself or on others:

1) Perceive and express emotions (Permit yourself to feel it).
2) Facilitation of feelings (How can I feel a different emotion).
3) Understanding (Why is this emotion coming up).
4) Emotional adjustment (Now I know why the emotion was felt...).

Once again, everything is a question of attitude (acceptance or refusal). **YOU CHOOSE!**

Advantages of managing of emotions:
- You recover better and faster from problems and setbacks.
- You achieve better and consistent professional performance.
- You are able to prevent those tensions from building up that destroy your relationships.
- You govern your impulses and conflicting emotions.
- You stay balanced and serene even in critical moments.

The first step towards get there is to **identify** your emotions and to **explore** them, which means to **permit their expression** and then **analyze** the problem that provoked them. Connect and talk to the emotion: breathe, relax, and relive the situation.

Questions:

1) Can you spot a "negative" emotion?
2) What symptoms do you feel and in what part of your body?
3) How do you feel? Be precise!

59
DO IT NOW!

"You cannot escape the responsibility of tomorrow by evading it today."
Abraham Lincoln

"Only put off until tomorrow what you are willing to die having left undone."
Pablo Picasso

Listen to Dr. Wayne W. Dyer when he says "Go for it now. The future is promised to no one." That unwritten e-mail, the old friend you want to reconnect with, the time you want to spend with your family: don't put it off any more. Do yourself a favor and stop the procrastination. It only causes anxiety! And most of the time you will find that things that you procrastinated for days causing you anxiety and a bad conscience are actually done in an hour or so and afterwards you feel so much lighter because you can forget about it.

Procrastinating is avoiding something that should be done. It's putting things off hoping that they magically get better without actually doing anything about them. But things don't get better on their own. Most of the time, the cause of procrastination is some kind of fear. Fear of rejection, fear of failure, even fear of success. Another cause is feeling overwhelmed.

We procrastinate in three different ways:

1) Doing nothing instead of what we are supposed to do.
2) Doing something less important than what we should be doing.
3) Doing something more important that what we are supposed to do.

As a freelancer and owner of his time, my client Marc struggled with procrastination a lot. It caused him a lot of anxiety and even cost him some sleepless nights. It was always the same pattern.

He procrastinated and felt burdened and anxious. In our coaching sessions he admitted that some of the stuff that causes this anxiety, he could actually finish in one hour! He became aware that he was paying a high price for procrastinating, and in the future when tempted to procrastinate he decided to ask himself: what price will I be paying for procrastinating this task? Is it worth it to be burdened by and lose my sleep over a task that I could have finished in one or two hours?

So do whatever it is that you have on your mind right now. **Don't start tomorrow or next week! Start NOW!**

Questions:

What are you procrastinating?

Are you productive or are you just being busy?

What is really important right now?

60
FAKE IT TILL YOU MAKE IT!

"If you want a quality, act as if you already have it."
William James

Act as if! Act as if you have already achieved your goal. Act as if you already have the quality of life, the lifestyle, the job etc. If you want to have more self-confidence act as if you already have it. Speak like a self-confident person, walk like a self-confident person, have the body posture of a self-confident person. (See Chapter 61).

Your subconscious can't differentiate between reality and imagination. Use this to your advantage by acting "as if" you already have a strength, a character trait, etc. In Neuro-linguistic Programming and coaching, this is called modeling.

A good way to become successful is to observe and copy already successful people. Use this for any character trait you want. Start acting "as if" and see what happens. Fake it till you make it!

Questions:

Which quality do you want?

How would you act if you already had that quality?

How would you speak, walk, behave, etc.?

61
CHANGE YOUR POSTURE

"Act the way you'd like to be and soon you'll be the way you'd like to act."
Bob Dylan

This is an exercise taken from Neuro-linguistic Programming which proclaims that changing your posture also changes your mind. People I tell this to usually think that I'm joking. But before writing this off as nonsense... try it out!

When you feel sad and depressed you usually look at the floor, keep your shoulders down, and adapt the posture of a sad person, right? Now try the following just for a moment: stand upright, shoulders up, chest out, and hold your head up high - you can even exaggerate it by looking up. How does it feel? If you smile, laugh and walk with your head held high, you will realize that you feel a lot better. It's impossible to feel sad walking around like that, isn't it?

And there has been more research conducted on this subject. A study by Brion, Petty, and Wagner in 2009 found that people who were sitting straight had higher self-confidence than people sitting slumped over!

There is also an amazing TED Talk by Amy Cuddy called "Your body language shapes who you are" about the research she did together with Dana Carney at Harvard University. The study has shown that holding "power postures" for 2 minutes creates a 20 percent increase in testosterone (which boosts confidence) and a 25 percent decrease in cortisol (which reduces stress). Imagine this. If you have an important presentation, reunion, or competition, just take on the posture of a confident person for two minutes. Put your hands on your hips and spread your feet (think wonder woman) or lean back in a chair and spread your arms. Hold the posture for at least two minutes...and see what happens!

Action Step:

Watch Amy Cuddy's TED-Talk "Your body language shapes who you are"!

62
ASK FOR WHAT YOU REALLY WANT

"Ask and you shall receive"
Matthew, 7, 7

Just ask! It's far better to ask and get rejected that to not ask and go along with the thought "if I had only asked". Ask for a better table in the restaurant, ask for the upgrade at the airport, and ask for the salary raise you have been waiting for. ASK! You already have the "No" for an answer, but maybe you will see some surprises. If you ask you at least have the opportunity to get what you want.

Ask your loved one for what you want. Your boss, your friends. **Don't expect them to read your mind!** Think about it! Aren't many things that hurt us based on the too high expectations that we had? This happened to me mostly in my romantic relationships. I was disappointed many times because my loved one just wasn't able to read my mind. That is, until I said, "That's it" and finally started asking for what I wanted.

Another example is our boss! We are putting in so much work and are waiting for this raise or promotion to come, but it doesn't come! Ask for it! What's the worst thing that could happen? You already don't have it. You already haven't gotten the raise or the promotion! If you don't ask it will probably stay like this. If you ask you will at least get an answer and know where you are at.

When you ask keep the following things in mind:
1) Ask with the expectation to receive.
2) Know that you can receive it.
3) Remember to keep your thoughts, feelings, and inner dialogue positive.
4) Ask the person who is in charge.
5) Be specific.
6) Ask repeatedly like you did when you were a kid.

Action Steps:

1) Write a list of all of the things that you want and don't ask for.
2) Start asking. Work on it.

63
LISTEN TO YOUR INNER VOICE

*"The intuitive mind is a sacred gift
and the rational mind is a faithful servant.
We have created a society that honors the servant
and has forgotten the gift."*
Albert Einstein

Albert Einstein already knew about the great gift our intuition can become for us! Listen to your inner voice, go with your hunches. It's not easy to distinguish your intuition from the "other" little voice in your head – the one that comes from rationality and often tells you what you should do or can't do.

You will need to practice a little. Start with little things. For example, which road to take to work each morning, or whether to take your sunglasses with you although it's a totally cloudy day. I remember practicing my intuition when I went to high school.

There were two ways to get to school and both had a train crossing with trains coming from different directions (both train crossings were very rarely closed at the same time). I made it a game to consult with my inner voice which way to go - sometimes following the intuition, and sometimes going against it - just to get to stop in front of the closed train crossing.

Some time ago I was driving on the German Autobahn and I had two options to get to my destination. I wanted to take one road,
but I had a very strong hunch to take the other one, even though it looked very crowded.

Thirty minutes later I heard on the radio that there was a 25 km traffic jam on the other autobahn! We would have been stuck right there! I thanked my inner voice right away…! You probably already have experienced intuition.

Did it ever happen to you that you thought of a person and just a second later the phone rings and it's that person? Or you think of somebody and a minute later you run into them at the shopping center? The more you practice and trust in this inner voice, the stronger it gets, the more results you are going to see, and the easier it will be to distinguish from the other little rational voice in your head. It's amazing! Meditation has been proven to be a great tool to get closer to your intuition. Just sit still for five or ten minutes and listen to what's coming up.

Once you've learned to listen to your intuition act on it immediately! It can be a hunch to write an e-mail, or to talk to somebody. If it comes in the form of an idea, act on the idea.

64
WRITE IN YOUR JOURNAL

"Everyone thinks of changing the world, but no one thinks of changing himself."
Leo Tolstoy

I wouldn't miss this exercise for the world! An important exercise that I recommend to all of my clients: have a journal and reflect on your days. This is about taking a couple of minutes at the end of your day and to take a look at what you did well, get some perspective, relive the happy moments, and write everything down in your journal.

By doing this, you will receive an extra boost of happiness, motivation, and self-esteem every morning and evening! It has the positive side effect that just before sleeping, you will be concentrating your mind on positive things, which has a beneficial effect on your sleep and your subconscious mind. Your focus is on the positive things of the day and gratitude instead of the things that didn't work well which probably would keep you awake, and by now you know how crucial that is! For my clients and also for myself this little exercise has led to enormous changes in our wellbeing.

Make an effort to answer the following questions each night before sleeping and write them in your journal:

- What am I grateful for? (Write 3 -5 points)
- What 3 things have made me happy today?
- What 3 things did I do particularly well today?
- How could I have made today even better?
- What is my most important goal for tomorrow?

Don't worry if the words don't flow right away when you start his exercise. Like all other things your journaling will get better with practice. If you are blocked and can't think of anything, just hold on for five minutes longer. Write what comes to mind without thinking and don't judge it. Don't worry about your style or mistakes. Just write!

Do this every day for a month and observe the changes that take place! A regular notebook or calendar should do. I'm using a lovely little book called THE FIVE MINUTE JOURNAL. Have a look at it my webpage.

65
STOP WHINING!

*"Never tell your problems to anyone...
20% don't care and the other 80% are glad you have them."*
Lou Holtz

"It is better to light one small candle than to curse the darkness."
Confucius

Complaining is poison in your desire to become happier. It's an absolutely useless behavior that encourages self-pity and doesn't accomplish anything. Complainers are not attractive at all. It's the mentality of a victim and that isn't you any more, is it? **Stop cursing the darkness and light a candle.**

Stop complaining about not having time and get up an hour earlier (Chapter 25). Stop complaining about your weight and start exercising (Chapter 75). Stop blaming your parents, your teachers, your boss, the government, or the economy, and take responsibility for your life (Chapter 3).

It's nobody's fault that you go on smoking, that you eat unhealthy food, or that you gave up on your dream, but your own. It's you who pushes the snooze button instead of getting up half an hour earlier and who chooses fear over risk. Don't blame others for not living a satisfying life. You own your life! You can do anything you want with it. The sooner you get this, the sooner you can move on in the direction of your dreams.

Remember where to keep your focus! Complaining about your present circumstances will put your focus on them and attract more of what you don't like. You have to get out of this vicious circle and concentrate on what you want instead (Chapter 12).

Look inside yourself, encourage your positive ambitions and your will to succeed. Now go and create the circumstances you want. Start taking decisions and start living.

Action Steps:

Make a list of all your complaints.
What have your complaints achieved?
Transform your complaints into requests.

66
BECOME A RECEIVER!

"I can live for two months on a good compliment."
Mark Twain

Do you find it difficult to accept a gift or a compliment? Well, this stops NOW! You have to become a receiver! It's very important to accept gifts and things with joy and it's also the secret to getting more of what you want.

If you get a present and you're saying "Oh. That's not necessary", you are taking away the joy of giving a gift from the other person, and the same thing goes for compliments.

Take a closer look at this behavior! Is there a hidden feeling of "I don't deserve this", or "I'm not worth it" behind the "That's not necessary?". There is no need for justification. Don't diminish the pleasure of giving for the other person. Just say "Thank you!"

From today on I dare you to practice your "receiving skills". If somebody gives you a compliment, accept it graciously with a "Thank you". Own it. Don't return it.

You may say: "Thank you! I'm happy you feel that way!" and let the other person enjoy the experience. It will help you a lot and take your self-esteem to a whole new level if you manage to eradicate the following behaviors:

- Rejecting compliments.
- Making yourself small.
- Giving credit to others although you have earned it.
- Not buying something nice because you think you don't deserve it.
- Looking for the negative if someone does something good for you.

Action Steps:
From now on just say "Thank you!" for every gift and compliment you receive! (Don't explain or justify)

Analyze if you have any of the five behaviors mentioned above. If yes, work on it/them.

67
STOP SPENDING TIME WITH THE WRONG PEOPLE!

"Whatever you do you need courage. Whatever course you decide upon, there will always be someone to tell you that you are wrong."
Ralph Waldo Emerson

"The person who says it can't be done shouldn't interrupt the person who is doing it!"
Chinese proverb

WATCH WHO YOU ARE SPENDING YOUR TIME WITH! Jim Rohn said that "You are the average of the five persons you spend the most time with", so you better take this seriously! Choose to spend more time with people who bring out the best in you, who motivate you, who believe in you. Be around people who empower you. **Remember that emotions and attitudes are contagious.**

People around you can be the springboard to motivate yourself, gain courage, and help you take the right actions, but on the other hand can also drag you down, drain your energy, and act as brakes in the achieving of your life goals. If you are around negative people all the time, they can convert you into a negative and cynical person over time. They might want to convince you to stay where you are and keep you stuck, because they value security and don't like risk and uncertainty.

So **stay away from the naysayers, the blamers, the complainers.** The people who are always judging or gossiping and talking bad about everything. And as Steve Jobs said at the famous Stanford address **"Don't let the noise of the opinions of others drown your own inner voice."**

It will be difficult for you to grow and thrive, if people around you want to convince you of the contrary.

And what do you do if it's people close to you? The only thing you can work on is becoming a better person yourself. If you grow and develop, soon negative people will turn away from you because you don't serve their purposes any more. They need somebody who shares their negativity and if you don't do that they will look for somebody else. If that doesn't work you seriously have to ask yourself the question if you should start to spend less time with them or stop seeing them at all. **But that's a decision you have to make.**

In my whole life I automatically separated people from my life that didn't support me and I never regretted it, although it wasn't easy! After my own coaching training - when I reinforced all the principles that you are learning in this book and changed myself - some of my colleagues had no other explanation than actually thinking that I had joined a sect!

Action Steps:

1) Make a list of all the people you have in your life and are spending time with. (Members of your family, friends, colleagues).

2) Analyze who is positive for you and who drags you down.

3) Spend more time with the positive people and stop seeing the toxic people (blamers, complainers) in your life, or at least spend less time with them.

4) Choose to be around positive people who support you.

5) Watch Steve Jobs' Stanford commencement address on YouTube.

68
LIVE YOUR OWN LIFE

"Your time is limited, so don't waste it living someone else's life. Don't be trapped by dogma - which is living with the results of other people's thinking. Don't let the noise of other's opinions drown out your own inner voice. And most important, have the courage to follow your heart and intuition. They somehow already know what you truly want to become. Everything else is secondary."
Steve Jobs

Actually the Steve Jobs quote already says everything! It's difficult to add something to his wise words. **Live the life you want and not the life other people expect of you.**

Don't worry about what your neighbors or other people think of you, because if you care too much about what they say, there will be a moment when you don't live your own life any more, but the life of other people. Listen to your heart.

Do the things you want to do, and not necessarily those things that everybody else does. Have the courage to be different! Paulo Coelho reminds us, "If someone isn't what others want them to be, the others become angry. Everyone seems to have a clear idea of how other people should lead their lives, but none about his or her own. "

Action Step:
In what aspect are you not living your life right now? Make a list!

69
WHO IS NUMBER ONE?

"No one can make you feel inferior without your consent."
Eleanor Roosevelt

Love yourself like your neighbor! Many times you see the good in others and fail to see it in yourself! The most important relationship that you have in this life is the one you have with yourself! If you don't like yourself, how can you expect others to like you? How can you expect to love others, if you don't love yourself first?

We are going to work on your most important relationship. Most of the problems my clients come to me for depend directly or indirectly on self-confidence. The salary raise they don't get, the appreciation they don't get, the relationship they don't find. So I usually work with them on their self-confidence while working towards their goal.

How do you gain more self-confidence? First of all **accept yourself as you are.** You don't have to be perfect to be great! **Learn to spend time with the most important person in your life – YOU. Enjoy going to the movies with the best company you can imagine: YOU!**

French writer and philosopher Blaise Pascal says "All of humanity's problems stem from man's inability to sit quietly in a room alone." Dr. Wayne Dyer adds "You cannot be lonely if you like the person you're alone with." Get comfortable with spending some alone time. Find a place where you can disconnect from the speedy everyday life.

It can't be mentioned often enough: **Accepting yourself is a key element of your wellbeing.** Recognize your value as a person. Know that you earn respect. If you make a mistake, don't beat yourself up over it, accept it, and promise yourself to do your best to not repeat it. That's it.

There is absolutely no use in beating yourself up about something that you can't change.

Be selfish! What? What am I saying? Yes you read right: Be selfish! I don't mean in an egocentric way, but by being well within yourself so that you can transmit this wellness to your whole environment. If you are not well within yourself you can't be a good husband, wife, son, daughter, or friend. But if you feel great you can transmit these feelings to your whole environment and everybody benefits.

Exercises to boost your self-confidence:
1) The Journaling Exercise from Chapter 64
2) Make a list of your successes and achievements.
3) Make a list of all of the things you are doing great.
4) Mirror exercise (Tell yourself how great you are in front of a mirror! It may feel strange at first, but you'll get used to it).
5) Increase somebody else's self esteem.

70
YOUR BEST INVESTMENT

"An investment in knowledge pays the best interest."
Benjamin Franklin

"If you think education is expensive, try ignorance."
Derek Bok

The best thing you can do for your further personal and professional growth is to invest in yourself. Commit yourself to becoming the best person you can be. Invest around 5-10% of your income in training, books, CDs, and other ways of personal development. Stay curious and eager to learn new things and better yourself.

A nice side effect of investing in your personal growth is that while you become a wiser person, you might also become more valuable for your company. There are so many possibilities: you could do training that improves your negotiating skills, time management, financial planning, and much more. In a two or four-hour workshop you can learn powerful strategies or tools that transform your life. Or you can decide to go all in and get a life coach and really start working on yourself.

One of my best investments in myself ever was hiring a coach. He helped me to get unstuck, get clear about what I really want from my life, and change my relationship with fear completely. You can also start in a less expensive way by reading more or listening to a learning CD or a course. I made it a habit to read at least one book a week, buy a new course every two months, and sign up for at least two seminars or trainings a year.

What are you going to do? Remember that baby steps count, too!

Action Step:
Write down what you will commit to in the next 12 months:

I, _____ will read __ book(s) a month, listen to __ learning CDs or audiobooks per month, and sign up for __ training(s) in the next six months.

Date: _____ Signature: _____

71
STOP BEING SO HARD ON YOURSELF

"Because one believes in oneself, one doesn't try to convince others. Because one is content with oneself, one doesn't need others' approval. Because one accepts oneself, the whole world accepts him or her."
Lao Tse

It's easy to fall into the habit of self-criticism because of past mistakes or because things didn't work out as we wanted them to. But does it serve you? No, NADA, zip!

It's time you accept something here: You are not perfect! You never will be, and - the best thing is - YOU DON'T HAVE TO BE! So once and for all stop being so hard on yourself! This is one of the top reasons that prevents people from living a happy and fulfilled life.

Did you know that a lot of the misery we have in our life is because we subconsciously think we have to punish ourselves for something? I'm glad I left the habit of exaggerated self-criticism and self-punishment behind a long time ago. **I'm just conscious that I'm doing the best that I can at any time.** That doesn't mean I don't analyze the many mistakes I made. If I can correct them I do; if I can't correct them - I accept them, let go, and promise myself not to repeat them, **because I know it's only a problem if I keep repeating the same mistakes over and over again.** Is that too difficult?

Do you want to know the magic recipe? It's not for sale in any pharmacy and it's free! Ready?

1) Accept yourself as you are!
2) Forgive yourself! Love yourself!
3) Take extremely good care of yourself!

That's it! Easy, isn't it? **Start NOW and ask yourself the following questions:**

In what areas of your life are you being too hard on yourself?
What benefits do you get from being too hard on yourself?

72
BE YOUR AUTHENTIC SELF

"We have to dare to be ourselves, however frightening or strange that self may prove to be."
May Sarton

"To be yourself in a world that is constantly trying to make you something else is the greatest accomplishment."
Ralph Waldo Emerson

The most successful people are the ones who are authentic. They are not playing any roles. They are who they are. What you see is what you get! They know their strengths and their weaknesses. They have no problem in being vulnerable and taking responsibility for their mistakes. Neither do they fear judgment of others.

Don't let the world tell you who you are supposed to be. Your fake self is who you are when you want to please everyone else. That's when you have a mask on and are keen to get feedback from the people who surround you such as colleagues, friends, neighbors, etc.

Don't play any roles! Stop thinking about what others want of you, or might think of you, and **give yourself permission to be your authentic self.** The rewards are awesome! Funnily enough, you will notice that the more you are yourself, the more people will be attracted to you! Try it out!

Questions:
1) On a scale of 0-10 how would you quantify your level of authenticity? An eight? Congratulations! You are quite close. Keep on improving! A four? Well there is some work to do, but goingmthrough the exercises in this book you will help you get closer!
2) How many roles do you play?
3) Who are you when you are alone?
4) When was the last time you felt authentic?

73
PAMPER YOURSELF

"You can change the way people treat you by changing the way you treat yourself."
Unknown.

This is one of my favorite exercises for my clients! Write down a list of 15 things that you can do to pamper yourself and then do one of them every other day for the next two weeks. This exercise is truly miraculous! (Examples: read a good book, go to the movies, get a massage, watch a sunrise, sit by the water, etc.) Once you start treating yourself well, it **will do miracles for your self-confidence and self-esteem! Start doing it NOW!**

1. _____
2. _____
3. _____
4. _____
5. _____
6. _____
7. _____
8. _____
9. _____
10. _____
11. _____
12. _____
13. _____
14. _____
15. _____

74
TREAT YOUR BODY LIKE THE TEMPLE IT IS!

"To keep the body in good health is a duty, otherwise we shall not be able to keep our mind strong and clear."
Buddha

Isn't it ironic? If you listen to people most of us say that health is the most important thing in our lives; nevertheless many people drink, smoke, eat junk food, or even take drugs, and spend most of their free time on the couch without any physical activity. Remember – it's easy!

A healthier life is only a decision away. Decide NOW to live healthier. Follow a **balanced diet, exercise regularly,** and **stay or get in physical shape** so that your brain has all the nutrition it needs to produce a positive lifestyle. Take care of your body, because if the body is not well the mind doesn't work well either. Here are some examples:

- Eat more fruit and vegetables.
- Reduce your intake of red meat.
- Drink at least 2 liters of water each day.
- Eat less!
- Stop eating junk food.
- Get up early.

Action Steps:
What will you do now for a healthier lifestyle?
Write down at least 3 things:

75
EXERCISE AT LEAST 3 TIMES A WEEK

"Those who do not find time for exercise will have to find time for illness."

Edward Smith Stanley

I think I'm not coming to you with breaking news here if I tell you how important exercise is for you. And even if we all know about the importance of exercise, there are many of us who just don't do it. The best excuse is always: "I have no time". But what if somebody were to tell you that your life depends on it? And if you don't start exercising right know you will be dead in a month? You will surely find time, wouldn't you? So time is not the problem.

I also won't put a lot of work into convincing you how important exercise is and how you can find time, because you already know that. I will just list the benefits that exercising three to five times a week will bring you. And then - if you want - you will find the time.

1. Exercising will keep you healthy.
2. Exercising will help you lose weight, which will improve your health and also make you look better.
3. Exercising will make you feel better and you will have a lot of energy.
4. Once the kilos start dropping there is a big chance that your self-esteem will go up. (I can confirm that one)
5. Problems with falling asleep? Exercise for 30 minutes a couple of hours before you go to sleep and see what it does for you.
6. Have you ever noticed that exercise significantly reduces stress? First of all there are the endorphins, but the other thing is that you just might get your mind off the things that were stressing you out.

Furthermore, studies show that regular exercise makes you happier, can reduce the symptoms of depression, reduces the risk of disease (heart, diabetes, osteoporosis, high cholesterol, etc.), lowers the risk of a premature death, and improves your memory, and many more. Are you in? One last thing: Don't force yourself to exercise. Enjoy it. Look for a recreational activity that fits you and that you enjoy doing such as swimming, for example. Even walking an hour a day can make a difference. (Chapter 34)

Action steps:

Find some studies about the amazing benefits of exercise on the Internet.

When will YOU start exercising?

If you think you don't have time, go back to the Chapters about finding time.

76
TAKE ACTION. MAKE THINGS HAPPEN!

*"Whatever you do, or dream you can, begin it.
Boldness has genius and power and magic in it."*
Johann Wolfgang von Goethe

"I am only one, but I am one. I cannot do everything, but I can do something. And I will not let what I cannot do interfere with what I can do."
Edward Everett Hale

One of the secrets to success and happiness in life is to make things happen. Just talking about it is not enough. It's the results that count or as Henry Ford said, **"You can't build a reputation on what you are going to do."**

Without action, there are no results. Without results, there is no feedback. Without feedback, there is no learning. Without learning, we can't improve. Without improving, we can't develop our full potential.

C.G. Jung said it correctly, "You are what you do, not what you say you'll do." **There are too many people who want to change the world yet never picked up a pen to start writing a book or an article or did anything about it.** It's a lot easier to complain about our politicians, than to start pursuing a political career or become more active in politics.

Your life is in your hands so start acting on your ideas. You don't have to go for the big challenges at once. By now you have learned that doing small things consistently on a daily basis can get you great results. Dare to do the things you want and you will find the power to do them.

But by all means START NOW! The biggest difference between people who reach their goals and people who stay stuck is ACTION.

People who reach their goals are doers who are taking action consistently. If they make a mistake they learn from it and go on; if they are rejected they try again.

People who stay stuck just talk about what they are going to do and don't walk their talk. Don't wait any longer! The right moment never comes! Just start with what you have and go one step at a time.

Do as Martin Luther King, Jr. said, **"Take the first step in faith. You don't have to see the whole staircase, just take the first step."**

Action Step:

What will you start TODAY?

77
ENJOY MORE

*The present moment is filled with joy and happiness.
If you are attentive, you will see it."*
Thích Nhât Hanh

"Real generosity towards the future lies in giving all to the present."
Albert Camus

It's very important to enjoy the present moment! If you don't then life goes by and you don't even notice it, because you are never right here, in the moment! When you're working you think of the weekend, on the weekend you think of all the things you have to do on Monday, when you're eating the appetizer you think of dessert, and when you eating dessert you think of the appetizer - with the result that you don't fully enjoy neither the one nor the other.

Living like this you never get to enjoy your point of power, the only moment that counts - the present moment. Eckart Tolle wrote an entire book about "The power of NOW" which I highly recommend to you. Think about it: Do you have any problem RIGHT NOW just being in the moment? Do you constantly live with guilt for your past actions and/or with fear of an unknown future? Many people are constantly worrying about things in the past that they can't change or things in the future that – even funnier - mostly never happen, and meanwhile they miss out on the NOW or as Bill Cosby puts it, **"The past is a ghost, the future a dream. All we ever have is now."** Just be present and enjoy the journey.

Action Step:
Remind yourself to be more in the present moment!
(My friend David wears his wristwatch on his right arm. This reminds him to be in the present moment whenever he watches his left arm for the time and notices it's not there.)

78
STOP JUDGING!

"Before you accuse me, take a look at yourself."
Eric Clapton

"Before you start pointing fingers, make sure your hands are clean."
Bob Marley

Judging goes hand in hand with the vices of blaming and complaining! On your way to a happier, more fulfilling life that's another bad habit you have to leave behind! Accept others without judging them, and without expectations.

I know that's easier said than done, but there is no way around it! **Think of it this way: each time you're judging somebody you are actually judging yourself.** Isn't it true that the things that bother us the most about others are actually the things that bother us the most about ourselves?

Action Step:

Make a list of what bothers you the most about others.

Put some though in it. What could this say about you?

79
A RANDOM ACT OF KINDNESS EVERY DAY

"One of the most difficult things to give away is kindness; usually it comes back to you."
Anonymous

"The smallest good deed is better than the grandest intention."
Anonymous

How can you make the world a little bit better today and every day? Why not be nice to a stranger every day? Be creative! Every now and then I pay for two coffees instead of the only one that I drank and tell the server to save it, in case somebody needs it and can't pay for it entirely. In the supermarket if I get a 10% discount voucher for my next shopping trip I usually give it to the person behind me in line.

You can offer your seat in the train or subway to somebody or even just gift somebody with a smile. Acknowledge people sincerely, treat people great, say thank you genuinely, hold the door open for somebody, help somebody whose hands are full to carry something, or store away somebody's heavy hand luggage on your next flight. Be creative! Start today!

The great thing is: "What goes around comes around." So when you start doing random acts of kindness, more kindness is coming back to you! Doing good begins to become the same thing as feeling good. The good that we do for others really does have the power to change us. **If you want to improve the world start with yourself! Be the change you want to see in the world! Do at least ONE random act of kindness every day.** Positively and significantly impact the lives of other people. **PAY IT FORWARD!**

Action Step:
Commit yourself to doing one random act of kindness a day for the next 2 weeks.
Observe what happens, but don't expect anything in return!

80
SOLVE YOUR PROBLEMS, ALL OF THEM

"Most people spend more time and energy going around problems than in trying to solve them."
Henry Ford

Solve your problems. Face them. Because if you are running away from them they will come after you. If you don't solve them they will repeat themselves over and over again until you learn something and are ready to move on. For example, if you change jobs because of problems with a colleague that you didn't face, in another job you may face the same challenge with another person. This will go on until you learn something out of the situation and solve the problem once and for all.

Did you notice that you may continue to encounter the same set of problems in multiple romantic relationships until you stop and solve the recurring problems? Another giant waste of energy is to dance around problems and responsibilities instead of somebody taking ownership and starting to solving problems.

I hear this over and over again from my clients: they procrastinate, they dance around the problem, and end up with a high level of anxiety and feeling really bad.

Once they decide to go against all their fears and confront and solve the problem, they feel much better and find out that it was a lot less painful to face the problem and solve it, than the whole process of dancing around it. Stop searching for the solution to your problems "out there", and start looking for it within you.

Questions:
How can you be different?
What can you do differently?
What can YOU do to solve the problem?
Action steps:
Make a list of all your problems and start working on their solutions.Examine your problems. Look for patterns (Do the same things happen to you over and over again?)

81
THE POWER OF MEDITATION

"All of humanity's problems stem from man's inability to sit quietly in a room alone."
Blaise Pascal

The benefits of meditation are widely known by now. More and more people have started practicing it. Its practitioners highlight its usefulness in calming the mind after a stressful day, and in warding off anxiety, anger, insecurity, and even depression.

Other studies point out that meditation can reduce blood pressure and pain response. It's an easy way of stress combat and quieting our information-overloaded mind. Just sitting still for 15 to 20 minutes once a day can already make a difference and help you to recharge. If you do it twice a day...even better! Here is how to begin your habit of daily meditation:

1. Look for a space, were you won't be disturbed and just be in silence for 15 to 2o minutes. Make it a ritual. It's beneficial to practice in the same spot and at the same time every day. Do you remember the magic of the early morning hours? Maybe that's also a good time for your meditation.

2. Before you start use the power of affirmations to get yourself in a relaxed state by saying for example, "I'm now focused and calm."

3. Set your alarm clock for twenty minutes so that you are not worried about when to stop your meditation, and are fully able to concentrate.

4. Sit or lie down and shut your eyes. You can also leave your eyes open and focus on one point in the room or on nature if you are sitting facing a window.

5. While focusing, concentrate on your breath and start relaxing.

6. When your mind wanders let it wander. Don't resist. See your thoughts passing by like clouds in the blue sky and just empty your mind. See your mind still like a lake without the smallest ripple.

Meditating for 20 minutes a day will surely provide you with great results once you have made it a habit. The six steps mentioned above are only a suggestion. **Meditation can't be done wrong and only you will know what works best for you.**

There is also a lot of information on the Internet, as well as classes and seminars that may be available close to where you live. **The most important thing is – as everything in this book –TO TAKE ACTION! Try it out!**

82
LISTEN TO GREAT MUSIC – DAILY!

"Life is one grand, sweet song, so start the music."
Ronald Reagan

An easy way to feel happy instantly is to listen to your favorite music! Make a soundtrack of your all-time favorites and listen to them, dance, sing! It might feel stupid at first, but doing this every day will be very beneficial! **What are your top 5 favorite songs of all time?**

1. _____
2. _____
3. _____
4. _____
5. _____

Why not make a playlist on your iPod, phone, or PC and listen to them right now! **Do it NOW! Come on!**

How did you feel after listening to your favorite song? **Any changes in your mood?**

What would happen if you made this a daily habit?

83
NO WORRIES

"If a problem is fixable, if a situation is such that you can do something about it, then there is no need to worry. If it's not fixable, then there is no help in worrying. There is no benefit in worrying whatsoever."

Dalai Lama XIV

Many people are constantly worrying. They worry about things that happened in the past that they can't change, things in the future that they have no influence over, or about economy, wars, and politics which they have no control over. Even funnier is that most of the catastrophes that you are worrying about turn out to be a lot less horrible in reality or just never happen.

Mark Twain was right when he said, **"I've had a lot of worries in my life, most of which never happened." Keep in mind: it doesn't matter how much you worry, it will change neither the past not the future!** Also, worrying usually doesn't make things any better, does it? Instead, it will drag you down and you will lose the present moment.

Can you already grasp what a waste of time and energy worrying is or shall I give you another example? This example is from Robin Sharma's book "Who Will Cry When You Die?" A Manager who did one of the exercises Robin suggests at his seminars identified the following: 54% of his worries were about things that would probably never happen. 26% were related to past actions that couldn't be changed. 8% were related to other people's opinions which he didn't even care about. 4% were personal health questions that he had already resolved. Only 6% referred to questions that needed his attention. Identifying his problems and dropping the ones he couldn't do anything about or which were just draining energy, the man eliminated 94% of the worries that had tortured him so much!

Action step:

Make a list of your worries:

Questions:

Which ones are related to the past?

Which ones are related to the future?

Which ones are outside your control?

Which ones can you actually do something about?

84
USE YOUR TRAVEL TIME WISELY

"Time is what we want most, but what we use worst."
William Penn

How much time are you spending every day in the car or public transport on your way to work? Statistics say it's between 60 and 90 minutes per working day! That means in a month we are talking between 20 to 30 hours.

Who said, "I don't have enough time."? We just found you another 20 to 30 hours to read (when on a bus or train), or listen to audio books in your car. What if you really spent that time listening to empowering CDs, mp3s, or reading inspirational books instead of listening to the negative news from the radio or reading about it in the newspaper?

Questions:

Are you ready to try it out?

When will you start?

Do it for two weeks and let me know how your life changed.

85
SPEND MORE TIME WITH YOUR FAMILY

"Family is not an important thing, it's everything."
Michael J. Fox

Walt Disney once said, "A man should never neglect his family for business." Yet I have to dedicate an extra chapter to this one. **Just to make sure that you don't skip it!** It's kind of sad that I have to mention it, but when I interview leaders and executives most of the time what comes up is that they just cannot (?) spend a lot of time with their families!

In Bronnie Ware's book (See also Chapter 94), one of the top regrets of the dying is to not have spent more time with their families and having spent too much time at the office! Don't become one of them and **start making time for your family NOW!** And if you are with the family…do everybody a favor and BE FULLY with the family. During our vacation in the Florida Keys last year I saw an absurd situation. A family was on a sightseeing walk with the father running ahead in the front making a business phone call, while the wife and daughter were following looking kind of sad which is understandable. It was even a Sunday! It seemed like something taken out of a comic book, and yet it was very real and sad to see.

WAKE UP! Value your family and friends. They are your constant source of love and mutual support, which increases your self-esteem and boosts your self-confidence.

Questions:
How are you going to find more time for your family? (Tip: Use the Time Management tips in this book) What will you stop doing to find more time?

86
DON'T BE THE SLAVE OF YOUR PHONE

"Men have become the tools of their tools."
Henry David Thoreau

Going back to the busy father mentioned in the last chapter, this tip comes in handy. **Don't always pick up your phone each time it rings;** your phone is supposed to be for YOUR convenience, not for those who call you. Give yourself the freedom to continue what you are doing and let the call go to voice mail.

Some time ago I always got very anxious when I didn't take a call. **I thought I had missed something.** My roommate Pol was much cooler about it. He only answered the phone when he wanted to, when he felt like it, and if not - he just went on doing what he was doing without bothering.

I started liking the idea and worked on adapting this "Zen-like" mentality telling myself that "They will call again." I also learnt that if it's a really important call the caller will not give up and probably call five times within 3 minutes...

Action Step:

Try it out! Don't be a slave of your phone and leverage voicemail.

87
HOW TO DEAL WITH PROBLEMS

*"Every problem has in it the seeds of its own solution.
If you don't have any problems, you don't get any seeds."*
Norman Vincent Peale

Do you have many problems? Congratulations!!! And I'm not kidding! You have many opportunities to grow, because a problem is always an opportunity to grow by learning from it! So let's have a better look at this. Over 20 years ago, when I started working at Disneyworld in Orlando, we – the newbies – were taught that the word "problem" doesn't exist in the vocabulary of a Disney Cast Member: "We don't have problems, we only have **challenges** here".

Dr. Lair Ribeiro writes that "Your problems are your best friends" and Leadership Guru Robin Sharma asks us to see our problems as blessings! So what are problems now? Challenges, blessings, friends? Or all three of them? Isn't life just facing one problem after another?

What makes all the difference is how you face it and how you learn from it! When you start learning from your problems life gets much better. Look back at the problems you had in your life. Didn't each one of it have something positive?

Maybe a loss in business saved you from an even bigger loss, because you learnt from it. In hard times it can be very beneficial for you to adapt the belief that life/God/the universe only puts a problem in your way if you are able to solve it!

Questions:
1. What problems do you have in your life right now that you haven't found a solution for yet? Make a list of your problems.
2. What would change if you see these problems as challenges or even opportunities?
3. How would it make you feel?

88
TAKE TIME OFF

"There is more to life than increasing its speed."
Mahatma Gandhi

With the stressful, fast paced life that we are living it becomes even more important to slow down your pace of life and take a break! Take some time off. Recharge your batteries by being around nature. You can start by scheduling some relaxation time into your weekly schedule which by now you are hopefully making time for (see Chapter "Manage your time"). If you dare - start with weekends in which you are completely disconnected from the Internet, TV, and your electronic games.

One of my best vacations ever - if not the best - was being on a houseboat in the Midi Channel in the south of France. No mobile phone, no Internet, no TV. Only ducks. The boat's top speed was 8 km/hr (= 5 miles/hr) so we were literally "forced" to slow down. It is also due to the fact that when you are floating on the channel, children on their bikes overtake you on the bike paths on the side of the channel. The villages you pass through are sometimes so small, that they don't even have a supermarket. So the whole trip comes down to the question, "Where will we get food?"

No worries! There is always a restaurant close by, but the charming thing is to cook your own meals on the boat and have dinner at the harbor watching the sunset or just being around nature. Once we had dinner in the middle of a vineyard! Priceless!

So is to walk into a tiny French village in the morning and get your baguette for breakfast from the only bakery in town. We got up at sunrise and went to bed two chess matches after sunset. Or as you could say "We got up with the ducks and went to sleep with the ducks."

Take time off and connect with nature! It doesn't have to be a long trip. Walk in the woods, on the beach, or in a park whenever you get the chance and observe how you feel afterwards. Or just lie down on a bench or in the grass and contemplate the blue sky.

When was the last time you walked barefoot on grass or on a beach? Did you get the idea of how important, relaxing, and reenergizing taking some time off is for you? I hope so! **What will you do?**

Action Step:

Schedule some relaxation time in your calendar right now!

89
HAVE A HIGHLIGHT EVERY DAY

"I believe the key to happiness is someone to love, something to do,
and something to look forward to."
Elvis Presley

Don't let routine and boredom crawl into your life. Create things you look forward to after a hard day at work instead of just ending up in front of the TV every evening. Here are some examples:

- Take some "alone time".
- Go for a walk in the nature with your spouse.
- Take a bubble bath or have a spa day.
- Celebrate something: a good job, family, life!
- Call a friend.
- Take somebody for lunch.
- Get a massage.
- Go for a drink.
- Go to the movies/theater/a concert.
- Get a manicure/pedicure.
- Movie night at home.
- Watch a sunrise, etc.

Remember to reserve some time for your special moments in your schedule!

90
STEP OUT OF YOUR "COMFORT ZONE"

*"As you move outside of your comfort zone,
what was once the unknown and frightening becomes you new normal."*
Robin Sharma

*"One can choose to go back toward safety
or forward toward growth.
Growth must be chosen again and again;
fear must be overcome again and again."*

Abraham Maslow

Have you ever heard of the saying, **"The magic happens outside of your comfort zone?"** But…what the heck is the comfort zone? The following metaphor describes it very well: if you put a frog into a pot of boiling water, it jumps out! But if you put it into a pot and start heating up the water gradually, it doesn't react and dies by being boiled! And that's what happens to many people who are trapped in their comfort zone without even knowing it.

Your comfort zone is the limit of your current experience. It's what you are used to doing, thinking or feeling based on your current level of knowledge. It's where it's nice and cozy and where we know most of the time exactly what is going to happen. It's where you live life on autopilot. It's also where change doesn't happen. Personal growth and development happen outside of your comfort zone. So if you want to change jobs, start an enterprise, be creative, get out of a relationship that has stopped working, you have to step out of your comfort zone.

Unfortunately it's more comfortable to stay where you are and your mind is doing everything to keep you there! When I was trapped in a job that I didn't like any more I caught myself saying the entire time, **"Well it's not that bad, it could be worse. Who knows, maybe in another job I would be even worse off."**

And so I continued in a job that no more made sense to me day in day out. On Monday I was already looking forward to Friday, and when I came back from my vacations I was already looking to the next ones. Can you imagine that? I should have watched Steve Jobs' commencement Address at Stanford some years earlier. (**Did you watch it yet?**).

Jobs had a great technique: each day he looked at himself in the mirror and asked himself, **"If this was my last day on earth, would I do what I'm about to do today?"** and if he answered "No" to himself for too many days in a row, he changed!

Be careful if you use that technique, **because once you start asking yourself this question everything changes.** When you step out of your comfort zone and start to venture towards the unknown, you start to grow. **You will start feeling uncomfortable and awkward. That's a great sign! That's actually a sign that you are growing and moving ahead.** Act in spite of fear and doubt!

Questions:

How can you challenge yourself to step out of your comfort zone? (Remember, small steps!)

Is there anything that makes you uncomfortable that you can do NOW?

91
WHAT PRICE ARE YOU PAYING FOR NOT CHANGING?

"The price of doing the same old thing is far higher than the price of change."
Bill Clinton

Another question that forced me out of my comfort zone when I was evaluating my situation was, **"What is the price you are paying for not taking action?"** I was on the worst possible way to being seriously burnt out. Of course it was very risky to just walk away from my secure job without putting up a fight in the worst economic crisis the world had seen, but what was the price I was paying to stay? Serious health problems? No thanks, buddy! I'm out of here. Since then I never looked back.

Many years ago my boss at Volkswagen in Mexico came to me - the intern – and said, "Marc, I don't know what to do any more. I'm close to a breakdown due to stress, but I'm on a three years Expat-contract and if I break it, I will be looked at as a failure at the headquarters in Germany. What would you do?" I told him, "Look, your health is the most important thing you have. If this job affects your health any more, leave. Because if you get a heart attack and die, the people that are now giving you the worst time will say what a great guy you were at your funeral in front of your wife and kid.

I'm talking from my own personal experience: the people that harassed my father the most at his workplace, actually wanted to speak at his funeral! Unbelievable! For now, I would hang in there and see what happens, because I really believe that life is a miracle, everything happens for a reason and in the end everything is always going to work out!"

Two months later he contacted me from Germany. He was still on his Expat-contract, however he had returned to Germany and was working on a new project with far better work conditions!

Life is a miracle – it always works out in the end! **But there is always a price you are paying and it's your decision if you want to pay it and live with the consequences.**

The price you pay if you want to get in shape is that you have to exercise. The price you pay for not exercising is getting overweight. If you want more time the price is getting up an hour earlier or watching less TV. The price you pay for procrastination is anxiety and feeling bad. **Choose your suffering wisely!**

Question:

Are you paying a price for doing the same old thing?

92
THINGS ARE ONLY TEMPORARY

*"You can't connect the dots looking forward;
you can only connect them looking backwards.
So you have to trust that the dots
will somehow connect in your future."*

Steve Jobs

"It does not matter how slowly you go as long as you do not stop."
Confucius

Everything is temporary. All triumphs, defeat, joy, sadness that happen in our life go by. What seems to be very important today is not important anymore in a month or three months. **And what seems to be a disaster today can be a great learning experience three months from now.**

When I was jobless for over nine months right after finishing college and was rejected by, I don't even remember how many companies, each one of my friends was pitying me and most of all I pitied myself, but somehow deep down inside me I knew that **all of the rejection is because something better is waiting** for me.

In the end, I started working in Barcelona, one of the most beautiful cities in the world with lots of culture, beaches, a fantastic climate, a great football team, and about 300 days of sun a year (very important for me). My friends went directly from pity to envy and from "poor Marc" to "lucky bastard!"

Look at life with a little more ease and sobriety knowing that misfortunes pass. Or as Rudyard Kipling in his fantastic poem "IF" says:

"If you can meet with Triumph and Disaster and treat those two impostors just the same; […] yours is the Earth

and everything that's in it, And - which is more - you'll be a Man, my son!"

Keep your attention on what you want and keep moving forward. Do you remember the saying, "In 6 months we are going to laugh about it!"?

Why not laugh already now? This phrase actually got me through my International Business studies. I remember many nights before the exams at 3 a.m. – a few hours before the exam – when I was totally stressed out in the dorm room of my friend Jorge and on the verge of a breakdown (failing those exams would have meant dropping out of college or worse still… be thrown out..) and he always just laughed and said, **"Marc, in 6 months we are going to laugh about tonight!"**

We actually even now – over 20 years later - still laugh about those stories. Try this technique! I hope it helps you as it helped me!

Action Steps:

Think back on other hard times in your life and how you got out of it and maybe even found something positive in it after some time.

MAPPING LIFE:
1. Make a timeline of your life. From birth until now. Mark every key
    event in your life on the line. All and any moments that changed your life.
2. Write the great moments, the successes above the timeline.
3. Write the challenges, the tragedies, the failures below the timeline.
4. Examine the events below the line and write the positive effects of
    them above the line.
(For example, somebody close to you died. A positive could be that you value your life more. Or perhaps you got fired from a job. This opened doors to an even better job that you have now.)
5. Have a close look at your timeline.

93
GET A COACH!

"Make the most of yourself....for that is all there is of you."
Ralph Waldo Emerson

After having a huge impact in business life, coaching is also becoming more and more available for private persons in the form of life coaching. Many people have the wrong concept that you only take on a coach when something is wrong, but leaders like Eric Schmidt actually take on coaches to get even better, or to have a neutral, objective partner with whom they can bounce back and forth their ideas and who keeps them grounded.

A coach can help you to achieve clarity on what you really want in life, encourage you to keep on going when you would normally stop, help set better and more rewarding goals for yourself, get results more easily and quickly, overcome fear, communicate much more effectively, experience a faster personal development, overcome self-sabotaging habits, find your true purpose, and to live aligned with your true values. During the coaching process you will learn to take responsibility for everything in your life and take better decisions.

Coaching achieves extraordinary results because you and your coach become a team, focusing on your goals and accomplishing more than you would do alone. You take more action, think bigger, and get the job done, because of the accountability the coach provides. A coach knows how to help you to make better decisions, set the best goals, and restructure your professional and personal life for maximum productivity. Coaching works because it brings out the best in you. A coach is trained to help you find your own best answers and will support you in the course of that process. Coaching is usually done during regular, weekly sessions by telephone, skype, or in person which last between 30 and 60 minutes.

In every session coach and coachee work on the coachee's goals, creating options and setting a plan of action for the coachee's next steps. While working towards the coachee's goal, the coach also works on the coachee's personal development.

You can find coaches, for example, in online directories of CoachU or the International Coach Federation (ICF).

Most coaches offer complementary strategy sessions. That's how you and your coach get to know each other and find out if you are comfortable working together. Chemistry is crucial in a coaching relationship.

There is no guarantee that coaching works. Your success depends on you! From my experience I can say that the coachees that attend their sessions, are committed to their coaching process, and do their work, end up being successful in their endeavors. That's why I even offer a 30 days money back guarantee (based on some ground rules). If you want to try out Coaching don't hesitate to contact me.

94
LIVE YOUR LIFE FULLY. DO IT NOW!

"Do not dwell in the past, do not dream of the future, concentrate the mind on the present moment"
Buddha

Most of us live like we have all the time in the world! We are so busy going after the big pleasures of life that we forget about the small ones.

When will you start to take better care of yourself, start exercising, learn something new, do the things you always wanted to do, spend more time with your family? Tomorrow? Next week? Next Monday? Next month? When you win the lottery? When you have another job? When the next project is finished?

Yes I know. There are so many other things you have to do right now. You just don't have time right now! A lot of people never discover the meaning of life until it's too late and they are just about to die. Bronnie Ware, an Australian nurse who accompanied the dying wrote down their top five regrets:

1. I wish I'd had the courage to live a life true to myself, not the life others expected of me.
2. I wish I didn't work so hard.
3. I wish I'd had the courage to express my feelings.
4. I wish I had stayed in touch with my friends.
5. I wish that I had let myself be happier.

Don't wait any longer. Live your life fully. NOW! Remember that failure is only feedback, that problems are opportunities to grow. Do the things you always wanted to do. Don't postpone them any longer. Don't fight life! Let it flow, because as Paulo Coelho says **"One day you will wake up and there won't be any *more time* to do the things you've always wanted to do. Do it now."**

The great Steve Jobs put it this way:

"Remembering that I'll be dead soon is the most important tool I've ever encountered to help me make the big choices in life. Almost everything--all external expectations, all pride, all fear of embarrassment or failure--these things just fall away in the face of death, leaving only what is truly important.

Remembering that you are going to die is the best way I know to avoid the trap of thinking you have something to lose. You are already naked. There is no reason not to follow your heart. No one wants to die. Even people who want to go to heaven don't want to die to get there. And yet, death is the destination we all share. No one has ever escaped it, and that is how it should be, because death is very likely the single best invention of life. It's life's change agent. It clears out the old to make way for the new."

Every day brings with it opportunities to move closer to what you want, every day contributes to the end result. Don't let these opportunities pass. **It doesn't take months or years to change your life; you change it step by step, day by day – starting NOW!** The results however, you will see for months and years.

Do yourself a favor and START LIVING NOW: not after the kids are out of the house, after you have finished the next project, after you have got the new car, after you have moved to the new house, or after you have got a better job. Don't be one of those people who say they don't have time, but spend 30 hours a week in front of the TV, playing video games, or going out drinking.

Do the things you always wanted to do NOW. Make plans NOW!

List 5 things you always wanted to do and set a date:
1. _____ Date: _____
2. _____ Date: _____
3. _____ Date: _____
4. _____ Date: _____
5. _____ Date:_____

THE
PRODUCTIVITY
REVOLUTION
Control your time and get things done!

MARC REKLAU

THE PRODUCTIVITY REVOLUTION

Control your time and get things done!

Marc Reklau

CONTENTS

Introduction..197

I - The Basics..201
  1. Self-Discipline and Commitment.............................201
  2. Set Your Productivity Goals....................................203
  3. Plan and Schedule..205
  4. Prioritize...209
  5. Focus..213
  6. Get Organized..215
  7. Distractions and Interruptions...............................219
  8. Procrastination...223

II - Productivity Habits...227
  1. Do It Now..227
  2. Work Against Time..229
  3. Develop a Morning Ritual....................................233
  4. Say No...235
  5. Arrive 10 Minutes Early..237
  6. Underpromise, Overdeliver...................................239
  7. Turn Off Your Phone..241
  8. Spend Time with Your Family..............................243
  9. Take Time Off...245
  10. Take a Power Nap..247
  11. Maximize Lost Time..249
  12. Keep a Journal...251
  13. Stop Watching TV..253

III - The Inner Game of Productivity..........................255
  1. Know Yourself..255
  2. Believe..259
  3. Visualize...263
  4. Increase Your Energy..265
  5. Celebrate Your Wins!..273
  6. Take Control...275
  7. Smile More..279
  8. Fake It Till You Become It...................................281
  9. Your Attitude...283
  10. Watch Your Words..285

IV - Recap..**289**
1. Burning Out..289
2. Tools Put into Practice.................................291
3. One Last Thing..295
Conclusion...299

INTRODUCTION

We say that time is the most precious thing we have and yet we waste it as if we were going to live forever. When you ask people why they don't go after their dreams or why they don't do more of what they love to do the usual answers are: "I don't have enough money" or "I don't have enough time." Rich people usually answer with "I don't have enough time."

With my friends and coaching clients, the most common excuse I hear almost all the time is "I don't have time," and even people that obviously have all the time in the world insist that they still never have enough.

I heard this so often in the last year after finishing my first two books that here I am, finally writing about Time Management and Productivity—with the hope and desire that you can finally find the time for yourself that you need and want to get things done and have more time to do the things you love. You can be a successful business person, entrepreneur, or employee AND have enough time to spend with your family. The time is out there. So let's go and find it.

"Ok Marc. That's nice...but what's the revolution here?" you might ask. The revolution is that we will not only have a look at the usual time management tools as listed in countless Time Management books over the years, but also at the "Inner Game of Productivity" which examines you, your attitude, your beliefs etc. and—and here's the real revolution—we will look at exercises that make you happier!
It has been proven that happier brains are more productive brains. So if you are happy you will perform another 20 to 30 percent better with the same tools, than a person in a neutral or pessimistic state. Now that's news, isn't it?

I'm still using the term Time Management, because we've been using it forever, although by now we know that time can't be managed. We can only manage how we spend the time we have, which is—unless you can bend time—24 hours a day like every other person on this planet. And of course we are not managing time, but our priorities. I'm still going to use the term "Time Management," because I like it.

Some concepts might repeat during the book. I didn't do that to be obnoxious or to stuff the book with unnecessary words. It happens because many concepts are interconnected and—okay, I admit—I also

hope that by repetition the most important concepts stick better.
I also used less exclamation marks. A couple of readers complained about the huge numbers of exclamation marks in "30 Days…" See, I'm taking your feedback seriously.

So why productivity? Easy. The more productive you are the more time you will have. Sounds boring? What about…the more productive you are the more money you will earn…either in your job, or starting a business on the side, or even earning money through a hobby of yours.

Do I have your attention now? I do hope so!

As always I only write about habits that I adopt in MY life to get things done and move ahead. Those habits helped me to write two more books, design various online programs and workshops in the last 12 months, to survive in my former job in a book printing Company (probably the most efficient one in Europe—with only eight people taking care of over 1200 book projects a year), cutting my working hours in half, and never have to work a weekend or spend extra time at work.

It's funny. My friends say "Oh Marc, now that you are a Bestselling author we probably have to ask for an appointment to see you." And yet I'm the one who always has time to see them and ends up asking them for an appointment…

Heck I'm so productive I don't even have an assistant and still answer every single email myself—which by the way is a joy.

I know it's "IN" to have a virtual assistant and play the "I'm-so-busy-and-have-so-many-clients-I-can't-even-answer-my-own-mails" card, but when I read that Personal Development Guru Brendon Burchard did everything himself until he had his first million in his bank account, I decided that I can also get my stuff done myself. I also noticed that the most successful people answer their own emails because they are mostly also the most productive.

Back to productivity…

Productivity at work is a process that we usually ignore. We don't actually analyze our personal work processes and—at best—just try to get things done and have the least possible fires to put out along the way. And that exactly is the mistake.

When we become aware of our work processes we can start analyzing them and seeing where we lose this precious time, make corrections, and finally have all the time we need to get things done and more.

Another problem is that people often don't see that there is a huge difference between being busy and being productive. We grew up in a culture where it was encouraged to be busy and work overtime and where being productive and organized was oftentimes seen as "not having a lot of work to do." And I'm not even talking about leaving work early or on time. You can be incredibly busy the whole day and not get any important work done.
But once you start going for results instead of being busy things will change and it will make a huge difference.

My clients usually don't find blocks of time of 30 minutes or an hour. They find a minute here and three minutes there but it adds up.
The tools and habits that you will learn in this book are not new and there are no new secrets revealed. You probably know most of them. But that's the point. **Knowing is not enough.**

If you are tired of not having the time to do what you want and being busy all the time **you have to start taking action** and use some of the tools to find time.

Not all the tools work for everyone all the time. Choose the ones you feel most comfortable with and start from there. Do them **consistently** over a period of time and analyze your results.

Most of what you will learn is common sense. But then again **common sense is not common action** or as others say **"Common sense is the least common of all senses."**

This stuff works, but only if you do! It's simple, but not easy. If it was easy we'd all have enough time in our lives…and most of us don't. It's time to change that and I will once again revert to **habits**.

As Aristotle already knew nearly 2500 years ago "We are what we repeatedly do. Excellence, then, is not an act, but a habit," and so is productivity. If you are working overtime all the time and don't get your work done then maybe it's time to change something or as Albert Einstein once said the clearest form of insanity is "doing the same thing over and over again and expecting different results."

I'll show you the tools and habits you need to be more productive. The best thing is: You don't need all of them to start gaining back your time and life. Only doing one or two things consistently every single day will do the job for you. The emphasis is on **consistency**. Don't worry if you miss a day. This is where a lot of people give up. Look at it like this: If you do it six out of seven days over four to six weeks that's still better than nothing and you will see results.

Remember: It's what you do every day that will change your life, not what you do every now and then.

Do the habits you choose over a period of 30 days and see what happens. I have seen enormous success with my coaching clients and if you do this your life will change too!
So how do we improve our productivity? In this book we will look at the usual Time Management techniques like "Setting Goals," "Getting Organized," "Prioritize," and "Planning and Scheduling." You will learn to identify distractions and interruptions and how to deal with them efficiently. We will have a look at what is procrastination and how to overcome it. In the second part I'll give you some simple habits to win more time and in the third part we will look at the the most important point: **"The Inner Game of Time Management"** which probably is even more important than the tools and techniques. If your beliefs and attitude are not correct all of the tools and habits will not be that effective. On the other hand if your beliefs and attitudes are correct you will see amazing results.

Sounds good? Then let's get to it!

I - THE BASICS

1
SELF-DISCIPLINE AND COMMITMENT

Let's do this! This is the first chapter, because you can only become more productive if you have the necessary discipline and are **committed to find time in your days no matter what**.

Don't be one of those people who say "I'd like to read more," "I'd like to exercise more," "I'd like to write a book," "I'd like to go out into nature more," and then don't do it.

Self-discipline and commitment are character traits that will decide whether you do what you said you would do and go through with it starting by making a schedule and sticking to it or planning your days ahead.

There's more: It's doing the things you need to do, even if you are not in the mood for it.

Not very self-disciplined? Don't worry. You can start training your self-discipline from this moment on! It's like a muscle. The more you train it, the better you get.

If your self-discipline is weak right now, start training it by setting yourself small, reachable goals like:

- Write a thousand words a day instead of writing a book
- Not answering the phone for one hour one day per week
- Not looking at your mobile phone, social networks, and emails in the first 90 minutes after waking up…and so on.

It's important that you keep your commitments—with others, but also with yourself.

Not keeping your commitments has a terrible consequence: You lose energy, you lose clarity, and even worse it affects your self-esteem!

Only make commitments that you really want. That can mean fewer commitments and more "NOs." You're already gaining time…If you commit—keep your commitment whatever it takes.

Saying "No" is so important and probably one of the best time management tricks of all, it will get a separate chapter all to itself further ahead.

On to the next chapter!

2
SET YOUR PRODUCTIVITY GOALS

If you are like most people you overestimate what you can do in a week and underestimate what you can do in month. If you go one step at a time and remain flexible, then over time you can achieve things that you couldn't even imagine before. It's like compound interest. The small steps with time, sum up to something really big

Write down your goals and they will drive you to take the right actions. Having clearly defined goals will be crucial on your way towards more productivity

Your goals are like a GPS system leading the way. But to be led, first of all you have to know where you want to go!

The first step to achieving your goals is to put them in writing. Until a little more than three years ago I wasn't a big goal setter. I was very skeptical. Then I started writing down my goals and incredible things started to happen. I became a lot more productive and focused and accomplished goals that weren't even imaginable just months before.

There's nothing like committing to your goals, writing them down…and achieving them or even exceeding them. (I wanted to sell 2,500 books in 2015 and sold over 12,000—imagine how I felt…)

Of course writing your goals down involves a certain risk: Suddenly you will be able measure what you achieve and what you don't achieve. Have the courage to do it anyway. It will be worth it!

Why write down your goals?

1) You declare to your mind, that out of the 50,000 to 60,000 thoughts you have a day, THE ONES written down are the most important ones.

2) You start concentrating and focusing on the activities that bring you closer to your goal. While written goals keep you focused on where you want to go, you also start taking better decisions.

3) You can look at your written goals everyday. This forces you to act and helps you to prioritize your actions for the day by asking yourself questions such as "In this moment, is doing what I'm doing bringing me closer to my productivity goals or should I be doing something else?"

Before starting the goal setting process, you have to be very clear about your goals. Be precise and formulate each goal as a positive statement. Then break them down into small, realistic, achievable action steps and make a list of all the steps that you will take to get there.

Calculate how long it will take you. Set a deadline for each action step and goal. Don't worry if you don't reach the goal by the exact date you set; it's just a way of focusing on the goal and creating a sense of urgency.

Create a clear vision of your goals in your mind. See yourself as already having achieved the goal: How does it feel? How does it look? How does it sound? How does it smell?

Another important point: When pursuing your goals, reward yourself for the effort put in, and not just for the results. If you won 10 minutes a day, you are improving. 10 minutes a day in four weeks are nearly two and a half hours! That's more than you have now, isn't it?

Some small things that will come in handy:
Put a little card with your time management goals written on it in your wallet and read it four to five times daily. The more the better
Keep a task list. Put your action steps on it as well as the time it takes to do the task and put the deadline for each task.
I recommend you to check your goals daily/weekly and monthly—this will boost your productivity enormously!

3
PLAN AND SCHEDULE

I'm sure you have heard phrases like "If you spend half of your time planning you will do everything twice as fast!" or "If you don't know where you are going you can end up anywhere."

They sound so trivial, but we all know there's some truth to them and yet…are you planning your days? Or are you just floating, fixing things as they turn up, putting out fires, and doing the same things every day?

The habit of planning alone will probably already completely change your life. It changed mine.

Planning your days, weeks, and even months ahead will help you to put the right priorities in place and plan you important work.

I have become an absolute fan of planning. I plan my coming week regularly on Sunday afternoon and "planning tomorrow today" has gained me a lot of time and peace of mind.

So how do you do this? Make task lists. Put all of your upcoming tasks on there and assign a time to every single action of that list. Always have the list close by and visible. This will help you stay focused during the day.

Another good idea is to work in blocks of time. I usually work in 90-minute blocks and then take a 30-minute break or if I'm in flow, three-hour blocks and then a two-hour break.

Ask yourself what are the five things that you want to get done tomorrow?
Choose things and actions that move you closer to the completion of your goals and designate the hours you need to complete each action.

Don't forget to schedule free time, fun time, and travel time into your calendar and always leave a little reserve of time for emergencies that might come up.

Problems that can come up planning your days and weeks:
- You don't have time to plan (Half an hour on Sunday afternoon to plan your week can do miracles).
- You are too optimistic with your time and have difficulties in estimating how long your tasks will take. So you always need longer that you scheduled and this builds up a lot of pressure that you are carrying around with you.
- You don't reserve time for unforeseen emergencies or tasks that come up and your schedule gets ruined every single day by those events.

Create a daily schedule
Schedule your day: Schedule in buffer time for unexpected things that WILL come up. Reserve blocks of time for your nap, free time, fun time. And remember: Don't be busy—go for results

Yearly planning
Divide your yearly goals into quarterly goals. What do you have to have accomplished by the end of March in order to be on track to your yearly goals?

Monthly goals.
Watch your goals for the week every day. What do you have to accomplish this week to achieve your monthly and quarterly goals?

Book your activities into your calendar.
Each evening watch your calendar and see what your goals, and actions for the next days are. This will make it so that the next day you know exactly what to do and get directly to work instead of wasting precious time figuring out what to do.

Keep score
Every now and then check on yourself: What did you get done? Were you doing the things you were supposed to be doing to move closer towards your goals or were you distracted?

Having a log of what you did will give you an overview of your productivity and also help you to see if the time you give yourself for every task is realistic or if you are too optimistic in your estimation. I have a friend who always thinks he can get tasks done in one hour and then takes two hours to complete them.

He not only "loses" one hour for every task—which can easily sum up to three hours a day, but there is also a heavy emotional weight bringing him down; A continuous feeling of not accomplishing stuff which naturally attacks his self-esteem.

One big secret of my productivity success is that I always give myself lots of time for the different tasks.

If I think I'll do it in an hour, I'll give myself two hours to finish the task. In comparison to my frustrated friend in the example above, I always have enough time and have experienced the success of finishing tasks earlier, paired with rewards and well-being. You'll hardly ever see me stressed.

You can download my yearly, quarterly, weekly, and daily planners on my webpage www.goodhabitsacademy.com along with some other coaching work sheets.

4
PRIORITIZE

Prioritizing actually is quite easy. You just have to separate the important from the unimportant stuff. Or as Victor Küppers, one of the best trainers and speakers in Spain says: "The most important thing is that the most important thing is the most important thing."

Unfortunately many times emergencies come up that have to be taken care of first. Asking yourself "What's my most important task for tomorrow?" will help you to get focused and give you a head start getting into action the next morning.

So how can we differentiate between what's urgent, what's important, and what isn't?

There are two helpful approaches when you want to prioritize: Number one is "The Time Management Matrix" which is usually attributed to Stephen Covey and is also known as Eisenhower's Urgent–Important principle and number two is "The Pareto Principle" which is also known as the 80/20 Rule.

The Time Management Matrix:
Stephen Covey introduced the idea of determining priorities by using four quadrants. The quadrants allow you to prioritize your tasks in relation to their urgency and importance.
Based on in which quadrant you put the task in, you decide if it's something you have to do immediately or if you can postpone it.

	URGENT	NOT URGENT
IMPORTANT	*Quadrant I:* Urgent & Important	*Quadrant II:* Not Urgent & Important
NOT IMPORTANT	*Quadrant III:* Urgent & Not Important	*Quadrant IV:* Not Urgent & Not Important

First of all we differentiate between important tasks and urgent tasks. The **important** tasks are those that contribute directly to the achievement of your goals, while the **urgent** ones are those that require your immediate attention. Not dealing with the urgent issues will cause immediate consequences although or because they are often tied to other people's goals.

Here's a summary of the meaning of each quadrant:
Quadrant 1 – urgent and important
Tasks that could have been foreseen, and those that couldn't go into this quadrant.
It includes only those activities that require your immediate attention like emergencies, extremely important deadlines, pressing problems, last minute preparations. (Could better planning have helped?)

Examples: Crisis, customer service, new business, delayed activities, health problems, paying debts, etc.

Quadrant 2 – not urgent but important
Tasks that don't have a high urgency, but play an important role in the future.

This is where you do your strategic planning, and anything related to education, health, recreation, exercise, and/career. The tasks in here might not be urgent in the present, but in the long term this quadrant is where you might want to spend most of your time. **The more time you spend here, the less time you'll have to spend in Quadrant 1 where the stress happens**. The better your planning is in Quadrant 2, the less future tasks will be found in quadrant 1.
Examples: Preparation, prevention, planning, building relationships, self-development, holidays with the family, important social activities.

Quadrant 3 – urgent but not important
Tasks that are not important, but appear to have high urgency go in this quadrant. Activities in this quadrant are often distractions with high urgency. They don't contribute any value and are rather obstacles than anything else. Minimize, eliminate, delegate, or reschedule these tasks.
If caused by another person, decline requests politely if possible. Stress often comes up because we confuse quadrant 3 tasks and think they are quadrant 1 tasks. I've had a lot of stressed clients that spent

their time in quadrant 3 thinking they were in quadrant 1. Once they became aware of the difference between the two, their life improved a lot.

Examples: Interruptions, unproductive meetings, unnecessary calls, reports, checking mails, redoing work, wasted time with people.

Quadrant 4 – not urgent and not important
If you spend most of your time in this quadrant you either are close to getting fired or very lucky that you aren't. The fourth quadrant contains tasks and activities that are absolute time wasters and do not contribute any value at all. These tasks are plain distractions. Eliminate all tasks from this quadrant or plainly avoid them!

Examples: Surfing the web without any purpose, watching TV or YouTube videos, surfing on Facebook, playing games, chatting and messaging, going shopping etc.

So where can the majority of your tasks and activities, both private and professional, be found? My guess is either quadrant one or three. Mostly quadrant two is neglected, although for your productivity it is the most important one. You should maximize time spent in quadrant two because the more time you spend in that quadrant, the less you will have to spend in quadrants one and three—which will boost your productivity enormously. The better you plan your activities and tasks, the less quadrant one activities will there be in the long term.

The time management matrix helps you to check whether a certain task or activity brings you closer to your goals or not. Once that is done, you will know exactly which tasks and activities to prioritize over those that cost you time, but contribute little or next to nothing to your results.

The Pareto principle or the 80/20 Rule
Pareto's principle from the beginning of the 20th century was based on the discovery that 20% of the Italian population owned 80% of the land, which seems quite outdated especially in a world where 1% of the population owns 99% of the wealth, but let's play with it for the heck of it. (Never underestimate the power of a good self-fulfilling prophecy: Millions of people believing in the validity of the principle may maintain it valid until today.)

Pareto researched this ratio and also found it in his garden, where 20% of his tomato plants produced 80% of his tomatoes and I have to admit that I spend 80% of my time in 20% of my house—usually the living and dining room.

Applied to business this would mean (and you can confirm this in your own business and personal life):

- 80% of your results will come from 20% of your actions
- 80% of your profits come from 20% of your clients
- 80% of your complaints come from 20% of your clients
- 80% of your sales come from 20% of your products
and so on…

So which of your clients bring you 80% of your sales? Wouldn't it be productive to concentrate most of your time on them? What about the 20% of clients that stand for 80% of your complaints? Getting rid of them would surely free up a lot of time that you can save by not having to handle their complaints—as long as they are not the ones who also bring 80% of your benefits of course.
Same goes for the 20% of your clients that account for 80% of your stress. If they are not bringing in 80% of the money…fire them!
Your business—and your available time—can grow exponentially if you can concentrate on the projects that earn the most money with the least time spent on them.
So sit down and identify—using Pareto's Principle—which projects are holding you back and which ones you should boost. Apply the 80/20 rule to every area of your business and your personal life.

Answer the following questions to yourself:
- Where should you invest more time?
- Where should you invest less time?
- Where are you getting good results investing relatively less time?
- Where are you spending a lot of time and getting few results?

5
FOCUS

One of the most important habits for improving your productivity is the ability to FOCUS.

When you are focusing you will get more work done than any other day when you are multitasking. I don't know who came up with the theory that multitasking is actually good for your productivity but it's a big lie. Do yourself a favor and stop multitasking right now! You are not gaining time with it; you're actually wasting time shifting from one task to another.

You are much better off doing **one thing at a time!**

The newest studies show that multitasking is actually less productive and that nothing beats doing one thing at a time with a concentrated effort. Some studies even imply that multitasking actually makes you slower and—careful now—dumber!

In any case, even if you think you are multitasking you are actually doing one thing at a time, aren't you? You might have five tasks on your hands, but I'm sure you don't do all five things at the same time. You are writing an email. You stop writing it and take a phone call. You hang up and continue writing the email. A colleague comes to you with a question. You stop writing your email and answer the question and so on. So forget about multitasking. **Focus on doing one thing at a time and do it with concentration!**

Batching

Batching is a great way to increase both your focus and your productivity. It means that you will concentrate on one only task for an hour or two. Do this during the time when you don't allow any interruptions or distractions—no email checking, no notification noises, no surfing the web, etc.

Did you ever notice that you get faster when you do the same thing for an hour? Batching things—like one hour of only writing emails, one hour of only answering calls etc.—is incredibly productive and will help you to do things more quickly because you'll get into the flow of the task and won't lose time in refocusing like when you are switching between tasks or being interrupted. Analyze your tasks and see which ones you can group together.

I usually combine the following tasks:

Planning, answering emails, reading, writing, phone calls, meetings, housework, shopping, etc.

6
GET ORGANIZED

You will earn an hour for every five minutes you spend on organizing. Period.So you are too busy to get organized, aren't you? You have post-its and mountains of paper all over your table? And if you just had a little bit of time to get organized you would do it, right?

I'm sorry that I have to be the one to tell you, but…
…it's not that you are too busy to get organized, it's because you are not organized that you are so busy!

Unfortunately, "being busy" doesn't mean that you are getting results! And the one with the messiest table in the office, is seldom the one who works hardest.
Studies say that today's executives spend between 30% and 50% of their time pushing around paper in search of the document they need. Scary, isn't it?

So, my overwhelmed worker, go on reading and TRY OUT these little tips, as they can change your life! I have been there and I turned it around using the little tips below:

- Spend the first 15 minutes of your working day prioritizing what to do.
- Spend one hour a week organizing and filing papers. If there is something you can do in less than five minutes, DO IT! If it takes longer put it onto your to-do or tasks list.
- Spend 15 minutes a day throwing away papers and clearing away your desk. Really throw away everything you don't need.
- Spend the last 15 minutes of your working day to go through your tasks for tomorrow. What's important? What's urgent?
- Bring order into your email inbox and delete old mails that you don't need any more. If you are not sure print the email out and file it to quiet your conscience.
- As an IT technician once told me, deleting your old emails not only makes you feel lighter, it also saves your company or yourself some money because hundreds or thousands of mails

stocked up in you inbox cost a lot more in energy—which translates into higher electricity costs.
- Don't accept any new tasks until you are in control.
- Do the job right the first time, so that it doesn't come back to haunt you and cost you more time later.

Organizing and filing paperwork:
- Collect all of your paperwork and process it as follows:
- If you need less than five minutes to do it, do it now!
- If you need more time, put it on your task list.
- Once you have completed it, archive it.
- If it's for another person, resend it.
- If it's for later, archive it or throw it away.
  (How many files do you have that you saved for later? How many of them do you actually need?)
- None of the above? Throw it away.

Organizing your email inbox:
- If you need less than five minutes to respond, do it now.
- If you can delegate it, delegate it NOW.
- If you need more time to process it, put it on your task list.
- Create folders and move finished tasks into them right away.
- Use your email inbox as a to-do list: Tasks solved get archived and tasks unsolved stay in the inbox.
- If you don't need it for future reference, DELETE it.
- Unsubscribe from every newsletter that you don't need—except from mine. Just kidding. For the sake of your productivity even unsubscribe from mine, although it would be hard to see you go.

Follow these steps until your email inbox is empty.
If you have a lot of emails, work on the ones from last month and archive the others in a folder named "Old emails."

Your work area:
- Put everything you need within your reach.
- Keep your folders close by and in order.
- Keep your work surface empty and clean.
- Keep things you need to use close by and in good condition.
- Put things you do not need often in a drawer.

- Keep work trays (Incoming, Outgoing, Pending).
- Put order in your head too. Do this by writing down your thoughts and ideas.
- Take time to organize your workplace every week.

Remember: If you lose five minutes a day looking for stuff that sums up to 30 hours per year! Having or not having this time makes a lot of difference.

Unclutter. PERIOD.

If you don't use it it's probably clutter. And clutter needs to go! It's all about energy. What goes for your work, goes for your home.
If you have too much stuff that you don't use in your house, it drains your energy! If you have less energy you become less productive. Start with your cupboard.

Here are some tips:

- If you haven't worn it in a year, you probably won't wear it any more.
- When you think "This will be useful one day" or "This reminds me of good times"—out it goes.
- Marie Kondo, Japanese uncluttering guru goes even further: "If it doesn't spark joy—out it goes." I highly recommend her book "The Life-Changing Magic of Tidying." It changed my life.

When I unclutter I usually give stuff away for free. It just makes me feel better and somehow I think life/God/the universe will reward me for it.

Once you are done with the cupboard take on the whole bedroom. Later move on to the living room, clean out your garage, and end up cleaning up your entire home & office. Get rid of everything that you don't use any more: Clothes, journals, books, CDs, even furniture, and so on. One of my clients uncluttered his whole apartment in one weekend. He felt so much better and lighter and got an energy boost that helped him to reach a whole bunch of his short term goals. He never looked back. When will you start uncluttering?

Remember those 30 hours you win if you don't have to search for things? Well having order at home will save you another 30 hours per year. We already found 60 hours! And counting…

Holy guacamole! It's just the beginning of the book and we already won around 100 hours a year for you. Please read on anyway. ;-)

Reminder:
Like everything else in this book, saying "That won't work for me" doesn't count as an excuse! Try it for at least two weeks and if it still doesn't work for you write me an email and complain to me!

7
DISTRACTIONS AND INTERRUPTIONS

How focused are you at your work? Or to put it in another way: What's the longest time you have focused on your work without getting distracted or interrupted? For most people it's not very long. My guess is that you get distracted every four to five minutes. The tone that notifies you that you just received a new email, the vibrating sound on your mobile that signals you that somebody just commented on one of your Facebook posts, your mom calls, Whatsapp or text messages, and so on and on and on.

There are two types of interruptions that knock you off your productivity path day after day: Internal and external interruptions. It's so important to ban all interruptions and distractions, **because it's not just the interruption or distraction time you lose**, you also lose your focus and studies show that it takes you seven to 15 minutes to refocus. Some people even say it takes you 25 minutes to refocus.

How many times do you get distracted or interrupted every day? 10 times? In the best case scenario, that's 70 minutes you lose and in the worst case, four hours…

This explains why disciplined and productive people can get done more in a day than other people in a whole week! If you want to control distractions you need to develop and build your self-discipline and the ability to let nobody and nothing distract you. But believe me it's going to be worth it.

Dealing with external interruptions is a another ball game and depends, to a great extent, on your ability and willingness to say NO without fear.

A small course in the art of saying "No":

Decide ahead of time how you are going to reject the request for a favor. Practice it! Always be nice and friendly, but firm when telling somebody that you can't help them right away. It's up to you if you want to explain or not why you are rejecting the person's request for immediate help.

My personal opinion is you don't have to explain anything. Funny enough, I was the guy always giving explanations until one day I didn't feel the need to explain any more. You can always offer other options or alternatives such as, "Sorry I can't help you right now. I could support you for an hour on Friday afternoon." Try to get to an agreement and find acceptable compromises when possible.

If you say "yes" to everything you will be the busiest person in the office, you will do extra time when your colleagues are going home, and you will get called on Friday nights or on the weekend.

How dare they call you on a Friday night or on weekends! Sorry it's not *"them."* It's *you* taking the call and thus indirectly signalling to them "It's okay to call me whenever you want."
It's you who has to set the limits.

How to deal with external interruptions

Interruptions by workmates or the boss:
Don't consider every petition as urgent. Take your time and think about when is a good time to act. If it's a valid interruption, schedule it in your task list, but don't let other people's priorities become your priorities. If the petition comes from your boss tell him or her how making this a priority will affect your other projects and tasks and renegotiate if necessary.
Keep an "interruptions log" for two weeks and write down who interrupts you.

Interruptions by phone:
I know. You have to take every phone call; if not you will lose the client/sponsor etc. If I got a dollar for every time I've heard this... Yet after putting it into action I never ever received any complaint about lost clients. In fact, one of my clients even improved his sales and got more clients! You'll read more of him later.

It's okay to not take every call or let calls go to voice mail at least for an hour a day. They will leave a message or call back and you will win a lot of time, because that hour without interruptions will be your most productive hour every day. You can also redirect it to a colleague who'll nicely tell the caller that you are in a meeting and take a message. Schedule a specific time for your outgoing calls and batch them to gain additional time.

Avoid distractions
"The major difference between successful people and the unsuccessful is their ability to not get distracted."

I know a lot of people who think and tell me that they are sooooo busy, work lots of overtime, and don't have any idea how and where to win time.
Once we look a little bit closer at their routine, we notice that they are checking their email every 20 minutes, getting notifications from people who saw their stuff on Facebook or Twitter, and are checking every new email that comes in every five minutes. Apart from this they are surfing on the internet and watching YouTube videos and cat photos on Facebook.

The Solution:
- Close your internet browser.
- Redirect your phone or take it off the hook.
- Turn off your mobile phone or at least turn the sound and notification sounds off. (I usually put my phone on airplane mode in order to work productively and without interruptions or distractions.)
- Close your email. Don't check your emails regularly. (Three times a day for half an hour should be enough.)
- Log out of your social media networks.
- Set fixed times to be on Facebook, Twitter etc. and stick to them.
- Close your office door.

Doing some of these things means an hour or two of time without being distracted by text messages or phone calls. Try it!
Once you start it you'll love it. You'll notice that you'll get more things done than ever before. Just one or two hours a day can do miracles for your productivity.
If you are working from home, think very well who you let distract you. The person who wants to have coffee with you or take you to

the mall will probably not be paying your bills at the end of the month when you wish back those hours that you lost being distracted and not doing what had to be done. Another advice…don't turn on the TV. You know it. Once it's on—gone is your productivity. You can use the TV as a motivation though: "If I get done what I planned for today I'm going to reward myself with my favorite series."

Reward yourself
Reward yourself when you get things done!
This can actually increase your focus and productivity. Setting up a reward can get you motivated to get things done fast.

For example: If I work on my book from 7 to 10 AM, I usually give myself a two-hour break to check my private Facebook account and watch one episode of my favorite series. But I can only get this reward if I write and produce until 10 AM sharp.

I usually reward myself in the following way: Meeting friends, taking a power nap, watching a movie or TV series, enjoying a nice bubble bath, walking on the beach, going to the beach bar and having a coffee, reading a good book, playing an hour on my xBox (needs a lot of discipline. ONE hour—not more…), a guided meditation. Distractions are everywhere. You just can't get rid of them. What you can do is get really good at recognizing them. Once you are aware of them you can take action to refocus.

Here's a list of the typical distractions that will keep you from being productive. Which ones are you guilty of?
- Watching TV
- Playing Video Games (or mobile games)
- Letting People interrupt you
- Checking emails every time you get one
- Watch your Phone all the time (Calls, Texts, Apps)
- Looking out the window
- Social Networking
- Surfing on Websites
- Looking at Photos
- "Researching"
- Eating & Drinking
- Worrying
- Thinking of the past or daydreaming

8
PROCRASTINATION

If you are working the whole day, but at the end of the day are not getting things done, or seeing any results of your work, there is a high chance that you are procrastinating the important stuff.

No worries. Everybody is procrastinating every now and then. It happens to the best of us.

Procrastination is a major thief of time and the goal is to minimize procrastination so that we can get more things done.

Read closely now—you might be procrastinating without even knowing it. Once you become aware that you are procrastinating and the methods that you are using to doing it, you can catch yourself and take counter measures like outsourcing tasks you don't like to do at all or not giving in to cheap excuses of your "inner saboteur."

So how do you notice that you are procrastinating?

- You are avoiding something that should be done.
- You are putting things off, hoping that they magically get better without actually doing anything about them. (Usually things don't get better on their own…and a lot of times the will get worse.)
- You are doing things that don't need to be done right now instead of doing what you are supposed to be doing—and it doesn't matter if those things you are doing are more or less important!

Yes. You read right. Even doing something that is more important than what we are supposed to be doing is procrastination.

Procrastination comes in a wide variety of forms:

- Getting distracted
- Putting off tasks
- Waiting until a task is perfect in order to complete it
- Leaving everything up to the very last minute.

Are you a delayer, a perfectionist, or easily distractible?

The most common reason for procrastination is some kind of fear: Fear of failure, fear of being judged, even fear of success to name a few. Even if we procrastinate because we are lazy or because we lack motivation there might be an underlying fear responsible for it. Sometimes feeling overwhelmed is the reason we procrastinate.

Excuses can be a form procrastination.
Whenever you use the following excuses watch very closely! You might be procrastinating:
- "I'm too tired."
- "I don't have time for it right now."
- "I need a break."
- "I don't feel like doing that now, I'll feel more like it later."
- "It's too late to start this today, I'll do it tomorrow first thing."

Whenever I catch myself talking like this I watch very closely what am I doing at that exact moment. What task am I doing and why does my mind want to distract me from it?

I use the trigger as fuel to do the task anyway telling myself **"If my mind wants to trick me into procrastinating this task it must be really important so I will stay here and finish it now,"** instead of giving in to the temptation of watching senseless videos on YouTube, cat photos on Facebook, or cleaning up my room (not so senseless, but a great way to procrastinate).

So when I'm on a task and suddenly feel the urge to do dishes and cleaning up the house, I clearly identify that as an intent to procrastinate and finish the task at hand. Unfortunately I wasn't that smart 20 years ago when I had this intense urge to clean up my apartment every time I was studying for an exam. Funnily this urge always showed up during exam time—never the rest of the year. So twice a year my apartment was super-tidy while I failed exams…

The easily distractible lose themselves in games, TV, on the internet, or going to the mall. **If you catch yourself playing Candy Crush you might just want to have a look at the task that you should be doing instead and analyze why you are not doing it.** Here are some more procrastination excuses and how to deal with them:

1) "I don't have enough time"
That's why you bought this book in the first place, isn't it? I hope you already found more time. Did you start making lists? When you have your task list, start working. Action is always and by far the best antidote do procrastination.

2) "I have to many things on my plate"
Who doesn't? There are always a lot of things to do and it probably will never stop but which are priorities? Which tasks will give you the best results?

3) "I can't decide what to start with"
Indecision arises when you are overwhelmed by too many options and don't know what to start with. The best is to start with the biggest, most overwhelming decision to take.

4) "It's not perfect yet"
This is one of the most dangerous excuses! It can be used to procrastinate for ever!

We don't see perfectionists as procrastinators, because they seem to be proactive and efficient. But are they really? If you are not finishing your book, your webpage, or your project because it's not "perfect" yet then you, my dear, might suffer from "paralysis by analysis" and are a procrastinator. For me the best tip I ever got was **"Done is better than perfect."**

Watch very closely how much of a difference putting in more effort really makes? Will your search for perfectionism steal away time that you need for other tasks?
A good trick for the perfectionists among us is to calculate how much your time is worth in money and then decide if what you are doing is beneficial. If you work 10 hours instead of two to finish a task, you are losing money. Especially when the additional eight hours only add little to the result.
Choose to finish the project NOW and then improve it along the way. Like for example, software companies do, right?

5) "It's not the right time," "I'm waiting for the right moment"
Oh dear, oh dear. If I had a dollar for every time I heard this one…
If you are waiting for the right moment to start your new business,

launch your new product, do your live event **you might as well wait for ever, because the right moment never comes.**

And neither does the sign from the universe you are waiting for. Maybe the universe is sending you signs all the time and you just can't see them. There is no "right time" to do something, or better said, **the right time to do something is always NOW.**

I don't know who said it first but the term "waiting for the right time to start something is like waiting in your driveway for all the traffic lights to turn green before going for a drive" has it about right. Usually procrastination ends in guilt, anxiety, self-loathing, or even depression and it's damaging to the procrastinator's self-esteem and inner peace. This is a price far too high to pay.

The worst thing is you lose twice. You don't do what needs to be done, but you also can't enjoy the activity you're doing instead of what needs to be done because of a bad conscience or because you are feeling guilty.

Become a doer! Do what needs to be done and afterwards enjoy the rewards without having a black cloud hanging over your head.

Solutions:
- Be absolutely honest with yourself. If tempted to procrastinate ask yourself "What price am I paying for procrastinating this task?"
- Dive straight in (Action is the best antidote to procrastination).
- Focus on the results you'll get by doing the task you are tempted to leave for later.
- Focus on the rewards.
- Work with others (Coach, Accountability partner).
- Set yourself deadlines.
- Analyze, divide, and conquer tasks.
- Do the most uncomfortable task first thing in the morning.
- Focus on the task that brings in money.

II - PRODUCTIVITY HABITS

1
DO IT NOW!

That unwritten email, the conversation with that annoying colleague or customer, the talk with your boss about that raise. Do it NOW. This habit will help you to really get stuff done. I'm sure you know the best time to finish a task is always NOW.

Do yourself a favor and stop the procrastination. It only causes anxiety! And most of the time you will find that things that you procrastinated for days causing you anxiety and a bad conscience are actually done in an hour or so and afterwards you feel so much lighter because you can forget about it.

Whatever it is that you have on your mind right now, don't start tomorrow or next week! Start NOW! I promise you—in one year you will be happy that you started today!
Same goes for every task that takes you less then five minutes to finish like answering short emails (batch it if you can), calling your mother back, calling your phone company, booking that dentist appointment, etc.
Do it now!

Do the uncomfortable tasks first thing in the morning. I know it's tough but it will improve the quality of the rest of your day. Because—as I mentioned before—if you postpone it you will carry it around with you all day anyway and your conscience will weigh you down. Do it now and forget about it.
The afternoon or other low-energy phases are good for doing simple stuff like organizing daily mail, cleaning your desk, easy reading, filling in excel sheets, following up, filing, etc.

2
WORK AGAINST TIME

A great productivity habit is to develop a sense of urgency and to work against time. Set yourself deadlines. If you have enough self-discipline to take your own deadlines seriously, fantastic! If not include other people that you don't want to let down.

Coaching for example is so effective and successful because the majority of clients don't want to let their coaches down. They do their stuff and thus, make progress from week to week towards their goals.

Back to time management…
Some people say you should punish yourself for not meeting your deadlines: Like not watching your favorite series on TV or not going out. If you have read my other books you know I'm not a big fan of any kind of self-punishment.

Why not reward yourself for making the deadline with watching your favorite TV series or going to the movies? A little change in perspective, but a whole new outlook. Two completely different approaches to the same result…The choice is yours!

The last day before vacation
Remember the last day before vacation when you suddenly get everything done? Why? Because it has to be done. Suddenly tasks get finished that haven't been finished for weeks. You have to take tough decisions right there and then and can't afford the luxury of procrastinating.
So why not pretend every day to be the last day before your vacation?

Parkinson's Law
Parkinson's Law states that "Work expands so as to fill the time available for its completion" which means whatever time you have to complete a project, you will need that time to complete it.

That's why you usually finish a two-week project in the evening of day 13 and if you had three weeks for the same project you'd finish in the evening of day 20.

Another reason is that deadlines force you to focus more on the task at hand. You concentrate on the essential, start cutting out any other superfluous activities, and get things done.

It's when you have a deadline that you start keeping your emails and phone calls short and suddenly win a lot of time. I see it over and over again: People tell me they don't have time, but then they spend hours on the phone.

I once worked with a colleague who worked a lot of overtime and never got her work done on time. Looking closer at her work process—she was a logistics manager—I noticed that when she booked a transport she called and stayed on the phone for 20 minutes with every freight forwarder to talk about her life when an email would have done the job. She talked to about five freight forwarders a day...You do the math.

Now don't misunderstand me, It's great and necessary to build great relationships with your suppliers, but if you are complaining about not having time...don't stay on the phone for 20 minutes. Make it 10 or even better—five minutes!

Phone calls
When you get called, get to the point quickly—it's best to already have an exit strategy when you pick up the phone... be polite but show that you don't have time to waste.

For example, tell your counterpart right at the beginning "Hi. Nice to hear from you. I'm just preparing for an important reunion. I have five minutes. What can I do for you?" Or something like that. It works. People get to the point much quicker when you start like this.

Email templates might be another possibility to win some minutes here and there. These minutes will add up.

Challenges
Set yourself little challenges such as "I'll get this done in one hour" and see how you are doing.

The curse of "being busy"
Many people are using the "I'm busy" excuse for never finishing things:
"I have to finish my webpage. It will be great, but I'm so busy and don't have time to do it."
"I have this great book inside me, but I'm busy and don't have time to write…"
"I have this great business idea, but I'm so busy I don't have time to look for alternatives and will stay in my dead-en job a little longer until I have time to send some CVs."

Stop using time as an excuse and start using your time better! Learn to get the important things done and stop wasting time doing useless stuff (a.k.a being busy) until you have built up some time reserves.
As I said before being busy doesn't mean that you are being productive and getting results.

Pomodoro Method
I don't know what impresses me more: The simplicity and efficiency of this technique or the fact that entire books have been written on how to set a timer to 25 minutes, work 25 minutes, and then take a five-minute break.

Basically it's another approach to the things mentioned earlier. Work 25 minutes **without interruptions**, then take a five-minute break. After four pomodoros (two hours) take a longer break of 15 to 30 minutes.

The Pomodoro technique should help you to focus and reduce the impact of external and internal distractions.

The fun starts when a whole department starts applying this technique. I've heard that productivity in such a department literally explodes. If you have experiences with the Pomodoro technique please let me know. I'm always interested in real-life examples.

3
DEVELOP A MORNING RITUAL

This is my favourite moment of each day and my morning ritual contributed a lot if not everything to my well-being, wealth, and productivity. This ritual alone might solve all of your time management problems.
One of the most important moments of your day is the 30 minutes after you wake up. This is when your subconscious is very receptive so it's of big importance what you do in this time.

The way you start your day will have a huge impact on how the rest of your day develops. I'm sure you have had days which have started off on the wrong foot and from then on it got worse and worse—or the opposite where you woke up with that feeling that everything will go your way and then it did.

That's why it's very important to begin your day well. Most of us just get into a rush from minute one after waking up and that's how our days unfold. No wonder most people run around stressed nowadays. What would getting up half an hour or an hour earlier every morning do for you?

What if instead of hurrying and swallowing down your breakfast or even having it on the way to work, you get up and take half an hour for yourself? Maybe you even create a little morning ritual with a 10- or 15-minute meditation? Do you see what this could do for your life if you made it a habit? Here are some activities for the morning ritual. Give it a shot!

- Think positive: Today is going to be a great day!
- Remember for five minutes what you are grateful for.
- 15 minutes of quiet time.
- Imagine the day that is about to start going very well.
- Go over your schedule for today. What's important? What has to get done?
- Watch a sunrise.
- Go running or take a walk.
- Write in your journal.

The last half an hour of your day has the same importance! The things you do in the last half an hour before sleeping will remain in your subconscious during your sleep. So then it's time to do the following:

- Write in your journal again.
- Now is the time for reflecting on your day. What did you do great? What could you have done even better?
- Plan tomorrow today. What are the most important things you want to get done tomorrow?
- Make a to-do list for the next day.
- Visualize your ideal day.
- Read some inspirational blogs, articles, or chapters of a book.
- Listen to music that inspires you.

I highly recommend that you NOT WATCH THE NEWS or MOVIES that agitate you before you are about to go to sleep. This is because when you are falling asleep you are highly receptive to suggestions.
That's why it's a lot more beneficial to listen to or watch positive material. The planning ahead of your day and the list of things to do can bring you immense advantages and time saving. The things you have to do will already be in your subconscious plus you will get to work very focused the next day if you already know what your priorities are.

4
SAY NO

This is one of those habits that will improve your productivity (and your life) a lot.
Did you know that the most successful people say no to nearly everything?

Here's what happened to me:
When I stopped wanting to please others and started being myself, a lot of it came with the word "No." Every time you say "No" when you mean "No," you are actually saying "Yes" to yourself!

Before learning to say "No," I often accepted invitations I didn't want to or went to events I didn't enjoy. The result was I was there physically but mentally I was in another place and honestly I was not the best company. Not to mention that I could have used the time for more important stuff.

If you say yes to everything you will never have enough time, because other people will decide your schedule and not you.

When I decided that a "Yes" is a "Yes" and a "No" is a "No," I felt much better. I accepted a lot less invitations (this already makes up for a lot of time) and although telling "NO" was hard at the beginning, the result was that when I accepted invitations to events or going out, I was fully there.

In my work life, the impact was even greater. Guess what happened when I said yes to every favor I was asked for…? I ended up being totally overwhelmed at work, because I was asked for a lot of favors and took on a lot of extra tasks—usually work nobody else wanted to do.

It took me a while to put my foot down, but finally I said "Enough." From then on, my first answer to all requests for favors was "**NO!** Sorry. Can't do it. Very busy at the moment"!

By starting to say "No" often, you will improve your work and personal life a lot and actually free up a lot of time.
But make sure you say "NO" without feeling guilty! You can explain to the person in question that it's not anything personal against them, but for your own well-being. You can still do your colleagues a favor, but only if you have enough time and decide to. If you do this, you will find that suddenly you are in the driver's seat.

Now you might say: "But Marc, what you are suggesting here is not what teamwork looks like." And you are right. But neither is going at half power knowing your coworker will save the day for you…I know you know that guy…he or she is in every office.

In one phrase:
Of course you can still do favors for your colleagues and you should—but under your conditions!
If I was up for it I would mention to the colleague in question that I'm only doing a favor and in no case do I want to end up doing the job.

Selfish? Yes! But keep in mind who the most important person in your life is. That's right! YOU are the most important person in your life! You have to be well! Only if you are well yourself, can you be well towards others and from this level on you can contribute to others, but first be well yourself. You can always buy some time and say "maybe" at first, until you come to a definite decision. Life gets a lot easier if you start saying "No"!

5
ARRIVE TEN MINUTES EARLY

Yes. This is a time management and productivity trick. Well kind of a mix. It might be more of a stress relief technique. Anyway it has done me so well that I want to share it with you. Being early for your appointments will take a lot of stress off your shoulders because you won't feel in a rush all the time. It might also give you some time to answer a quick email or a phone call.

I noticed it especially when coming in to work 10 minutes earlier. I had time to sit down, relax, look at my task list and then go full speed ahead into my work day, when before I arrived just in time or maybe even late and was then stressed out all the time from minute one at work. If you're not doing it already, try it out and let me know how it works for you.

Being 10 minutes early is also a good habit for business meetings, lunches, or dinners. There's a french proverb that is always on my mind that says **"While we keep a man waiting, he reflects on our shortcomings."**

Punctuality is a sign of discipline and respect for others. Without it, you might come across as slightly offensive, even if you are the nicest person in the world. Of course there are cultural differences. For example, while in Mexico and Spain people are very relaxed about punctuality, in Germany not being punctual is seen as highly unprofessional and might ruin your chances in any endeavor.

I have made being 10 minutes early to every appointment a habit —not to be especially polite, but instead I do it for myself. Those 10 minutes will make you feel a lot better and will give you a lot of peace of mind. When you arrive at a place, you aren't in a rush and you actually have 10 minutes to compose your thoughts and prepare for the interview or meeting. Instead of feeling rushed arriving at the last minute, you'll feel very relaxed.
Being 10 minutes early shows professionalism and politeness. Try it and see for yourself if it adds to your life or not!

6
UNDERPROMISE, OVERDELIVER

This is another biggie. A great time management technique that changed my professional life in an extraordinary manner and reduced stress at work to virtually zero!

Most of my stress at work came from deadlines and I, or we as an enterprise were always struggling, which made those days when our products were shipped to the clients—which was every day during high season—horrible and very stressful.

We were always just in time or sometimes maybe a couple of hours late and I had to calm down angry and sometimes hysterical clients... until I started to under-promise: I figured out that over 90% of our late deliveries were just a question of a couple of hours, so I got permission from my boss and started my own delivery schedule that only I had access to.

If production gave me a delivery date of April 5th, I told the client April 10th. So if we delivered on April 7th instead of an angry client threatening to fine or sue us for being two days late, I suddenly had extremely grateful clients that thanked me for delivering three days early. Within a short time we reduced late deliveries from nearly 50% to virtually 0% over the next three years.

I found out later that a great side effect of controlling our own deadlines was a diminished risk of coronary heart desease by a whopping 50%—at least. (A study found that people who feel little control over deadlines imposed by other people have a 50% higher risk of coronary heart desease.)

You can apply this to your entire life. When your boss gives you a project that takes you three days, you could tell him or her that you are going to need five days. If you have completed it after four days you'll come off as a great worker and if you take a little longer you are still on time. For me this worked out great.

In my whole life as an employee I never had to stay a weekend at the office.

Of course you have to customize this technique and and adapt it to your work place and environment. I don't want you to get fired for lying to your boss…

If you are struggling with deadlines at your work, trying this and making it a habit is definitely worth a shot. I also apply it to my private life: If I know that it takes me half an hour to get to a meeting place, I tell my friends I'll be there in an hour and by showing up half an hour early I see happy faces and convey to the people I meet "You are important to me, I rushed to see you."

I don't know about your friends and family but mine prefer this a thousand times over telling somebody "I'll be there in half an hour" and then showing up after an hour.

7
TURN OFF YOUR PHONE

Do you think you have to always pick up your phone each time it rings? Well…Don't! Your phone is supposed to be for YOUR convenience, not for those who call you. Give yourself the freedom to continue doing whatever you are doing and let calls go to voice mail every now and then.
I know. I know…You might lose a client. Every single one of my clients thought that. Guess what: You probably won't lose the client.

Leave a nice message on your voice mail in the sense of the good old "Sorry I'm busy and can't get your call right now. I'll call you back as soon as possible." If it's important they will call again. Or they will leave a message. Or you'll see their number on your display and call them. The only thing that's really bad is not calling them back right after you have finished what you are doing or even forgetting them.

One of my clients, a very stressed sales manager, let's call him Steve, came to me at the edge of being seriously burnt out. He received 60 to 80 calls a day and didn't have time to do his real job which was selling his product and visiting customers, because he was on the phone all the time fixing everyone's problems and continuously putting out fires.

I laid out all of the different time management tools for him that you find in this book. He had to choose the one which fits best for him.

He decided to let calls go to voice mail for at least an hour every day and changed the message of his voice mail. "Hi. I can't get to the phone right now. I'll call you back as soon as I can. If it's urgent send me a Whatsapp message." That's it.

The first two weeks there were no big changes. In the third week he suddenly received only half the calls and by the time he called back 80% of the problems people called for in the first place were fixed.

After a month he was relaxed. He thought he might have received fewer calls because vacation time was close by or work was slow.

Three months later he had to admit to himself that he did it! He was in control of his time. He also improved his free time with his family on the weekends because he wasn't thinking about work all the time and had time to think about fun stuff to do with his family.

Further he went on to break his sales record for that year (2015) and this year (2016) he expects to increase his sales by another 20%....if he decides to stay in his job that is, because Steve got a very good offer from a big competitor to join their sales team! **All this nine months after his first step: Changing the message of his voice mail. Mind-boggling!**

Not picking up the phone every time it rings and telling myself "They will call again" has been working for me for years and I think I didn't lose a lot of clients by it. I WON a lot of time though. I also learnt that if it's a really important call the caller will not give up and probably call like eight times within three minutes...

8
SPEND TIME WITH YOUR FAMILY

"Family is not an important thing, it's everything," says Michael J. Fox. Be smart and listen to the man who went to the future and back three times.
This is a very important habit. **There are various studies that prove that the biggest and most powerful predictors of success and happiness in our life are our relationships!**

Nevertheless, when I interview leaders and executives most of the time what comes up is that they just cannot (?) spend a lot of time with their families or that when they are stressed, the first hours to cut are the ones they spend with their family and friends—when they should be doing exactly the opposite.

Value your family and friends. They are your constant source of love and mutual support, which increases your self-esteem, boosts your self-confidence and—as I just said—even makes you happier and more successful.
In Bronnie Ware's book "The five regrets of the Dying," one of the top regrets of the dying is to **not have spent more time with their families and having spent too much time at the office**!

Don't become one of them and start making time for your family NOW! And if you are with the family... do everybody a favor and BE FULLY PRESENT.

Believe it or not, this habit will also make you more productive. It's not only about the work—it's also about how you spend your free time. But as with everything in this book, you can only find out if you put it into practice.

9
TAKE TIME OFF

You didn't expect that here, did you? Same as taking a power nap, taking time off actually boosts your productivity instead of damaging it!
With the stressful, fast-paced life that we are living it's more important than ever to slow down your pace of life and take a break! Take some time off. Recharge your batteries by being around nature.

Start by scheduling some relaxation time into your weekly schedule which by now you are hopefully making time for.
If you dare, completely disconnect from the Internet, TV, and your electronic games for a whole weekend. If that "scares" you... start with a Saturday morning, then a whole Saturday, and then the whole weekend.

One of my best vacations ever was being on a houseboat in the Midi Channel in the south of France. No mobile phone, no Internet, no TV. Only ducks. The boat's top speed was eight km/hr (= five miles/hr) so we were literally "forced" to slow down.

There's few things more relaxing than a couple of six-year olds riding their bikes overtaking you on the bike paths on the side of the channel while you are floating. The villages you pass through are sometimes so small, that they don't even have a supermarket. So the whole trip comes down to the one and only simple question: "Where will we get food?" No worries! There is always a restaurant close by, but the charming thing is to cook your own meals on the boat and have dinner at the harbour watching the sunset or just being around nature. Once we even had dinner in the middle of a vineyard! Priceless!

So is it to walk into a tiny French village in the morning and get your baguette for breakfast from the only bakery in town. We got up at sunrise and went to bed two chess matches after sunset.

Or you might say "We got up with the ducks and went to sleep with the ducks."

Take time off and connect with nature! It doesn't have to be a long trip. Walk in the woods, on the beach, or in a park whenever you get the chance and observe how you feel afterwards. Or just lie down on a bench or in the grass and contemplate the blue sky. When was the last time you walked barefoot on grass or on a beach? Did you get an idea of how important, relaxing, and reenergizing taking some time off is for you? I hope so! Go put it into practice. You will double your productivity with this habit!

10
TAKE A POWER NAP

"When you can't figure out what to do, it's time for a nap."— Mason Cooley

There's nothing like a power nap! It's scientifically proven that a power nap at midday reenergizes, refreshes, and increases your productivity.

I made my nap a daily habit. That allows me to sleep around six hours a night without worrying about my sleep. I know that come afternoon I will get my 45 to 90 minutes nap.

Since I changed my sleep rhythm I'm much clearer, more focused, and yes… more awake.

During my most stressful period at my old job I started taking a power nap and the change was extraordinary. I was far less stressed and a lot calmer while being yelled at by angry clients and much more concentrated and efficient in finding solutions.

For a while, I slept for 25 to 30 minutes on a bench in a park close by, and later I just put two chairs together in the office and slept there.
It felt as if my working day suddenly had two halves and midday was halftime. I started the "second half" always fresh and I also performed a lot more productively because the typical tiredness after lunch between 2 and 5 PM was gone.

As absurd as it sounds you will find more time if you nap 30 to 40 minutes every day. You will be better rested and thus much more productive.

11
MAXIMIZE LOST TIME

If time is what we most want, why are we using it so badly?

How much time are you spending in the car or public transport on your way to work every day? Statistics say it's between 60 and 90 minutes per working day! That means in a month we are talking between 20 to 30 hours.
Who said, "I don't have enough time"? We just found you another 20 to 30 hours to read (when on a bus or train), or listen to audio books in your car.

What if you really spent that time listening to empowering CDs, mp3s, or reading inspirational books instead of listening to the negative news from the radio or reading about it in the newspaper? How much could you learn in one year? It would be like going to university again!

Do you maximize your "lost time"?

I work a lot on the train and wrote half of my last book "From Jobless to Amazon Bestseller" on the train and writing this chapter I'm actually on the train between Barcelona and Premia de Mar where I live!

Another thing I do on public transport is listening to motivational speeches, or guided meditations and connecting on social media. The supermarket queue is also a great time to go through your social media or answer some quick emails—all the stuff I don't do when I'm productive. When I'm on the train surfing on Facebook or the web, depending on what I'm doing, I often even credit it to myself as work time.

Other possibilities are: Listening to a webinar while doing the dishes, watching TV while folding your clothes, and many more.

So now the question is: How will you maximize your lost time?

12
KEEP A JOURNAL

This is another one of these habits that will have a crucial impact on your productivity. Write in your journal and reflect on your days.

It's about taking a couple of minutes at the end of your day to get some perspective, relive the happy moments, reflect on the work done, and write everything down in your journal.

By doing this, you will receive an extra boost of happiness, motivation, and self-esteem every morning and evening. Writing in you journal has the positive side effect that just before sleeping, you will be concentrating your mind on positive things, which has a beneficial effect on your sleep and your subconscious mind.

Journaling will shift your focus to the positive things of the day and gratitude. It will make your brain scan the last 24 hours for positive things, the result of which will be a higher level of happiness and optimism for you which… surprise, surprise… as countless studies from the field of positive psychology prove will make you more productive! Those studies show that happy people are around 20% more productive than their neutral or unhappy coworkers.

For my clients and also for myself this little exercise has led to enormous changes in my well-being.
Make an effort to answer the following questions each night before sleeping and write them in your journal:

- What am I grateful for? (Write 3 to 5 points)
- What 3 things have made me happy today?
- What 3 things did I do particularly well today?
- How could I have made today even better?
- What is my most important goal for tomorrow?

Don't worry if the words don't flow right away when you start his exercise. Like all other things you will get better with practice.

If you are blocked and can't think of anything, just hold on for five minutes longer. Write what comes to mind without thinking and don't judge it. Don't worry about your style or mistakes. Just write! Do this every day for a month and observe the changes that take place! By the way these five questions also make for a great conversation with your spouse and kids over dinner!

13
STOP WATCHING TV

You want to gain time fast, don't you? Here is the tip that will let you gain a lot of time! How many hours a week do you sit in front of the "box"? The average American or European spends four to five hours a day in front of the TV!

That's between 28 and 35 hours a week! Here you have it. You just won 20 hours, supposing you cut down you daily TV time to an hour. Yes and count in YouTube also.

Apart from gaining time there is another beneficial side effect! TV is one of the biggest energy robbers, if not the number one! Do you ever feel renewed or reenergized after watching TV? Turn off your television!

Why would you expose yourself to so much negativity? Don't expose yourself to too much of the garbage that is out there on TV. Substitute your habit of watching TV for a healthier habit like taking a walk, spending more time with your family, or reading a good book.

I stopped watching the news many years ago when I became aware that while on the train to work I got upset over things heard and seen on the morning news and I thought to myself, "I can't go to my stressful workplace being already stressed, simply because of what politician A said or banker B did or because there is a war in C." Just one week after I stopped watching the news I felt a lot better! Don't believe me? Just try it for yourself! Don't watch the news for a week and see how you feel.

You will still be up to date with the "important stuff," because your family, friends, and colleagues will keep you updated. Just choose and be selective how much garbage you expose your mind to.

And nope—you won't become ignorant because you stop watching TV. **A recent study even shows the opposite! People who**

don't watch TV are actually better judges of reality than people who are influenced by the daily news programs. Now that is NEWS, isn't it.

If you need more reasons to stop watching television read one of the great books that are out there about how the media manipulates us and how nearly everything is fake! Control the information that you are exposed to.

Make sure it adds to your life. Instead of watching trash TV, watch a documentary or a comedy. Instead of listening to the news in your car, listen to an audio-book or motivational CDs.

III - THE INNER GAME OF PRODUCTIVITY

1
KNOW YOURSELF

The first step before changing your life is becoming aware of where you are and what's missing. You might remember this questionnaire from my book <u>30 Days - Change your habits, change your life</u>. The reason is simple. Every process of self-improvement—**including your productivity**—starts with getting to know yourself better.

Whatever your goals and dreams are you won't get around answering these questions to yourself honestly. So the earlier you start - like NOW - the better.

This questionnaire is also the starting point of all my coaching processes. So even if you did it before, **please take some time to answer the following questions**.

What are your dreams in life?
_____
_____
_____

At the end of your life, what do you think you would most regret not having done for yourself?
_____
_____
_____

If time and money were not factors, what would you like to do, be, or have?
_____
_____
_____

What motivates you in life?
_____
_____
_____

What limits you in life?
_____
_____
_____

What have been your biggest wins in the last 12 months?
_____
_____
_____

What have been your biggest frustrations in the last 12 months?
_____
_____
_____

What do you do to please others?
_____
_____
_____

What do you do to please yourself?
_____
_____
_____

What do you pretend not to know?
_____
_____
_____

What has been the best work that you have done in your life until today?
___
___
___

How exactly do you know that this was your best work?
___
___
___

How do you see the work you do today in comparison to what you did five years ago? What's the relationship between the work you do now and the work you did then?
___
___
___

What part of your work do you enjoy the most?
___
___
___

What part of your work do you enjoy the least?
___
___
___

What activity or thing do you usually postpone?
___
___
___

What are you really proud of?
___
___
___

How would you describe yourself?

_____
_____
_____

What aspects of your behaviour do you think you should improve?

_____
_____
_____

At this moment in time, how would you describe your commitment level to making your life a success?

_____
_____
_____

At this moment in time, how would you describe your general state of well-being, energy, and self-care?

_____
_____
_____

At this moment in time, how would you describe how much fun or pleasure you are experiencing in your life?

_____
_____
_____

If you could put one fear behind you once and for all, what would it be?

_____
_____
_____

In what area of your life do you most want to have a true breakthrough?

_____
_____
_____

2
BELIEVE

"Be not afraid of life. Believe that life is worth living and your belief will help create the fact." Science is now catching up with what William James knew a long time ago: Your beliefs create your reality. Period. You create what you believe and your world is only your interpretation of the reality.

In other words, you don't see the world how it is, but how you were conditioned to see it and your perception is only an approximation of reality.
Your maps of reality determine the way you act more than reality itself and each one of us sees the world through the lenses of their own beliefs. If you believe you don't have enough time, imagine what will happen...

This is not just hocus-pocus. There are countless studies in the field of Positive Psychology and Medicine that prove the power of your beliefs such as Placebo Effect, The Pygmalion Effect, and Self-Fulfilling prophecies.

These studies show that the Placebo effect is 55–60% as effective as medicine. For example in an experiment with poison ivy mentioned by the New York Times in 1998, researchers rubbed the arms of their subjects with a harmless plant and told them it was poison ivy. Following that, all of the 13 subjects showed the typical symptoms of poison ivy rash! When they rubbed their arms with REAL poison ivy and told the subjects that it was just a harmless plant only two of the participants showed symptoms!

They drew the following conclusions:
　1. Your belief becomes a self-fulfilling prophecy.
　2. Our brains are organized to act on what we **expect** will happen next.

But it gets even better! In the late 1960s, Robert Rosenthal and Leonore Jacobson did the following experiment in an elementary school. They gave intelligence tests to the students to research their academic potential.

Then they told the teachers that the data had identified some students as academical superstars. Further they told the teachers that they should not disclose the results, or treat these students differently and to drive their point home, they added that the teachers will be observed!

At the end of the year they repeated the test and the identified students had extraordinary results. Not a surprise you might think. The fun thing is though that those students were absolutely average and ordinary and randomly picked by the researchers for the first test!

This is proof of the Pygmalion Effect which states that **our belief in a person's potential brings that potential to life!** This goes for other areas of your life. Your expectations about your colleagues, spouses, or children can make these expectations a reality… so you better always expect the best from others!

Robert Dilts defines beliefs as judgments and assessments about ourselves, others, and the world around us. A belief is a habitual thought pattern. Once a person believes something is true (whether it's true or not) he or she acts as if it were—collecting facts to prove the belief even if it's false.

Depending on your belief-system you live your life one way or another.

So to finally find time you also have to change your belief that you don't have time! Once you start believing that you have time, you'll start finding it everywhere.

As I mentioned before, your beliefs are like a self-fulfilling prophecy. They work like this:

Your beliefs influence your emotions, your emotions influence your actions, and your actions influence your RESULTS!

I've worked with people that had all the time in the world and still couldn't see it. They were convinced that they had no time at all while they spent hours browsing the internet, watching videos on YouTube, or playing games.

You not having time is a reflection of your beliefs, thoughts, and expectations of you not having time. So if you want to change that you first have to change your patterns of thinking.

Remember that for many decades it was thought impossible that a man could run a mile under four minutes. There were even scientific papers and studies on the subject. These studies could all be shredded on May 6th 1954, when Roger Bannister proved everybody wrong at a race in Oxford. From then on over a 1000 people have done it.

I highly recommend that you let go of limiting beliefs such as:

- I don't have time
- Whatever I do, I never get my work done
- The more I work, the more work comes up
- I'll never finish this on time

And pick up some empowering beliefs such as:

- I don't know how I do it, but it seems I always find time
- Every day I get my work done
- I'm in total control of my work day and always have a reserve of time
- I'm so productive I do in two hours what my colleagues do in six.

Here's a little exercise.
Ask yourself the following question:
What do I believe about time?

To change a belief follow this exercise and say to yourself:
1) This is only my belief about reality. That doesn't mean that it is the reality.
2) Although I believe this, it's not necessarily true.

3) Create emotions which are opposite to the belief.
4) Imagine the opposite.
5) Be aware that the belief is only an idea that you have about reality and not reality itself.
6) For just 10 minutes a day ignore what seems to be real and act as if your wish has come true.
   (See yourself relaxed having all the time in the world.)

3
VISUALIZE

Visualization is a fundamental resource in building experiences. The subconscious part of your brain cannot distinguish between a well-done visualization and reality.

This means that if you visualize that you are very productive with a lot of emotion and in great detail, your subconscious mind will be convinced that you really are. You will then be provided with motivation, opportunities, and ideas that will help you to transform yourself into a more productive person.

Does this sound like woo woo to you? Can for example sports be practiced by pure visualization? Well, actually YES. There are various studies that confirm the power of visualization. As early as in the 80s, Tony Robbins worked with the U.S. Army and used visualization techniques to dramatically increase pistol shooting performance.

There have also been other studies done for improving free throw shooting percentages of Basketball players using the same techniques. The results were amazing! If you look closely at athletes they all visualize their races and matches. If it works for the best professional skiers, Formula One drivers, golfers, tennis players, and soccer players who visualize in-game situations, days and hours before the actual match, why shouldn't it for your productivity goals?

Greats like Jack Nicklaus, Wayne Gretzky, and Greg Louganis, to name a few, are known to have achieved their goals with visualization. Thanks to the newest technologies Neuro-Scientists have found that the same neurones light up in your brain when you imagine something (for example eating a lemon) as when you are actually doing it!

See yourself as already having achieved the goal of productivity. See it through your own eyes and put all your senses into it: Smell it, hear it, feel it, taste it. Can you feel how you relaxed you are, now that you have your day under control and enough time for everything that's on your plate?

The more emotions you put into it, the more of an impact it will have. If you do this for 15 minutes every day, over time you will see enormous results. Make time for you daily visualization either in your morning ritual or in the evening before going to bed.

4
INCREASE YOUR ENERGY

To be productive you need lots of energy. Here's a chapter with lots of recommendations of how to increase you energy and become super productive. It seems like common sense, but once again **"Common sense is not common action."** You're probably already doing most of these habits, but there is nothing like a good reminder.

Surround yourself with the right people

Watch who you are spending your time with. The famous quote "You are the average of the five persons you spend the most time with," once said by Jim Rohn and since then cited in thousands of workshops and books around the world has now been proven to be more than just an empty mantra. Numerous scientific studies in the field of Positive Psychology have proven that emotions actually ARE contagious!

It's said that when you put three strangers in a room together, the one who expresses most emotions will transmit his or her mood to the others in just two minutes. Did you notice that when you feel anxious or are in a negative mood these feelings are affecting every interaction you have, whether you want to or not? Similarly, you can be affected by overtly negative persons in an instant! Imagine spending lots of time with them. If this can happen in two minutes, imagine what it can do to you in an eight-hour working day or at home!

Luckily it works the same way with positive emotions. There was an experiment at Yale where while on a group task one member of the group was instructed to be overtly positive. The experiments were video taped and researchers tracked the emotions of each team member before and after the session. Later the individual and group performances were studied.

Guess what happened… **whenever the positive team member entered the room his mood instantly infected everybody around him**. More than that, thanks to "happy guy's" positive mood each individual team member improved their performance and their ability to accomplish their task as a team.

In another experiment, students with bad grades who were rooming with better students improved their grade point averages. Even sports teams can improve their performance having one happy player on their team—and the happier they are, the better they will play!

So you better choose to spend more time with people who bring out the best in you, who motivate you, who believe in you, who empower you instead of people who drag you down.

Stay away from energy vampires. The naysayers, the blamers, the complainers. The people who are always judging or gossiping and talking bad about everything. People around you can be the springboard to motivate yourself, gain courage, and help you take the right actions, but on the other hand can also drag you down, drain your energy, and act as brakes in the achieving of your life goals and productivity.

Don't spend a lot of time around people who have nothing to do and want to convince you to do like them, mostly to justify their own laziness. ("Let's go for a three-hour lunch, let's finish early today and go for some beers.") Nothing against going for some beers with your friends. Just be on the lookout and analyze if it's for socializing or if you are wasting your time.

If you are around negative people all the time, they can convert you into a negative and cynical person over time. They might want to convince you to stay where you are and keep you stuck, because they value security and don't like risk and uncertainty.

Steve Jobs put it in one short phrase:
"Don't let the noise of the opinions of others drown your own inner voice."

It will be difficult for you to grow and thrive, if people around you want to convince you of the contrary. Unfortunately often times it's the people closest to you who drag you down, because they want to protect you. So what do you do if it's people close to you?

The only thing you can work on is becoming a better, energy-loaded person yourself.

Fortunately the contagion of emotions works both ways. If you are happy and energy-loaded you might infuse that spirit in people around you.
If that doesn't work and you grow and develop, negative people soon will turn away from you because you don't serve their purposes any more. They need somebody who shares their negativity and if you don't do that they will look for somebody else.

If all of that doesn't work you seriously have to ask yourself the question if you should start to spend less time with them or stop seeing them at all. But that's a decision you have to make.

I always automatically separated people from my life that didn't support me and I never regretted it, although it wasn't easy!
One of my favourite phrases is, "If your friends and family don't think that you are totally crazy, your goals aren't big enough!"

Here's a little exercise:
Make a list of all the people you have in your life and are spending time with (members of your family, friends, colleagues).
Analyze who is positive for you and who drags you down.
Spend more time with the positive people and stop seeing the toxic people (blamers, complainers) in your life, or at least spend less time with them.
Choose to be around positive people who support you.

Treat your body like a temple

Most of us say that health is the most important thing in our lives; nevertheless many people drink, smoke, eat junk food, or even take drugs, and spend most of their free time on the couch without any physical activity. Now isn't that ironic?

If you adopt some of these little healthy habits into your life your productivity will probably at least double. Follow a balanced diet, exercise regularly, and stay or get in physical shape so that your brain has all the nutrition it needs to produce a positive lifestyle.

- Eat more fruit and vegetables.
- Reduce your intake of red meat.
- Drink at least two liters of water each day.
- Eat less!
- Stop eating junk food.
- Get up early.

Exercise

We all know it's great, and yet few of us do it. In one mind-boggling study it was proven that exercising three times a week had the same impact on depressed people as taking anti-depressants. But not only that: The relapse rate among the people that exercised was only 9% compared to over 40% of the study group that took pills.

I guess I'm not coming to you with breaking news here if I tell you how important exercise is for you. The best excuse is always: "I have no time." Funnily enough if you invest time in exercising you will improve your productivity and end up having more time.

Here's a list the benefits that exercising three to five times a week will bring you.
1. It will keep you healthy.
2. It will help you lose weight, which will improve your health and also make you look better.
3. It will make you feel better and you will have a lot of energy.
4. It will improve your self-esteem.
5. You will sleep better.
6. It will reduces stress.

Furthermore, studies show that regular exercise makes you happier, can reduce the symptoms of depression, reduces the risk of disease (heart, diabetes, osteoporosis, high cholesterol, etc.), lowers the risk of a premature death, improves your memory, and many more. **Are you in?**

One last thing: Don't force yourself to exercise. Enjoy it. Look for a recreational activity that fits you and that you enjoy doing such as swimming, for example. Even walking an hour a day can make a difference.

Listen to your favorite music

An easy way to feel happy and motivated instantly is to listen to your favorite music! This will boost your productivity instantly. Make a soundtrack of your all-time favorites and listen to them. Why not make a playlist on your iPod, phone, or PC and listen to them? This will boost your productivity. Give it a try! I don't know about you, but I work a lot better with music. If I'm writing I listen to classical or instrumental music and sometimes while translating I listen to energy-loaded electronical music of my favorite Trance DJs.

Wake up early

The first benefit of getting up an hour earlier is that you gain around 365 hours per year. 365! Who said "I don't have time"? When clients come to me telling me that they don't have time, the first thing I ask them is how many hours of TV are they watching. This usually provides them with the time they need. Those who stop watching TV and still don't have enough time can gain time by getting up an hour earlier.

There is a very special energy in the morning hours before sunrise. My life changed completely ever since I started getting up around 5.30 or 6 AM.
I usually go for a walk half an hour before the sun rises so that on my way back I see the sun rising "out of" the Mediterranean Sea. This is absolutely fantastic and already puts me in a state of absolute happiness. As a consequence I feel much more clear, focused, calmer, and relaxed and don't start the day already running around stressed.

And for those of you who don't live next to the sea: A sunrise "out of" fields, forests, or even a big city is just as exciting. Just go watch it and let me know! Starting your day like this is very beneficial for your happiness and peace of mind. Another great advantage of getting up earlier is that it reinforces self-discipline and you'll gain self-respect.

All of these benefits will have a tremendous impact on your productivity! Many successful leaders were and still are members of the early birds club: For example, Nelson Mandela, Mahatma Gandhi, Barrack Obama, and many more.

It's scientifically proven that six hours should be enough sleep per night paired with a 30- to 60-minute power nap in the afternoon.
Your freshness depends on the quality of your sleep, not on the quantity, but you have to try and figure out for yourself how many hours of sleep you need. Give it a try, because once you figure it out, it will improve your quality of life a lot.

Don't forget that getting up early is a new habit, so give it some time and don't give up after the first week if you still feel tired after getting up earlier. The habit needs at least three to four weeks to kick in. If you absolutely can't get up one hour earlier, try half an hour.

And don't forget that your attitude, thoughts, and beliefs about getting up an hour earlier play a big role, too. To me it was always intriguing how it was so difficult for me to get up at 6.45ish to go to work after seven or eight hours of sleep, but before every vacation I usually slept four hours and woke up before the alarm clock went off and I was totally refreshed and energized.

In the end, getting up or hitting the snooze button is a decision you make. It's up to you. How important is a better lifestyle and more time for you?

Read

"The man who doesn't read has no advantage over the man that can't read" says Mark Twain. If you read for half an hour a day that's three and a half hours a week and 182 hours a year! That's a lot of knowledge at your disposal. One of my first written goals during my coaching training was "to read more" (not very specific, but it worked). That was at a time when I hadn't read a book in years. Now I'm devouring an average of two books a week. I have learnt more in the last two years that in the whole 30 years before including my International Business studies.

So always have a book with you. If you substitute the habit of watching TV or, even worse, the news by reading a good book just before going to bed, you will derive the additional benefit of peace of mind.

Another side effect is that you increase your creativity. So what are you waiting for? Make a list of six books that you will read in the next three months! If you don't know what to read, check out my webpage for recommendations. But make that list NOW!

Take breaks

You might think you don't need breaks and would rather work 10 hours every day to become more productive. Think again! If you deny yourself free time, you'll actually be less productive because when you are tired you are a lot less efficient. You'll also be less creative and make poorer decisions.

Take a break every now and then and see what it does for you. You will notice that you will be much more productive that way. It's recommended to take a five-minute break every hour. I usually take half an hour every two hours or two to three hours after working four hours in a row when I'm in a flow state.

Change your posture

This is an exercise taken from Neuro-linguistic Programming which proclaims that changing your posture also changes your mind. People I tell this to usually think that I'm joking. But before writing this off as nonsense... try it out!

When you feel sad and depressed, you usually look at the floor, keep your shoulders down, and adapt the posture of a sad person, right? Now try the following just for a moment: Stand upright, shoulders up, chest out, and hold your head up high—you can even exaggerate it by looking up. How does it feel? If you smile, laugh, and walk with your head held high, you will realize that you feel a lot better. It's impossible to feel sad walking around like that, isn't it?

And there has been more research conducted on this subject. A study by Brion, Petty, and Wagner in 2009 found that people who were sitting straight had higher self-confidence than people sitting slumped over! There is also an amazing TED Talk by Amy Cuddy called "Your body language shapes who you are" about the research she did together with Dana Carney at Harvard University.

The study has shown that holding "power postures" for two minutes creates a 20 percent increase in testosterone (which boosts confidence) and a 25 percent decrease in cortisol (which reduces stress). Imagine this.

If you have an important presentation, reunion, or competition, just take on the posture of a confident person for two minutes. Put your hands on your hips and spread your feet (think Wonder Woman) or lean back in a chair and spread your arms. Hold the posture for at least two minutes... and see what happens!

You can watch Amy Cuddy's TED-Talk "Your body language shapes who you are" here. It does miracles for me before presentations or being on radio or TV.

5
CELEBRATE YOUR WINS

"Celebrate what you want to see more of," says Thomas Peters. On your way forward to more productivity and reaching your goals, it's also important to be aware of your progress!

Stop every now and then and celebrate your wins! Celebrate that you have come further than you were last week. Celebrate that you have crossed a lot of things off of that to-do list of yours. Celebrate that you don't pick up your phone on Tuesdays for two hours and work super focused during that time.

If you want to write a book celebrate for every 2000 words you have written. Don't let your small victories go unnoticed! This will help you to stay motivated. Every action step completed is worth celebrating.

It doesn't have to be big stuff. You can celebrate with a walk among nature or take a morning off and go to a museum. Or a night at the movies alone or with your sweetheart. Be creative. But celebrate!

6
TAKE CONTROL

It's scientifically proven that you'll be more successful and therefore more productive if you adopt the belief that have control over your life. If you are a student you will be happier, get better grades, and more motivation to pursue a career you really want; if you are an employee feeling in control will have you do a better job and be more satisfied with your job.

There is only one person that's responsible for your life and that is YOU! You are the designer of your life and of your productivity. Not your boss, not your spouse, not your parents, not your friends, not your clients, not the economy, not the weather. YOU!

If you don't have time in your life you are making the wrong decisions. It's not THEM who call you whenever they feel like it, **it's YOU taking the call**. It's not THEM always giving you extra work, **it's YOU being too afraid to put your foot down** and say "I'm sorry I can't take on this task."
It's not THEM who distract you from work, **it's YOU letting them distract you**.

The day your stop blaming others for everything that happens in your life, everything changes! Taking responsibility for your life is taking charge of your life and becoming the protagonist of it. It's one of the most liberating experiences you can have.

Science has proven that believing you are in control leads to success in nearly every aspect of your life and not just at your work. You'll be much happier, will have less stress at work, and be more motivated, which is the perfect formula to boost your productivity.

The fun thing is that psychologists found out that to reap all these benefits it doesn't even matter a lot if you **really** have that control; it's more important that you think you have it. That's no surprise keeping in mind how your beliefs, expectations, and attitudes shape your experience of the world.

Instead of being a victim of your circumstances, you obtain the power to create your own circumstances or at least the power to decide how you are going to act in the face of circumstances that life presents to you.
It doesn't matter what happens to you in your life; it matters what attitude you adopt towards what happens to you. And the attitude you adopt is your choice!

If you blame others for not having enough time, what has to happen to make you find more time? All of the others have to change! And that my friend, I tell you, is not going to happen. If you are the protagonist, YOU have the power to change the things that you don't like in your life! You are in control of your thoughts, actions, and feelings. You are in control of your time and the people you spend your time with.

If you don't like your results, change your input—your thoughts, emotions, and expectations. Stop reacting to others and start responding. Reaction is automatic. Responding is consciously choosing your response.
You don't depend on external factors. Life happens, but you choose your behaviour. The solutions of your problems are not on the outside—thanks to options and the power of choice. Your success only depends on you. The sooner you can embrace this the better it gets.
Yes. Bad things happen to good people. You can still choose to make the best out of the circumstances.

Act where you have control and accept where you don't have control, and above all don't lose your time on subjects that are out of your control.

The victim says: Every bad thing in my life is the fault of the others, but if you are not part of the problem, then you also can't be a part of the solution or—in other words—if the problem is caused by the outside, the solution is also on the outside.

So once again: Even if you don't have control over the stimuli that environment sends you continuously, you have the liberty to **choose** your behavior of how you will face the situation.

The person with a "victim mentality" only reacts, is always innocent, and constantly blames others for his or her life situation, while using the past as justification and putting their hopes on a future which will miraculously bring solutions to problems or a change in others who are causing the troubles. This is pretty risky and almost probably neither one nor the other is going to happen.

Protagonists know that they are responsible, choose adequate behavior, and hold themselves accountable. They use the past as a valuable experience from which to learn, live in the present where they see constant opportunities for change, and decide and go after their future goals.
The most important question is: **"Who will you choose to be—by your actions—when life presents you with these circumstances?"**

Choices and decisions

Your life is the result of the decisions you made. How do you feel about that? Is this true for you? It's important that from now on, you are aware of the power you have over your life by making decisions!

Every decision, every choice has an important influence on your life. In fact, your life is a direct result of the choices and decisions you made in the past and every choice carries a consequence!

The most important thing is to make decisions. Whether the decision is right or wrong is secondary. You will soon receive feedback that will help you to progress. Once you have made a decision, go with it and accept the consequences. If it was wrong, learn from it and forgive yourself knowing that at that point in time and with the knowledge you had, it was the best and the right decision to take.

YOUR ATTITUDE + YOUR DECISIONS
=
YOUR LIFE

Victor Frankl was a Jewish psychologist imprisoned in Germany's concentration camps during the Second World War. He lost his entire family except his sister.

Under these terrible circumstances, he became aware of what he named "the ultimate human freedom," which not even the Nazi prison wards could take away from him: They could control his external circumstances, but in the last instance it was him who CHOSE HOW these circumstances were going to affect him!

He found out that between STIMULUS and RESPONSE there was a small space in time in which he had the freedom to CHOOSE his RESPONSE! This means that even if you may not be able to control the circumstances that life presents to you, you can always choose your response in facing those circumstances, and by doing so have a huge impact on your life.

In other words, what hurts us is not what happens to us, but our response to what happens to us. The most important thing is how we RESPOND to what happens to us in our lives. And that is a CHOICE!

Do you want to have more time? Make better choices about who you surround yourself with, how you plan your work, how many favors you do for others, which phone calls you take, and so on. You now have the knowledge you need to become a productivity machine and find lots of time. The decision to apply this knowledge is yours to take. There are no excuses!.

7
SMILE MORE

Smile! Even if you don't feel like it! Smiling improves the quality of your life, health, and relationships… and your productivity! It's proven that every little shot of happiness improves your work performance and productivity.
If you don't do it already, start to smile consciously today. It's confirmed that laughing and smiling is extremely good for your health! Science has demonstrated that laughing or smiling a lot daily improves your mental state and your creativity. So laugh more!!

Make it a point to watch at least an hour of comedy or fun stuff a day and laugh until tears roll down your cheeks! You will feel a lot better and full of energy once you start this habit. Give it a try!

Tara Kraft and Sarah Pressman at the University of Kansas demonstrated that smiling can alter your stress response in difficult situations.
The study showed that it can slow your heart rate down and decrease stress levels—even if you are not feeling happy. It's proven that not only do your emotions influence you physiology, but also the other way around. Smiling sends a signal to your brain that things are all right.

Just try it next time you feel stressed or overwhelmed, and let me know if it works. If you think you have no reason at all to smile, hold a pen or a chopstick with your teeth. **It simulates a smile and might produce the same effects.**

If you need even more incentives for smiling, search for the study by Wayne University on smiling which has found a link between smiling and longevity! When you smile your entire body sends out the message "Life is great" to the world. Studies show that smiling people are perceived as more confident and more likely to be trusted. People just feel good around them.

Further benefits of smiling are:
- Releases serotonin (makes us feel good).
- Releases endorphins (lowers pain).
- Lowers blood pressure.
- Increases clarity.
- Boosts the functioning of your immune system.
- Provides a more positive outlook on life (Try being a pessimist while you smile...).

8
FAKE IT TILL YOU BECOME IT

There is a lot of truth in William James' words "If you want a quality, act as if you already have it."

Act as if! Act as if you already are productive. Act as if you already have the quality of life, the lifestyle, the job that a productive person has.

If you want to be more productive you have to start acting as if you already are. Speak like a productive person, walk like a productive person, have the body posture of a productive person. Your subconscious cannot differentiate between reality and imagination. Use this to your advantage by acting "as if" you already have the strength, the character trait, etc. In Neuro-linguistic Programming and coaching, this is called modeling.

A good way to become successful and productive is to observe and copy already successful and productive people. If they have made it, you can do it too. If you look very closely, the most successful persons are oftentimes also the most productive ones.

This works! It's actually what I did. I became productive using all the tricks successful and productive people explained in their books and talks. And look at me: Six, seven years ago I was not productive and not organized at all and today I'm writing a book about productivity…

Start acting "as if" and see what happens. Fake it till you become it!

9
YOUR ATTITUDE

Your attitude is crucial for everything including your time management! It can change your way of seeing things dramatically and also your way of facing them. You will suffer less in life and at your work if you accept the rules of the game. Life is made up of laughter and tears, light and shadow. You have to accept the bad moments by changing your way of looking at them. Everything that happens to you is a challenge and an opportunity at the same time.

Always look at the positive side of things in life even in the worst situations. Sometimes it might take some time to discover it, but there is something good hidden in every bad. Take a moment and look back. Isn't it true? Your partner left you and you were destroyed, but today you are happier than ever with your new love. A business deal went sour, but today you are happy it did, because an even better opportunity came up…

Remember: It's not what happens in your life that's important; it's how you respond to what happens to you that makes your life! Life is a chain of moments—some happy, some sad—and it depends on YOU to make the best of each and every one of those moments.
Many years ago all of the success teachers and positive thinkers described it this way: "If life gives you a lemon, add sugar to it, and make lemonade out of it." Younger readers might say that "If life gives you a lemon, ask for some salt and Tequila." You get the point, don't you?

So allow yourself to make mistakes and learn from them. Admit that there are things you don't know. Dare asking for help and let other people surprise you with the help they offer you.

Differentiate between what you have done in your life until now and what you want to do - or better still - will do from now on! Now go out and get your life back. You can do it and above all—you've earned it!

10
WATCH YOUR WORDS

"The only thing that's keeping you from getting what you want is the story you keep telling yourself."

Tony Robbins

Watch your words! Don't underestimate them! They are very powerful! The words that we use to describe our experiences become our experiences. You probably encountered a situation or two in your life, when spoken words did a lot of damage. And this is true not only in talking to others, but also talking to yourself. Yes, this little voice in your head—the one that just asked "Voice, what voice?"

Words can affect your performance, and also the performance and mindsets of others. Remember the Pygmalion Effect? What you expect from yourself and/or other people is transmitted by your words, and your words have a very powerful effect not only on your results, but also on the results of your friends, colleagues, or family.

You are what you tell yourself the whole day! Your inner dialogue is like the repeated suggestion of a hypnotist. Are you complaining a lot about not having time? What story are you telling yourself?
If you run around telling yourself that you'll never have time I'm afraid that's what you will find in your world.

On the other hand, if you say you always find time and are a super productive person, you will reflect that and the outer environment will fall into place. Of course talking alone is not enough. You have to take action and apply some of the time management tricks you have learnt by now.

Your inner dialogue has a huge impact on your self-esteem. So be careful with how you describe yourself: Such as "I'm lazy," "I'm a disaster," "I'll never be able to do that," "I just don't get things done on time," or my personal favourite "I'm tired" because of course the more you tell yourself that you are tired, the more tired you will get!

Watching your inner dialogue is very important! The way you communicate with yourself changes the way you think about yourself, which changes the way you feel about yourself, which changes the way you act and this ultimately influences your results and the perception that others have of you.
Keep the conversation with yourself positive such as "I want to achieve great productivity," "I want to have a lot of free time," "God, I am good," because your subconscious mind doesn't understand the little word "NO." It sees your words as IMAGES. Don't think of a pink elephant! See? I bet you just imagined a pink elephant.

And—I will repeat myself—please focus on what you want. Keep in mind that your words and especially the questions you ask yourself have a huge influence on your reality. I tell my coaching clients to never tell me or themselves that they have no time, but instead always ask "How can I find more time? or "How can I get more done?"
If you ask yourself "how," your brain will search for an answer and come up with it. The good thing is that you can really change your life by changing your language, talking to yourself in a positive way, and starting to ask yourself different questions.
Why wait? Start asking yourself different questions now!

The powerful two words"What if?"

"Our expectancies not only affect how we see reality but also affect the reality itself."—Dr. Edward E. Jones
Always expect the best! Life doesn't always give you what you want, but it sure gives you what you expect! Do you expect success? Or do you spend most of your time worrying about failure? Your expectations about yourself and others come from your subconscious beliefs and they have an enormous impact on your achievements. Your expectations influence your attitude and your attitude has a lot to do with your productivity. They also affect your willingness to take action and all of your interactions with others.

Many of us know all this and yet most of us expect negative outcomes when asking one of the favorite questions of the mind: The question "What if."

By asking it, we are often focused on what doesn't work: "What if it doesn't work out?," "What if the stuff Marc writes about doesn't work?," "What if I don't get the job done?," "What if I never find time?"

However neither does that feel good, nor is it good to focus on what we fear. Why not turn this around and ask yourself for every limiting or negative thought, **"What if the opposite is true?"**, "What if this works out great?", "What if this little book changes my life?", "What if this stuff works?", "What if I finish this project on time?", "What f I finally find time"?

The single adjustment in how you ask your questions transforms you, your energy, and the answer you get. It changes your thinking and your inner dialogue.

Suddenly you start asking positive "What if" questions in your head, rather than negative ones. The benefits of shifting your thinking will be:

- Less stress, fear, and anxiety.
- You will feel more peaceful.
- Your energy level will go up.
- It allows you to be the inventor of your own experience.

Try it out! How did you feel just now reading it? Write a list of all of your fears and negative "What ifs" and then turn it around.

IV - RECAP

1
BURNING OUT

Burnout creeps into your life silently. Watch very closely if you notice the following symptoms:
- You work more and more hours and get less and less done.
- You don't sleep very well any more.
- You start hating what you do and questioning yourself if it's all worth it.
- You sit in front of your computer the whole day and notice at the end of the day that you got nothing done.
- What normally took you hours, now takes days.

There is only such a small line between working a lot on your business or career being motivated to do it all and slowly burning out so that you don't even notice it at first. When you notice that you just drag yourself from day to day and have lost the joy of working on your business or in your job you might be at the point of crossing that line.

Ask yourself the following questions:
- Have you lost your enthusiasm?
  Do you get much less done now than before?
- Did you run out of ideas and momentum?
- Is it difficult for you to get up in the morning and get to work—or do you even hate it?

If you answer one or more of those questions with a YES, then you might want to have a look at whether your are burning out. Many people think that in order to build their business or their career they have to work 20 hours a day and can't take a day or a weekend off. There's some truth to it, but unfortunately it's the fast lane to burnout.

As we have learnt now, taking breaks every now and then and on weekends will not damage your productivity. It will actually boost it! **Don't work 60 hours a week thinking that once you are successful you can cut down your hours. Start cutting down your hours and take breaks to become successful quicker.**

I bet that most of my readers can cut their hours in half. Use as many tricks as you can from this book. Of course you have to work a lot, but being productive, you might not have to put that many hours in, just make the most of the hours (Remember Pareto & Company).

There is a huge different between putting in hours and wasting them. Taking short breaks every now and then revitalizes you and you'll get a lot more work done afterwards. You will also become more creative, get new ideas, be happier, and therefore better able to cope with obstacles in your way. I'd even go as far as to say that not taking time off is wasting working time! When you notice that you are not getting as much done as you should, forgetting things, or feeling like you are simply staring at your computer screen for hours without getting anything done, it's time to take a break.

How to prevent burning out:
1. **Take time off every week.** At least one day.
2. **Get enough sleep.** Most of the time it's better to go to bed before midnight and get up early the next day. If you work until 2 am in the morning you are usually less productive the next day. However, this also depends on your rhythm. If you are a night owl it might just work out great for you. That's something you have to try out for yourself. Lack of sleep will definitely accelerate burning out.
3. **Take good care of yourself.** Read a good book, go to the movies, get a massage, watch a sunrise, sit by the water, go for a walk, take a bubble bath, etc. Treating yourself well will do miracles for your productivity with the positive side effect of lifting your self-confidence and self-esteem!
4. **Ditch projects.** Remember Pareto? Find out which 20% of your projects are bringing 80% of the money and ditch the rest. Ditch the projects that are very time intensive, demand too much effort, and bring in relatively little money. Be selective about what new projects you accept. There's nothing better than a project that you don't really want. Double the price. If you still get the project, outsource most of it.

2
TOOLS PUT INTO PRACTICE

Managing your time

- Invest a few hours in defining exactly what you want to do
- Plan—take 15 minutes the day before or 15 minutes before you start your day to plan
- Prioritize
- Do the uncomfortable first
- Block time and learn to say "No"
- Group similar tasks ("Batch")
- Use a task list
- Keep an Interruptions log
- Keep track of your time for at least a week

Conflicts

- Listen with the intention of understanding—not with the intention to answer
- Negotiate "win-win situations"
- Go for collaboration rather than confrontation
- Be willing to take the first step
- Explain what you need and why and let the other person know how they can help
- Take a deep breath
- Remember—"We see the world not as it is but as we are"

Organize your email

- Set aside the time needed for a "BIG" inbox organization
- Organize or create files according to your needs
- Move all emails that are older than a month to a "temporary file" (if you haven't touched them in six months... delete them)
- Divide the project into smaller tasks—work on your emails an hour every day
- Commit to go home with a clean mailbox every evening
- Remember: Do it now, file it for later, delegate it, file for reference, delete
- The more you postpone this task, the uglier it gets...
- Handle emails that come from other parts of the world first thing in the morning
- Educate your team to copy you only on emails that are really important

- Use Skype (or similar) to handle things that are typically distributed in several emails
- Assign at least one morning or afternoon to work without interruptions

Work fast

- Set goals and allocate time for each one
- Commit to keep given times
- Avoid distractions
- Group similar tasks (Batching)
- Block time for your tasks, do not allow interruptions
- Learn to say "NO"
- Focus on your goals, visualize results, prioritize
- Remember the Pareto principle: 20% of your effort will give 80% of your results

Too much work?

- Define priorities—Time Management Matrix
- Allocate time for your most important tasks and stick to it
- Check if all you have to do is really necessary. Can you delegate? Automate?
- Do you need to talk to your boss about your workload?

When you are relying on others

- Write down what you need from the other person
- Write how the person impacts your delay
- Think in advance about how you might reach a solution. Present alternatives
- Use positive language
- Have a meeting or private call with the person
- Be honest, polite, and understanding
- If the person ignores your request, talk to your boss

How to deal with interruptions

- Learn to say "NO" in a friendly manner and schedule time for later
- Inform people that from now on you would be grateful if your time "without interruption" is respected
- Use headphones
- Go to a place where you cannot be interrupted
- Let calls go to voicemail
- Negotiate with a coworker to redirect the phone while you're busy
- Analyze if it's really necessary to attend all the meetings you are invited to
- Help others, but do not make it a permanent habit

Everything is urgent

- Prioritize and check the importance of each task
- If you get to the point where everything is urgent, your workload must be revised
- Analyze why all of your tasks are urgent: Are you procrastinating? Are you organized? Are your coworkers organized? Are there any technical problems?
- Avoid jumping between tasks
- Explain in a calm voice that you are ending task # 1 and when it's done you will go to task # 2…
- Explain politely WHEN your task will be completed. People do not want to hear that you're busy; they just want to know when you'll be done with their stuff

Managing distractions

- Make a list of things you have to do during the day
- Prioritize
- Commit to finishing your tasks before the day is over
- Reward yourself for finished tasks
- Ask a colleague to help you achieve your goal of the day
- Disconnect your phone
- Disconnect everything that distracts you. Work without distractions for at least one hour a day

Inconsistency and lack of commitment in the implementation

- One small step every day—if you fail, do not beat yourself up. Try again the next day
- Remember, no one else will do it for you
- Do the most uncomfortable task first thing in the morning each day for a week and check results
- Reward yourself
- Use the tools that are easy for you (list, group tasks, etc.)

Multitasking

- Avoid it—many studies show that multitasking is less productive
- Use the Time Management matrix and do one thing at a time
- You need discipline: Avoid looking at your emails constantly; don't answer messages/private calls; don't get distracted into doing things that are not important
- Plan your day in "time blocks" that you will devote to specific tasks and follow through
- Every time you have completed a task, take a break and go to the next one

Loud environment
- Ear plugs
- Change your workplace to a quieter space
- Headphones
- Do important things very early in the morning, at noon, or at night
- If things get really bad, take a walk to "gather your thoughts"

Afraid to make mistakes
- We are all in a constant learning process, therefore, ask for help! Your boss will appreciate it
- Remember: It's better to be nervous once than regretting later
- If the worst happens… think philosophically: We learn more from our mistakes
- Talk to your boss and explain what areas need help (training, mentoring, coaching, etc.)

Difficulties in follow-up/forgetting the customers' problems
- Use an electronic calendar
- Schedule the follow-up the same way you'd program a meeting or any other task
- Set a phone alarm
- Write down the "problem" as a task and be sure to follow up

Too curious to not check incoming emails
- Disconnect the sound of incoming email
- Assign specific times during the day for accessing your email
- Commit to not check emails. Nobody can make you do what you do not want to do
- Reward yourself when you refrain from taking a look at the inbox
- Keep track of the time you spend going back and forth to look at your emails and compare it with the time you spend when you focus on your tasks and agree to check emails only a few times per day

Too many meetings
- Evaluate whether you really have to attend all meetings
- If you attend… Do you have to stay for the entire meeting?
- Try to schedule days without meetings where you can concentrate on your other tasks
- Delegate attending meetings or other tasks

3
ONE LAST THING

I want you to have all the time wasters in one chapter. This is a little summary of the most "dangerous" time robbers and how to manage them and I added this section to make sure you really get your productivity to the next level. If you manage those time drains effectively they won't harm your productivity.

Email

Turning off email notifications will boost your productivity (remember that every beep or vibration is a distraction that costs you between seven and 25 minutes)

More tricks:

- Set yourself a fixed time during the day and set a time limit for checking your emails. For example, three times a day for half an hour, in the morning, afternoon,and evening.
- For emails that you need longer to respond to, send the prson a quick message like: "I received your message and will send you a detailed reply later." Add this to your task list.
- Organize your email inbox.
- Have different accounts for you personal and work emails so that personal emails don't distract you.
- Create an "away" message that tells the sender that you received their email and that you'll get back to them as soon as possible.
- Create email templates for similar emails that you send.

The Internet

Oftentimes you go online to research some information and before your know it it's lunch time and you have been looking at random YouTube videos for the last two hours. It's very easy to get lost in the endless space of the internet.

- The best solution is to stay away from the web! If you have to go online anyway keep your goal in mind! What specific bit of information are you looking for? Which task are you looking to accomplish?

- Log out of your social media accounts. Period.
- Turn off notifications from social media apps on your phone.
- Use free time or down time for your social media. For example, waiting in line at the supermarket while responding to messages via your mobile device. I usually do my social media on the train to Barcelona. If you use social media for your job, schedule time for it, stay on task when using it, and stay away from it when it's not scheduled.

Phone Calls

Not all phone calls are important and you don't have to pick up the phone all the time. Every now and then you may have no choice but to answer the phone though.

- Maximize productivity by keeping your calls short and focused on important business.
- Let the call go to your voice mail and let people know when they can expect a reply.
- Schedule a time to call the person back later.
- Redirect the incoming phone calls to a colleague for a determined time. The colleague can inform the caller when it is okay to call you. Do the same for your colleague so that they can also become more productive.

Meetings

My personal opinion: Skip 'em or don't have 'em. (I'm clearly damaged by unproductive meetings.) If that's not possible, keep meetings to a minimum and keep them as short as possible.

- Have a clear starting and ending time.
- Let everybody know what the goal of the meeting is.
- Stay focused on the important stuff and let people know what they need to do before attending the meeting.
- Hold standing or walking meetings. They usually end quicker.
- Use google hangouts or skype if possible instead of meeting in person.

Colleagues

There are several ways to handle coworkers if they present a distraction.

- Isolate yourself physically. Close your door. Use headphones (like me—writing this chapter on the train again...).
- Say "No" to requests until you have your tasks under control.
- Tell people when you are busy and when they can interrupt you.
- Offer them help at a later time.

Mundane Tasks

There are some tasks that just have to be done. Here are four ways to get rid of them:

1. Eliminate
2. Delegate
3. Outsource
4. Automate

And by all means don't run any errands for your colleagues, family, and friends. If you are the one running the errands for everybody you will never find time. Period. Running errands for others in a huge time waster and if you are the good guy that does many favors everybody will like you, but you will never have time and if you are an entrepreneur you'll probably go bankrupt. So watch closely which errands you run and for whom. *(If you run errands for everybody and still are successful and have all the time in the world, please le me know. I have never met anybody like you!)*

Mindless Entertainment

While examining my clients' time, I found that many times they are losing a lot of time on mindless entertainment: TV, video games, social media, YouTube videos, online games, etc.

On one hand it's important to take your mind off your work every now and then and distract yourself a little. The problem starts when you lose control of it or when you just cannot differentiate anymore between relax time and work time.
Set clear rules and times for work and fun. When you work you work and when you play you play.

CONCLUSION

This is it! I hope you had fun and that you now have a lot of tools and habits that can help you increase your productivity and thus help you getting more done, having more time for your family, more free time in general, or more time to make money.

Whatever you decide, the choice is yours. There are no more excuses. You now know that "I don't have time for you," most of the time means "You are not important enough for me."

Remember you don't have to do it all. You can start with one or two habits from this book and you don't even have to do big things. As you saw from the example of Steve, the stressed Sales Manager, just changing small things on a daily basis can gain you enormous amounts of time.

The important thing as always is **doing it!** Remember that small steps constantly done can bring huge results. Don't wait for the future to solve your time management problems magically. Take control. Start **NOW** and I assure you in one year you'll be grateful you started today.

For starters work the basics such as planning, scheduling, prioritizing. Adopt two or three productivity habits and be very aware of the inner game of productivity. You've got this!

Please let me know what you think about this book. As you saw at the beginning I really take your feedback seriously. Constructive critics are always welcome and will help me to improve future books or even future editions of this one.

Get in touch with me over facebook, twitter, or send me an email at marc@marcreklau.com. I like to be in touch with my readers. :-)

It would be great if you could take the time to leave an honest review on Amazon. This helps other people find the book and if it's five stars…even better ;-)

All the best and I wish you lots of time!

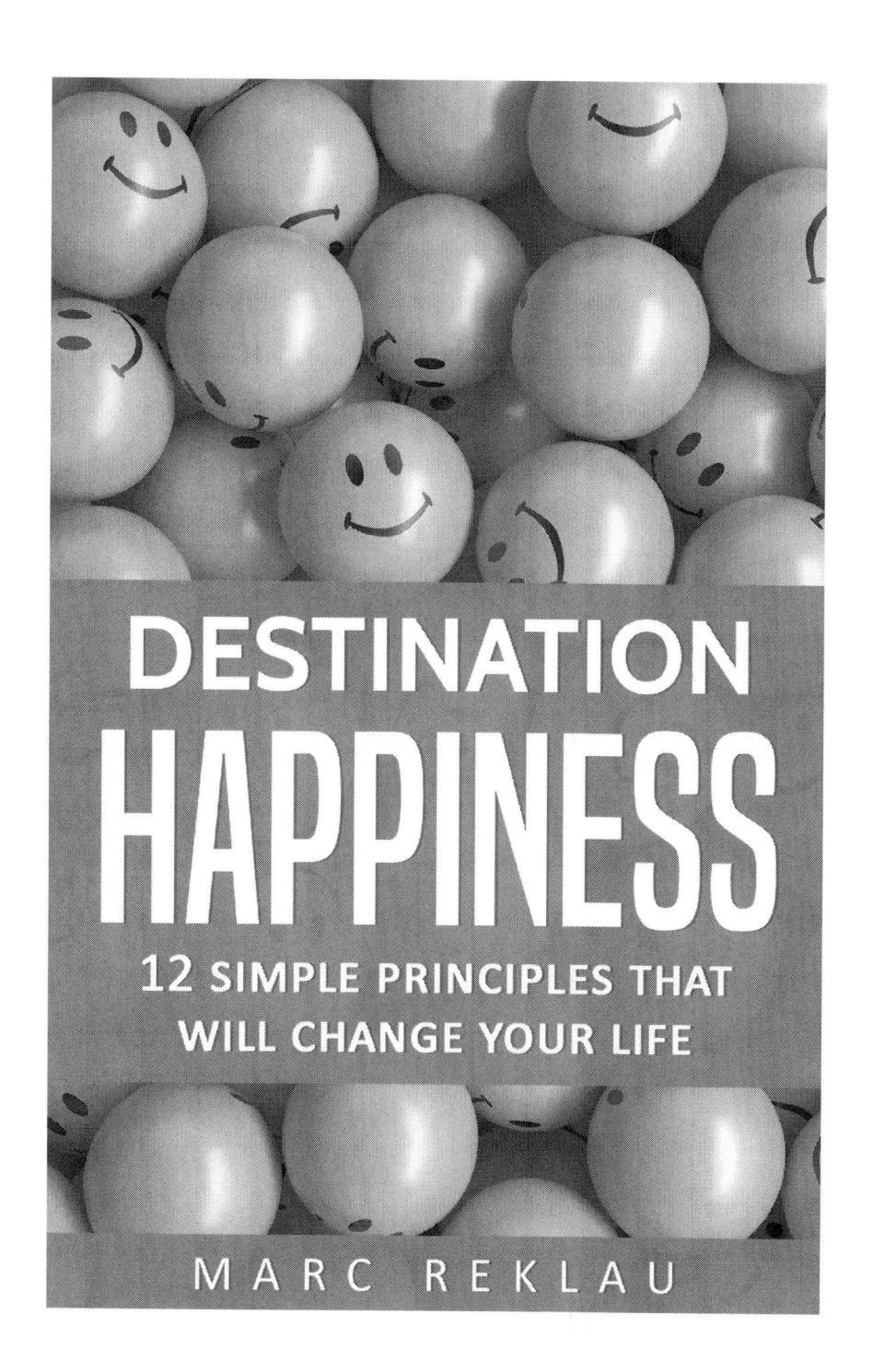

DESTINATION HAPPINESS

12 SIMPLE PRINCIPLES THAT WILL CHANGE YOUR LIFE

MARC REKLAU

Marc Reklau

DESTINATION HAPPINESS

12 Simple Principles that will change your life

If you want to make the world a happier place, start with yourself :)

Contents

Introduction..311

1. The Basics..**321**
Applying the science..321
Believing that change is possible..321
The Power of One 323
Which factors influence our happiness......................................324
Accepting our emotions 326
Making 'Happiness' the ultimate goal.....................................328

2. The Power of Belief..**333**
Beliefs create reality..333
Creating a positive situation...336
Believe in yourself..337
Changing your performance by changing your beliefs...................337
Being an optimist helps...340
The three keys to success..343

3. The Power of Focus..**347**
Health benefits..350
Why aren't we all optimists?..351
The Power of Gratitude..352
Focus on the positive...355
Are some people just lucky?..355
Train your brain on focusing on the positive..............................356

4. The Power of Choice...**359**
Choose your thoughts...359
Choose your emotions..360
Choose to take responsibility for your life................................362
More choices… 366
Do you have to or do you choose to? 368
Stop these toxic habits..369
Take control...370
Feeling in control is good for your health................................372

5. Change is Possible..........373
Face your fears and do it anyway..........373
Be the change..........375
Step out of your comfort zone..........376
How does change work? The Power of Habit..........377
Why is change so difficult?..........380
Changing emotions..........381
Changing behavior..........382
Self-discipline is overrated..........384
How to create habits?..........387

6. The Power of Goal-setting..........389
Why set goals?..........390
Goals and focusing on the present..........392
Learn to enjoy the progress..........393
Write down your goals..........394
Examine your values..........397
Find your Purpose..........399
Purpose at the workplace..........401

7. The Ugly Twins – Perfectionism & Failure..........405
Learn to fail or fail to learn..........407
The characteristics of perfectionism..........411
The consequences of perfectionism..........413
The sources of perfectionism..........414
How to overcome perfectionism..........414
Can we help others to overcome perfectionism?..........415
How to deal with perfectionism..........416

8. Overcoming the Silent Killer..........417
Overcoming stress..........417
Stop multitasking..........419
Procrastination..........420

9. Raising Your Self-Esteem..........423
Definitions of self-esteem..........423
The benefits of self-esteem..........424
Critics..........425
More criticism..........427
How to cultivate self-esteem..........428
The importance of independent self-esteem?..........430
How do we enhance our self-esteem?..........432

10. Habits to Boost Your Self-esteem..........433
Stop being so hard on yourself..........433
Raise your standards..........434
Self-love is #1 435
Live your own life 436
Become a receiver 436
Invest in yourself..........437
Be authentic..........438
Honor your past achievements..........438
Listen to great music (Yes, it's important)..........439
Celebrate your wins 440
Have a highlight every day..........440
Pamper yourself..........441
Forgive everyone..........441

11. The #1 Predictor of Happiness: Relationships..........443
Know yourself..........444
How can we create relationships that thrive?..........444
How do we sustain love? 448
The importance of asking the right questions..........453
Relationships at work..........454
The most important relationship at work..........456

12. The Power of the Mind-Body Connection..........459
The Magic of physical exercise..........460
The Power of Meditation..........465
Mindfulness: be here now..........467
Breathe right and conquer..........471
The Importance of Sleep..........472
Physical and Psychological need of sleep..........473
The Importance of Touch..........474
Smile like your life depends on it..........476

13. What now?..........479

About the Author?..........483
I Need Your Help..........484
Bring the simple steps of 30 DAYS to your Organization..485

Acknowledgements:

Thanks to Natalia Montolio, my partner in life and business, for her constant support, and for brightening my days with her smiles and always-cheerful mood. Thanks to my family; my mother, Heidi; grandmother, Hilde; my uncle Dieter; and my cousin, Alex and his wife Yvonne (our joint vacations in the beautiful city of Naples, Florida, always inspire me).

Olaf, Paola, Sophie and Adrian for you hospitality in FTL. It's always a pleasure to visit.

My friends Claudio, Christian, Pol, Inma, Oscar and all the new people who came into my life in this amazing last two years.

Stefan Ludwig, my mentor and sounding board for over 15 years.

Big shout out to Jaime Avargues, the first publisher who discovered my first book, '30 DAYS', took a chance and bought the Spanish rights for Latin America even before the book became a bestseller.

Pilar Zaragoza de Pedro, who had the brilliant idea to write a book together, which led to the birth of our own publishing label.

I also want to thank David H. Morgan for his valuable inputs and feedback over the years.

Dr. Steve Mallon, Carlos Moreno Gonzalez, and Lisa Williams for giving me the chance to teach happiness at the Geneva Business school. Also, thanks to Paloma Garcia from GBS and my fabulous bachelor students.

Thank you to my German teacher from high school, Mrs. Gabriele Krohm for believing in me, while your colleague Mr. Scheuthle strongly advised me to not major in German and take Biology instead. Also, thank you to you Mr. Scheuthle for your honesty.

Thank you Angel Miro for applying the Pygmalion Effect with me and making me a better student.

Thanks to everybody who continuously supported me and for believed in me when not a lot of people did. I also want to thank the people I parted ways with. You were very important to me at one point of time. Things just didn't work out. I appreciate your presence in my life once, and wish you all the best.

But above all, thank you to the following people whose work has had a huge influence on my own work in the last few years, and which, in a lot of ways, made this book possible.

Thanks to Martin Seligman for starting a revolution in Psychology and changing the questions.

To Tal Ben Shahar, for teaching the "Happiness Class" at Harvard University and opening doors for hundreds (or even thousands) of other teachers teaching the subject all over the world.

Shawn Achor, for translating the fantastic studies from the field of Positive Psychology into everyday language that we all can understand.

A huge thank you also goes out to the researchers of the hundreds of studies that provide us with fantastic insights about the power of our mind

And last, but not the least, a HUGE thank you to you, dear readers. Without YOU, this book wouldn't exist. Your e-mails and comments encourage me to continue writing and give me strength in moments of doubts and darkness.

Thank you!

Introduction

I've believed in all the things that I've written about since I was 16 years old. When I started getting into self-help and personal development, most of the things that were taught like "Your Beliefs create your reality" or "You attract what you concentrate on" were mere philosophical concepts that you could believe, or not. There was no scientific basis for it.

However, I still believed.

When I found the science that supports most of the concepts that are introduced in my first book "30 Days– Change your habits, change your life" I became immensely happy, because I knew that thanks to science, I can now even convince the skeptics, at least most of them.

I felt like I was given a superpower, because now – apart from showing that the exercises work by *doing* them – we have science as proof. This, hopefully, will motivate more people to give it a shot. We are quickly running out of the excuses that keep us from doing them.

While 30 Days is primarily a practical book, this book looks more at the scientific side of happiness and the huge impact it has on our life and our potential – at home as well as at work.

The book stems from the classes I taught at the Barcelona Campus of Geneva Business School, which was in most parts, based on my book "30 Days– Change your habits, change your life" and the works of Martin Seligman, Tal Ben Shahar, and Shawn Achor among others. These three men made hundreds of studies in the field of Positive Psychology accessible by "translating" them into a language that everybody could easily understand.

The fact that Tal Ben Shahar taught the "Happiness-class" (Positive Psychology) at Harvard University – which went on to become the most-demanded class at Harvard with over 1,400 students – helped me and hundreds (or even thousands) of other teachers to make this subject an integral part in universities, business schools, and even workplaces– something quite unthinkable till a little over a decade ago.

"Why teach happiness at Harvard?", one may ask. Well, in 2004, the Harvard Crimson Poll found out that 4 in 5 Harvard students suffer from depression at least once during the school year, and nearly half of all students suffer from continuous depression so debilitating that they can't function. Fast-forward to a couple of years later, these numbers were confirmed by a nationwide study of universities in the U.S.

This book looks at the base question of all questions: How can I become happier?

You will learn how to cultivate the habits and mindset that have been scientifically proven to fuel greater success and fulfillment.

The original formula that my generation and the ones before were taught was the following:

Study hard, get a job, work hard, become successful, and once you are successful, you will be happy. So tell me, my friend, how did that work out for you? For me, it didn't, and when we look around us, we have to admit that this formula obviously doesn't work for most of us.

After more than a decade of research in the fields of Positive Psychology and neuroscience, today we can say that it's actually the other way round: We become more successful when we are happier and optimistic.

Another false concept we were taught was that reaching certain goals fuel happiness. That once when we have the perfect body; once we have a great job; a promotion; a new car; a great house in the most-affluent locality in town; once we have the fattest bank balance; and the worst – once we find the perfect partner – *then*, we will be happy.

But did that work for you? Well, I have good news for you– this too was proven wrong, but worry not, as science also gives the solution of how to find real happiness.

Once again it's not about the information and theory of how to live a happier life.
I want you to use the scientific basis as an additional motivation to apply the material and do the exercises.

But first… why happiness?

Nobody ever teaches us how to find meaning and happiness, and that's why there's lots of trouble in Happiness-Land:

Divorce rates are at 50-60%, and that doesn't mean that the other 40-50% of marriages are just peachy. Because it doesn't include the number of marriages that are intact due to habit, a sense of duty, or due to the fear of change.

Depression rates are ten times higher than it was in the 1960s, and the average onset age of the first depression has dropped from 29.5 years to 14.5 years!

Suicide rates are rising.

Turn on the news and all you see is corruption, murder, terrorism, accidents, war, and abuse. What's worse is that this constant focus on the negative tricks our brain into believing that reality actually looks like this – that most part of life is negative.

Unfortunately, looking at traditional Psychology as late as in the year 1998, the ratio didn't look much better. For every one study on happiness, there were 17 studies on depression and disorder.

And then – thank god – came Martin Seligman, the President of the American Psychological Association, who officially launched the field of Positive Psychology, or the scientific study of optimal human functioning, in 1998.

Seligman concluded that instead of studying what's broken, "we have to study what works." We have to look at what makes some people thrive and succeed even in the most difficult of circumstances. What are successful people doing differently from the others?

We have to focus on what works by looking at the questions we ask because what we focus on creates our reality. So we better start focusing on and cultivating the positive.

And that changed everything...

Being happy is much more than the absence of sadness. Today, thanks to over 200 studies on 275,000 people worldwide, we know that happiness leads to success in nearly every domain of our lives. Being happy improves our health, our marriage, our friendships, our social life, and especially our jobs, careers, and businesses.

It starts with making changes within ourselves. Later on, we can bring the benefits of happiness to our complete environment, such as in our teams, our organizations, and in everyone around us.

The examples and studies shown in this book will bring you proof that happiness and optimism enhance your performance and achievement, providing you with the competitive edge.

Martin Seligman, for example, found out that optimistic salespeople sell a whopping 56% more than their pessimistic counterparts. Further studies show optimism can make CEOs 15% more productive and not only that, they also have healthier teams that perform better. Happy and optimistic managers can improve customer satisfaction by 42%.
And, happy workers have higher levels of productivity, get higher sales figures, perform better in leadership positions, and receive higher work performance ratings.
They are also paid better, and are less likely to take sick leaves.

To summarize, the benefits of happiness are countless. Positive emotions flood our brains with dopamine and serotonin, which make us feel better, make us better at organizing information, and make us able to retain information for longer. We become faster and better creative thinkers. We see new ways of doing things, subsequently making us better at problem-solving.

As I already mentioned, there are countless studies about happiness. One study reveals that the happiness levels in students as freshmen in college predicted how high their income was as much as 19 years later, regardless of their initial level of wealth.

Talking about health. In the famous "Nun-Study" researchers studied the level of positivity in journal entries of nuns and found out that the nuns with joyful and content journal entries lived nearly ten years longer than the ones that were negative or neutral entries. Another study shows that happy employees are healthier and therefore more productive on the job (did we really need a study for that?), but not only that, the Gallup Healthways Wellbeing Index 2008 showed how unhappy employees take more sick leaves, stayed at home 1.25 more days a month than their happy colleagues. This sums up to 15 days a year!

A recent study by the German government shows that employees in Germany missed more workdays due to sickness than in the years before.

How did researchers show the correlation between happiness and health anyway? Easy. They injected people with a cold virus (why didn't we think of this earlier). Happy people felt better at the start of the cold, and even after a week they had fewer symptoms than their unhappy counterparts.
So, let's drill down to what this book really is about.

You have already heard of a lot of things that I've mentioned in this book. I'm not going to tell you anything new. You already know it, and I'm just reminding you.

A lot of times people tell me: "Marc but what you are writing or teaching is common sense!"
And I answer: "Yes it is, but then again common sense is not common action. If it were, we would all be at our ideal weight, working our dream jobs, and living our dream lives, wouldn't we?"

The "Science of Happiness", as Positive Psychology is often called, has built the bridge between the self-help movement with its accessible books, speakers, and workshops, (do phrases like "The 5 steps to a happier life", "3 keys to success" and so on, sound familiar?) but unfortunately, in many cases promise results that are difficult to achieve. On the other hand, we have scientific studies that confirm that these things work, but just very, very few people read them – or can read them. I tried a couple but failed miserably; I just couldn't understand them.

This book, then, is about connecting the best of the two worlds – the scientific studies and the accessibility of self-help.

The important and the most difficult thing is, and I'm not getting tired of repeating this, that it's not the information that determines the quality of your life, it's the application of the information and the putting in practice of the exercises that will make all the difference.

Will this book make a difference in your life? I don't know. If you apply some of the things you learn here, it almost definitely will, and your life will never be the same. Applying these exercises made all the difference in my life. It won't be easy, there will be setbacks and hardships, but it would be worth it.

It's been a bit more than four years since I was fired from my job after being there eleven years. I've made it to best-selling author, with my book read by over 170,000 readers; business school teacher; mentor coach, and I can now earn in a day what I once earned in a month. It was not a walk in the park. It took time, effort, patience, and persistence. There was pain, sadness, doubt, fear, and the temptation to give up numerous times, and above all, a failed marriage, but I kept going on. I hope you do too.

What will you learn after reading this book?
- You'll learn how to overcome for example the fear of failure.
- You'll learn how to overcome perfectionism, which is only debilitating and hurts your progress and peace of mind.
- You'll learn how to improve your relationships

We will look at the importance of gratitude, the importance of physical exercise, and the importance of spending time on relationships and you will read about some mind-boggling studies that hopefully will convince you to give the exercises in this book a shot.

We will look at the importance of perception, interpretation, and focus, which makes all the difference between people that seem to have everything and yet are unhappy and those who enjoy life to the fullest; between those who have nothing and yet never cease to be happy and those who have very little and see themselves as victims of the circumstances

When John Carter studied extraordinary successful people, he found that it came down to only two characteristics that they had, that less successful people didn't have. Only two things mattered, and it wasn't their IQ or their external circumstances, or where they came from.

People who were extraordinary successful had two things in common: firstly they believed in themselves, they believed they are going to make it, and secondly, they kept asking questions. They always wanted to learn.
Please keep just one thing in mind and I will repeat this over and over again:
THERE IS NO QUICK FIX.

If you are looking for a quick fix, a magic pill, a proven system that will fix your life in no time, this book is not for you. This stuff works, but it will take some time. Just like how learning to play tennis or any other sport takes some time.

Another warning:
After reading this book, you will NOT be on a constant high and free of pain or succeed in everything you do. That wouldn't be

normal. Pain and getting over it, failure and getting up again, ups and downs in life, success and its celebration, victories and losses are all part of life. These are essentials that lead to experiences, learning, and growing.

What you will learn is how to bounce back from hardships quicker, how to deal with failure, how to get over pain faster, and how your focus and your interpretation of events can and will elevate your base level of happiness.

If you don't apply what you learn in this book, it will be just one more book on the shelf.
If you do – this book – or any other about the subject can change your life forever. Although many people might tell you otherwise, truth remains that THERE IS NO SECRET. The secret, however, if you at all want to look for one, is APPLICATION!

Yes! Happiness can be learned. Resilience can be learned. Bouncing back can be learned. Optimism can be learned. Thanks to neuroscience, we know today that our brain is not a fixed thing. It can actually change.

So how can we become happier and through that, help other individuals, communities, and societies as a whole to become happier? What is happiness and how do you measure it? Is happiness really a destination? Or is it rather a life-long pursuit, or a process of continuous learning?

The first step on the journey is looking within ourselves, introspecting, and making the effort of applying what we learned by introducing behavioral changes in life, which by the way is the only way to bring about real, lasting change.

Are you in? Then let's do this…

1. The Basics

Let's look at the basics, the foundation that we have to lay first, the conditions that have to be in place to begin our journey towards happiness.

1. Applying the science

Good intentions are not enough. We have to take the studies of Positive Psychology and apply them. We need more teachers to know about the Pygmalion effect. They have to know that their expectations are self-fulfilling prophecies, meaning that if they see the greatness in their students, that greatness is much more likely to come alive.

We need more psychologists and doctors to know about the mind-body connection. Who knows about the studies that show that yoga in jail reduces the possibility of second-time offenders? That meditation literally transforms our brain? How many doctors know that 3 x 30 minutes of exercise has the same effect as the most powerful psychiatric drugs?

2. Believing that change is possible

To make changes in your life, first of all, you have to believe that change is possible. But first, here's an interesting question – do genetics matter and if yes, then to what extent?

Lyken and Tellegan, in their famous Minnesota twin study in the 1980s, looked at identical twins that were separated at birth and were brought up and lived in radically different circumstances. The study revealed significant similarities such as:
The twins had wives with the same names, enjoyed drinking the same beer, called their children the same names, had an incredibly similar personality, and similar happiness levels.

They came to the following result: "It may be that trying to be happier is as futile as trying to be taller and is, therefore, counter productive." While this was a very famous quote at the time, it was bad news. **It was also wrong!**

Imagine an unhappy person reading an article like that. He or she's unhappy and reads that we can't become happier, starts believing it, leading it to becoming a self-fulfilling prophecy.

Many years later Lykken said to TIME Magazine. "I made a dumb statement. It is clear that we can change happiness levels, up or down".

There is a lot of evidence that show that people actually do change, for example, through coaching or therapy.
So what happened to Lykken and Tellegen? They made "the error of the average." On an average, when you look at a group of twins, they are just the same.

In reality, many of them are the same, but not all. Those who are not the same are the outliers, and very often it's these outliers that are the most interesting. When researchers started studying the outliers, that's when they got new results.

Genes do matter a lot, science says around 50%, but change is possible! Sometimes it's a sentence or a book that can change your life. We have seen people change as a result of their experiences (PTSD, Post Traumatic Growth – yes, it exists).

So our question shifts from "Is change possible?" to "How is change possible?" and "Why do some individuals succeed despite the circumstances?"

When scientists shifted from studying the average people who hadn't changed to studying the happiest people, they learned that everything changed. When we study what works, when we study the best, that's when we can come to understanding the potential in each one of us.

3. The Power of One

Unfortunately, we underestimate our power to bring about a change. But yes! One person can make a significant difference. Why? Because all change begins in the mind of a single individual, and then it expands, or as Margaret Mead puts it: "Never doubt that a small group of thoughtful, committed citizens can change the world. In fact it's the only thing that ever will."

We underestimate our capacity to bring a change because we underestimate the potential of the exponential function and change happens exponentially. Think, for example, about the exponential nature of social networks. It's said that within six degrees of separation, we are connected to everyone on this planet.

Or think of smiles. Smiles are contagious. If you make three people smile and these three people each make three other people smile and so on, then within 20 degrees of separation, the whole world would be smiling. The same happens when you make people feel good.

We actually influence people every minute of our life. The only question is: In which direction are we going to do it? Will we be a force for change by applying our knowledge or will we just have good intentions, will we just talk about change without actually putting in the effort?
So yes! Change is possible. It's now proven that we can change our brain through mere practice.

We can rewire our brains to be more positive, creative, resilient, and productive – to see opportunities wherever we turn to look. Our brains can be changed by our thoughts and our daily behavior. We can learn to become happier. Pessimists can learn to become optimists and stressed negative brains can be trained to become relaxed and see more opportunities. But as all training, it takes EFFORT.

4. Which factors influence our happiness

Most of us think that the influence of external factors on our happiness is huge.
For example, who do you think is happier? People who won the lottery or people who got paralyzed after an accident? This was a groundbreaking study with surprising results…

Yes, the lottery winners were very happy, but not for very long. After six months they went back to their previous levels of happiness. The accident victims were sad, but surprisingly after six months, they went back to their previous levels of happiness.

The same studies were done with professors. They were asked how happy would they be if they got tenure, to which they answered "very happy for the rest of my life." And others were asked how unhappy would they be on not getting tenure and they answered "very unhappy for a very long time." When researchers went back to them three months later, every person had gone back to their previous level of well-being. If they were happy before, they were happy six months later, and if they were unhappy before, they were unhappy six months later. Whether it was the lottery winner, accident victim, or the professor, everybody went back to their base level of happiness. This shows that it's very difficult to change happiness based on external factors, and there's a lot of research supporting this. It also shows that we all gravitate around a base level of happiness. The goal then becomes to raise this base level, and it can be done with the exercises I'm going to mention later in this book.

Now you could criticize this research because, until recently, most of it was conducted using questionnaires, which were subjective. But with advancement in technology, like brain-scans, FMRIs, and EEGs, psychologists found that there is a very high correlation between the objective measuring like brain-scans and people's evaluation of their well-being through questionnaires.

Ed Diener found that once our basic needs are met (shelter, food, and basic education) income makes little difference in our levels of happiness, except in extreme situations. A homeless person surely might become a lot happier if you pay him or her 2,000 USD a month.

Also when we look around us, we find that our generation is much wealthier than our parents' and grandparents', yet depression and anxiety levels have gone up significantly.

What about your place of residence? Does it make a difference? Well actually it makes very little difference to your happiness. "If I move to Italy, will I be happier" Yes, for a while, before you go back to your base level.

Science confirms that it makes very little difference to our happiness where we are, where we live, what we earn, if we win the lottery, if we get the promotion, or even if we get the dream job. (One thing that does matter is if you live in a democracy or a dictatorship) And you might say: So why do I work so hard if it doesn't make a difference? Well, it doesn't make a difference, but that doesn't mean that you cannot increase your levels of happiness and well being. And that's the good news: You can increase your basic level of well being.

Another misinterpretation is that a lot of people think that the problem with general levels of happiness and unhappiness is that people have extremely high expectations. So if you lower your expectations, you lower your stress levels, and you will enjoy life more. Wrong again! You will probably be happy for a while but not in the long term.

The problem is not low versus high expectations; the problem is right versus wrong expectations:

It's a wrong expectation that going to a new place, getting a raise, finding your idea of a dream partner is responsible for your happiness. These things will not raise your base level of happiness.

The right expectation is to believe in change from within. Our happiness is mostly dependent on our state of mind, NOT on our status or the state of our bank account. It's about changing our perception, our state of mind, our interpretation of the world, of what's happening to us, of our achievements, and of our failures.
Scientifically speaking, happiness is about what we choose to pursue and what we CHOOSE to focus on.

5. Accepting our emotions

The last thing I want you to think about after reading this book is that you will experience a constant high and never have any problems anymore. That won't happen. Tal Ben Shahar says that "There are two kinds of people who don't experience painful emotions such as anger, envy, disappointment, sadness, unhappiness or depression: Psychopaths and dead People."

If you experience these emotions, it's a great sign! You are not dead, and you are not a psychopath. However, in our culture, we don't give ourselves what Tal Ben Shahar calls "the permission to be human". We don't give ourselves the freedom to experience these painful emotions as well, although they are an undeniable part of human nature.

As babies and children, we give ourselves the permission to be human. Later, society becomes important for us, and we realize that other people are watching and evaluating us constantly. That's when we stop giving ourselves the permission to be human. The consequences are that our energy levels, our well-being, our happiness, our creativity, and ultimately also our success suffer.

Give yourself the permission to experience painful emotions when you experience it and accept it. That's it. It's human. The worst thing you can do is to suppress an emotion. When we suppress an emotion, the emotion only gets stronger.

It's like when you say "Don't think of a pink elephant." I bet you just visualized a pink elephant, right? The same happens with your emotions. For example, if you are nervous when speaking in front of a crowd and you tell yourself "I'm not nervous, I'm not nervous, I'm not nervous", but when you finally start to speak, you are more nervous than ever. If you are sad and tell yourself "I'm happy, I'm happy, I'm happy", chances are that you end up even more sad and frustrated. You can't trick your emotions, so accept them.

Painful emotions are as much part of the human nature as the law of gravity is part of physical nature or as rain is a part of the climatological nature, and rejecting our nature leads to bad performance. Envy, anger, sadness, depression are part of human nature. There's nothing good or bad about it. They just are. Find a place where you can give yourself the permission to be human. This can be your "me-time" that you use for journaling or being with friends and family.

Giving yourself the permission to be human doesn't mean that you won't have painful emotions anymore. It means that your psychological immune system will get stronger. A stronger immune system doesn't mean that you won't get sick any more (as I always thought), it means that you'll get sick less often and when you do get sick, you'll recover much faster.

The difference between extremely happy and extremely unhappy people is not that unhappy people get sad, upset, anxious or depressed and the happy ones do not. It's how fast you can recover from these painful emotions.

Stop pretending that you are doing fine, when in fact you aren't doing so well. Be honest and say "I'm having a hard time right now. I'm really stressed". Give yourself the permission to be human; there is nothing wrong with you if you experience painful emotions. Happiness doesn't mean that you have to be happy all the time.

6. Making 'Happiness' the ultimate goal

Another fundamental part to make this whole thing work is to give happiness the highest importance. We have to make it the ultimate end that we pursue. Stop for a moment, take a break from your busy life, and analyze your thoughts. Aren't we spending a lot of time thinking about happiness for ourselves as well as for others?

Aristotle said more than 2,500 years ago: "Happiness is the meaning and purpose of life. The whole aim and end of human existence." William James concluded that "If we were to ask the question 'What is human life's chief concern' one of the answers we should receive would be 'It is happiness'. How to gain, how to keep, and how to recover happiness is, in fact, for most men at all times and the secret motive of all they do."

Last but not the least, the Dalai Lama states "Whether one believes in a religion or not, whether one believes in this religion or that religion. The very purpose of life is happiness. The very motion of our life is toward happiness."

Happiness, or the search for it, transcends cultures, religions, and classes. In my class at the Geneva Business school, there were Christians, Muslims, and Atheists, there were nearly as many nations as students in one room, and we all had one thing in common: wanting to learn how to become happier.

One thing is for sure, and I will show you the scientific proof for it – in case you need it to be convinced – happiness contributes to our life and to our relationships. Happiness helps us to think beyond everyday things, build relationships, and build capacities

In her studies, Barbara Fredrickson found that "Through the experience of positive emotions, people transform themselves to become more creative, knowledgeable, resilient, socially integrated, and healthier individuals."
Yes! Positive emotions do help us overcome negative emotions. While negative emotions narrow and constrict our focus – which is a good thing when you encounter a wild animal and the question is "fight or flight?" – it's not a good thing if it continues beyond the threat.

Positive emotions, on the other hand, broaden, build, and expand our peripheral line of vision.

If for example, my girlfriend or wife leaves me, it's normal that I dwell on it and feel sad for a while. But if after a few months, I still think. "Oh she left me, poor me, how could she do that." I'll spiral down into more sadness and other negative emotions. And if I don't snap out of it, and this feeling starts to persist, then it can turn into depression.

The same goes for positive emotions. Positive emotions can take us out of the downward spiral and create an upward spiral. We can enhance the positive emotions by watching a funny movie, having a good talk with a friend, taking deep breaths, remembering good things from the past, and even by changing our body posture.
It doesn't really take long, but we have to be willing to try it instead of writing it off as nonsense.

In a study conducted by scientists at the University of Toronto revealed that we even see more of what is around us if we are in a positive mood. The scientists primed people for either positivity or negativity and then let the subjects look at a series of pictures. The results were stunning: People in a negative mood were missing substantial parts of the pictures, while people in a positive mood saw everything.

In another experiment, four-year-old children were asked to put blocks of different shapes together as quickly as they could. One group of the children was asked to think about something that makes them happy. Those kids significantly outperformed the group of children that weren't primed to be positive, they were quicker and had fewer errors.

And here is one study that I often remind my friend Marc, a doctor. In one experiment by Estrada, Isen, and Young, happy doctors came to a diagnosis much faster (twice as fast as a neutral controlled group) and exhibited much more creativity.

So what about other people? How can we talk about or act in our life pursuing OUR happiness? Is that selfish? YES, IT IS! "I want to be happier" That's selfish. But it only becomes bad and immoral in a society where selfishness and immorality have virtually become synonymous.

The number one cause of unhappiness, subconsciously or not, is the feeling of guilt associated with pursuing happiness. A lot of times, we are *taught* to feel guilty about feeling good about ourselves. This has to stop! Because it's only when you are happy that you can contribute to other people's happiness and well being. Happiness is the only thing that grows when you give it away, or as they say "You can light thousands of candles with one single candle" This makes happiness a positive addition game. Your happiness is not taking away from other people's happiness, as a matter of fact, most of the time it adds to other people's happiness! Helping others is also helping ourselves, and it feels good to feel good.

If you want to spread happiness, work on your own happiness because then you lead by example and people tend to follow what you do rather than what you say.

2. The Power of Belief

Beliefs create reality

"Your beliefs create your reality." The first time I read this was nearly 30 years ago in the Seth-Material written by Jane Roberts who was channeling Seth. Adventurous and as metaphysical as it gets – I know – nevertheless, over the last 25 years, we've seen a lot of the things that Jane/Seth "wrote" proven by science. And yes, today science can prove that our beliefs really create our reality, and that they are self-fulfilling prophecies.

Remember the study of the most successful people? One of the two characteristics they had was that they believed in themselves. They knew they were going to make it…and the best part is one can *learn* to believe in themselves.

Let's start by looking at beliefs in detail a little later in this chapter. First, here's taking a look at some of the most amazing studies supporting this claim.

Robert Dilts defines beliefs as "judgments and assessments about ourselves, others, and the world around us. A belief is a habitual thought pattern. Once a person believes something is true (whether it's true or not), he or she acts as if it were – collecting facts to prove that belief even if it's false." So each one of us sees the world through the lenses of our own beliefs.

It works like this:
Your beliefs influence your emotions, your emotions influence your actions, and your actions influence your results. So if you want different results, you have to follow the chain backwards. To get a certain result, how do you have to act? And to act in a way to get the result, how do you have to feel?

And to feel in a way that makes you act in the way to get the result, what do you have to believe?

Until 1954, it was thought impossible that man could run a mile under four minutes. Doctors and scientists said that it was impossible. There were even scientific papers and studies on the subject. These studies were all shredded on May 6, 1954, when Roger Bannister proved everybody wrong at a race in Oxford when he ran the mile in under four minutes. Just six weeks later, an Australian, John Landy, did the same. In 1955, 37 runners ran the mile under four minutes, and in 1956, over 300 runners. What happened?

It was the power of their MIND. As long as they believed that it was impossible, their subconscious mind prevented them from running faster. Once one man broke the four-minute barrier, the others saw that they could do it too. And they did it.

Our beliefs determine how we perform, how good or bad our relationships are, and a lot of other things. They are the number one predictor of life's successes as well as well-being. So how does it work? How can we raise our beliefs? How can we turn a dream into reality?

"If we treat people as they ought to be, we help them become what they are capable of becoming."

What Goethe already knew hundreds of years ago was proven by the Pygmalion effect. **Our belief in a person's potential brings that potential to life.** When Robert Rosenthal and his team went to an elementary school and did some intelligence tests on the students, they told the teachers that students A, B, and C had extraordinary results and were academic superstars.

The teachers could not mention this to the students, nor treat them differently, and to make them understand the seriousness of the project, they were even told that they were being observed.

At the end of the year, the tests were repeated and, to no one's surprise, A, B, and C posted off-the-chart intellectual ability again. Again? Well, the fun thing was that the researchers lied to the teachers the first time around. When tested the first time A, B, and C were absolutely ordinary and randomly picked by the researchers. They concluded that the mere belief of the teacher in the potential of the students brought that potential to life.

Remember this, because the Pygmalion effect can happen anywhere. The expectations you have about your co-workers, your children, your friends, and spouses – whether or not they are ever mentioned – can turn that expectation into reality.

Another amazing experiment was conducted by Ellen Langer in 1979. Langer put a group of 75-year-old men on a one-week retreat in a hotel. These men had to pretend they were 20 years younger. They could bring anything from no later than 1959. There were books, magazines, newspapers, TV shows, news, and pictures from 1959. They dressed like 1959, walked like 1959, even their ID badges had their photos from 1959.

Just before the retreat, they were tested for physical strength, posture, cognition, and short-term memory. So they went on this one-week-retreat, and the results of that experiment were staggering. After the retreat, all of them improved significantly.

Their eyesight improved up to 10%; their hearing and their memory improved significantly; their physical appearance changed; and they became more flexible, stronger, healthier and happier! Both their mental and their physiological age decreased!

All of that just because they entered a powerful positive situation!

Creating a positive situation

You can create a positive situation for yourself. Scientists call it priming.
Priming is when somebody consciously or subconsciously plants a seed, belief, or a picture in your mind and how this, then, influences your behavior.
For example, elderly people who get primed with "old words" like "stick," or "Florida" perform worse on memory tests than people who aren't primed that way. Observers of the experiment even see them walk slower and walk like they were older.

On the other hand, when they are primed with words of achievement like "achievement," "persistence," or "success," they do better in intelligence and memory tests and persist longer in a difficult task

In another experiment, subjects had to describe a typical day in the life of a soccer hooligan, a secretary, and a professor and then did memory and intelligence tests. Guess who performed the worst? The "hooligan" group, while the "professor" group performed the best.

You can use the power of priming and the power of our beliefs by creating a positive environment that brings out the best in you. Here are some examples of how to do that:

- Put up photos of people or places you love
- Put your favorite objects around you (flowers, souvenirs, art, etc.)
- Have your favorite quotes in sight.
- Have your favorite books around you
- Listen to your favorite music
- Watch movies or conferences that inspire you

Believe in yourself

I have great news for you: Self-belief can be learned! It might take some time and some training, like everything else, but you can work on it. Albert Bandera found out that 56% of the success as an athlete is determined by the athlete's levels of hope, and by how much they believe that they are going to succeed. If that works for an athlete, why shouldn't it work for YOU?

Nathaniel Branden, the leading researcher on self-esteem, came to the conclusion that "the level of our self-esteem has profound consequences for every aspect of an existence, how we operate in the workplace, how we deal with people, how high we are likely to rise, how much we are likely to achieve, with whom do we end up falling in love, how we interact with our spouse, children and friends, and what level of personal happiness we attain."

Changing your performance by changing your beliefs

You have a choice. You can see pain, negativity, stress or you can look at things with the lens of optimism, gratitude, hope, resilience, and purpose. You might not be able to change reality, but you can and should use your brain to change how you process the world around you, and that will change how you react to what happens to you. It's time that you use the power of your beliefs to change your reality.

Do you need more proof for the power of your beliefs? Here we go:

Take for example, the **Placebo Effect.** It works like this: You have a headache, you see a doctor, the doctor prescribes you a pill, you take the pill, 30 minutes later, the headache is gone. No surprises, until now. But what if the doctor gave you a sugar water pill (placebo) instead of an Aspirin. What got rid of your headache? Right, your belief that the pill would cure you. As a matter of fact, a placebo is 55-60% as effective as medicine.

Herbert Benson took it a little further. He treated pregnant women who were nauseous with a placebo and surprise, surprise, they felt better after taking the pill. They cured themselves with their belief alone. But Herbert didn't stop there. The next time around he gave them a small dose of ipecac, a pill that induces vomiting. So the pregnant women should feel even more nauseous as they already felt. But they didn't know that they were taking an ipecac, so they got better!

This doesn't mean that drugs don't have any effect, but it shows the enormous power of the mind, and we shouldn't discard it.
The most incredible experiment though was mentioned in the New York Times and was done by some Japanese researchers – and I have no idea how they got permission for this. The researchers rubbed the arms of thirteen unknowing students with a harmless plant and told them that it was poison ivy. All 13 showed symptoms (a mean rash). In the next round, they rubbed their arms with real poison ivy but told them it was a harmless plant, and only two students showed symptoms. Based on these incredible results, the researchers came to the conclusion that our brain is organized to act on what we expect what will happen next.

So yes, our beliefs turn into fulfilling prophecies. They can actually change the concrete results of our efforts and our work. That's why "self-concept is destiny."

A.J Crum and E. Langer show this best in an experiment they did with the cleaning staff of different hotels. They formed two groups. Group one was told to think of their work as exercise, while group 2 was told nothing. After only six weeks, the members of group 1 had actually lost weight and their cholesterol levels dropped. The only difference between the two groups was in how their brains perceived the work they were doing!

We learn from these studies that your beliefs about our daily activities define our reality more than the activities themselves. Amazing, isn't it? How much more productive and efficient could you be if you changed the way you see the hours in your work day?

Be careful! If you believe that time with your family or free time is not productive, you will make it, in fact, a waste of time. Train yourself to adopt better beliefs about your time, like for example, looking at it as a chance to learn new things, a time to recharge your batteries, or to connect with others. If you manage it, you will return stronger and more relaxed than ever before.

And there is even more! Applying the placebo and the Pygmalion effect, it's safe to say that the more you believe in your ability to succeed, the more likely you are to do so. It's even more important that you believe that you can improve them, that you can enhance your basic qualities through training and effort, and therefore, maximize your potential. This is what psychologists call a "growth mindset."

On the other hand, you have the "fixed mindset." People with a fixed mindset think that their capabilities are already set and that they can't change them. People who think like this usually miss opportunities for improvement and underperform consistently.

So remember: If you believe you'll do well, you'll probably do well. I'd love to make it more complicated, but it really is that easy. The hard part is the daily work and training you have to do to reach that level of self-belief.

Our reality really depends on how we view it. Shawn Achor mentions in his book "The Happiness Advantage" that positive psychologists found out that external circumstances predict only 10% of our happiness! 10%!

That means that if I knew everything about you. Where you live, in which country, in a house or an apartment, where you work, your salary, the car you drive, etc. I could still only predict 10% of your happiness.

Once again: The way you perceive these external circumstances is much more important for your happiness than the circumstances themselves. By changing the way, you perceive your circumstances, your work, and yourself, you can dramatically improve our results.

Being an optimist helps

Even if you think that you are born an optimist or pessimist, being an optimist or a pessimist ultimately comes down to one thing: How do you interpret events?

Do you interpret an event as permanent (never) or as temporary (one step closer)?
Do you see failure as a catastrophe and give up or do you see it as an opportunity for success?

In the last two years, I failed more than in the total 41 years of my life. Really, I had at least one failure a week for the last two years. It's also no coincidence that this was the two best and most successful years of my life. Because with a lot of failures automatically comes more success. It's a numbers game. If I have to be rejected 15 times to get a well-paid speaking gig, I take this equation any time.

Back to interpretations, I'm sure you have heard the story about Thomas Edison who considered his 10,000 failed attempts to create the light bulb not as failure, but as showing 10,000 ways of what doesn't work.

When Dean Simonton studied the most successful scientists and artists through history, he found out that they were also the ones who failed the most.

Many remember Babe Ruth as one of the greatest baseball players of all times and for his home run records, but few people know that the seasons where he had the most home runs, were also the seasons when he had the most strikeouts. He said it himself: "Every strike brings me closer to the next home run."

If you can internalize that way of interpreting failure, nothing can stop you. Twenty phone calls to make one sale. I take it. Fifteen rejections for one speaking gig. I take it. Thirty job interviews to score my dream job. I take it. There is no other way to learn. There is no other way to succeed.

That's how you learn to walk, that's how you learn to eat. Learn to fail or fail to learn. Fail often. Fail fast.

Learning to interpret events optimistically leads to much higher success. It also strengthens our biological and psychological immune system. And last, but not the least...Optimists live longer, which doesn't mean that all pessimists die young because there are more things to factor in. It also doesn't mean that all optimists live long. If you smoke 40 cigarettes a day, being an optimist might not help a lot.

And there is another crucial thing to be careful about: **False optimism, sooner or later, leads to disillusion, anger, and hopelessness.** We need to train to become "realistic optimists." Positive thinking alone is not enough. You also have to add optimism, passion, and hard work to the success formula.

Why did nobody ever teach us this? It might be because the countless studies about the influence of happiness in our success are only surfacing now. As I said in the beginning, twenty years ago, you could either believe it or disregard it. Now you have science to back it up, which is hard to deny.

Another reason is that our parents are often concerned about us, about our happiness, and about our self-esteem. They don't want us to be disappointed. They think that too high expectations will lead to disappointment, but that is totally wrong. False expectations lead to disappointment.

In this case, the false expectation is that events can make us happy or unhappy. That's wrong. **Science found out that there are ups and downs around a base level of well being. These ups and downs in life are inevitable, how you deal with them is your choice.** The good news is that you can take more risks. If you cope instead of avoiding, if you confront things, if you take risks, if you deal with things, if you go out and try, your base level of happiness increases and that's what it's all about.

The self-perception theory states that we derive conclusions about ourselves the same way we derive conclusions about others: By looking at behavior. So if we behave like people with self-esteem, our self-esteem rises. We think of ourselves "I must be a self-confident person" and then it becomes a self-fulfilling prophecy, and we become more self-confident.
We'll talk about failure in another chapter a little later, but let me just mention: The pain that comes with failure is far lesser than the pain that we *think* comes with it. Once we realize this, we become more confident telling ourselves "I can deal with this. I can handle it. I'm actually more resilient than I thought I was".
Your self-esteem increases, your happiness increases, and finally, success comes. There is no other way to succeed.

The three keys to success

First of all, you HAVE to take ACTION. There is no way around it. If you find a way to succeed without taking action and hard work, please let me know. I've worked 40 to 60 hours per week in the last three years, including weekends. I think hard work is the only way to succeed, but I'm open to your feedback. Hard work and coping inevitably lead to success.

Taking actions is important. If you only talk about what you will be doing but don't take actions, you will not accomplish anything. It can actually even harm you. Even positive self-talk and positive affirmations can harm. If you only talk, but then avoid challenges, or constantly avoid difficult experiences and don't give yourself the permission to fail, you end up creating a downward spiral regarding your self-esteem, which affects your success and well being. Only talking and not doing sends a message to yourself that says "my word isn't worth anything, I'm not worth anything" and this will definitely affect your self-esteem. So take actions instead of just talking.

The second key is visualizing your success. The three components of success are optimism, believing in yourself, and loving what you do.

Stephen Kosselyn found out that whether you look at your hand or whether you imagine it, the same neurons are firing. This means that for your brain there is no difference! That's incredible and was even promoted by self-help gurus for a long time. Now it's scientifically proven, and YES I'll say it one more time: For our brain, there is no difference between imagination and the real thing.

Athletes use visualization, sales people use it too, and so can you. If you are imagining success, you are fooling your mind into believing that it's the real thing. For me personally, I visualize only the outcome; the destination I desire, while I leave the rest to destiny, God, the universe, life or whatever you want to call it. There is some fascinating science about this subject though.

Shelley Taylor from UCLA did the following research:
She took two random groups. Group 1 was imagining themselves over and over again getting an A. Group 2 was imagining themselves getting an A, but also seeing themselves work and persist in the library, prepare for the exam, and then get an A. In this experiment, the second group was much more successful!

Last, but not the least, remember that thoughts drive emotions. If you want to change the emotion, you have to change your thoughts

EVENT —> EVALUATION (Thought) —> EMOTION —> ACTION

A lot of times, in our evaluation of a situation, we distort reality and have irrational thoughts. There are three traps of irrational thoughts, which we should closely look at when they surface.

1. **Magnifying** (overgeneralizing)– For example, you fail one exam, and because of that, you think that you are stupid. Or one person says no to you, and that makes you think that nobody wants you, or your product. You had one bad experience on a Tuesday afternoon, and you think you had a terrible week.

2. **Minimizing** (tunnel vision)– This happens when you focus on the one person that is asleep in your presentation and not at the 200 that are highly interested. You concentrate on one critical comment and not on the ten people that praised you. If you catch yourself with these irrational thoughts, look at the bigger picture and zoom out.

3. **Making up** (fabricating)– This unfortunately often happens to abused people. They think it's their fault because they have not been behaving appropriately. Which it is of course NOT true! Another example would be failing an exam and blaming your girlfriend/boyfriend for that, which is utter nonsense.

The following questions can help you deal with irrational thoughts:

- Is my conclusion tied to reality?
- Is it rational?
- Am I ignoring something important?
- What important evidence do I still have to take into consideration?
- What am I magnifying?
- What am I minimizing?
- Am I ignoring something that's going well?
- Am I ignoring something that's not going very well?
- What is the big picture?

As always, it comes down to choice. Whatever we do with our beliefs, we can create an upward or a downward spiral!

3. The Power of Focus

As I already mentioned, one of the most decisive influences of your daily happiness is your focus. You can retrain your brain to see more of the good things in life. Doing this, will help you see more opportunities, more possibilities, feel more energetic, and lastly, succeed at higher levels.

Where is your focus? In the past or the present? On problems or solutions? Do you celebrate your successes or do you take them for granted? How do you see failure? Is it a disaster, an opportunity to grow, or a learning experience? Everything depends on where you put your attention.

Does this sound familiar to you? You are thinking about buying a new car, and suddenly the car you're considering to buy is everywhere? You are pregnant, and suddenly there are pregnant women everywhere. Or you have a cast, and suddenly everyone seems to have a cast? When we look for something, we see it everywhere.

Or you hear a song once, and suddenly every radio station starts playing it. You buy new clothes – suddenly everybody seems to be wearing something similar. This is how focus works. Once your focus is on something, you start to see it everywhere. This is great when you focus on the positive, on opportunities, on things that make you happy; and not so great when you focus on worries, problems, and sadness.

Two people can view the same situation and actually see different things depending on what they are expecting to see. They don't just come away with different interpretations of the event – they have actually seen different things in their visual field.

Ed Diener describes the power of focus in the following way
"How we perceive the world is much more important to happiness than objective circumstances. It's not the external that matters;
it's the internal. It depends on our state of mind – on what we CHOOSE to focus on."

In the end, how we experience our life is a matter of interpretation, a matter of choice, and it's up to us what we choose.

When we complain about life and how things are horrible and awful for us, we often do not realize that we are causing this. We imagine the worst, and then the Pygmalion effect kicks in and our beliefs become self-fulfilling prophecies, or we focus on what's not working and then we see more and more of what is not working. It seems like we are attracting it.

WE ACTUALLY CREATE OUR REALITY.

The questions you ask determine your reality, they change the way you perceive reality. You transform your reality by changing your focus on what's working, and by asking new questions. These new questions will create a new reality for you.

Tal Ben-Shahar distinguishes the following type of people in his classes at Harvard.

On one hand, there is the "Benefit Finder," whose focus is always on what works, always looking on the bright side of life, making lemonade out of lemons, finding the miracle in the common, and respecting reality. The benefit finder knows that sometimes we are not responsible for things that happen, but we are responsible for how we deal with what happens to us. Simply said: Shit happens, but it's up to us what we do with the experience.

The "Fault Finder" on the other hand always focuses on what doesn't work, on things that are not going well, on problems. "Fault Finders" are constant complainers who find faults even in the best of situations. This is very dangerous because it can lead to resignation. They do not recognize that they create that reality.

They think that the terrible reality is out there and that they are victims of their circumstances. So they feel miserable most of the time. No matter what job they find, they always have a horrible boss. No matter what partners they have, they are always awful and inconsiderate. No matter what restaurant they go to, the service is always terrible. And when the service is excellent, the food is terrible. There is always something. They accept that reality as given and their existence becomes a very painful self-fulfilling prophecy.

The good news is: We can learn to become "Benefit Finders" by training our brains to focus on the positive, by learning to interpret things optimistically. As Tal Ben Shahar always says: "Things don't happen for the best, but some people are able to make the best of things that happen." Yes, there are some people who accept the situation and then are able to make the best of it. Become one of such people.

A "Benefit Finder" always knows: "This too shall pass," "It's going to be alright again," and "Been there done that." The "Benefit Finder" accepts reality as it is, makes the best of it, and therefore reaps the benefits of this behavior like feeling better, being happier in the long term, experiencing more positive moods, and being less likely to feel anxious.

Health benefits

Being a "Benefit Finder" is also healthier for you. Glen Affleck was studying people who had a heart attack. Some of the patients interpreted their health problems as a catastrophe, or at the end of the world, while the "Benefit Finders" saw it as a wake-up call, as a sign to take better care of themselves, and revise their values. The second group was more likely to survive and less likely to have a second heart attack.

Another study on AIDS patients revealed that those who found benefits in their situation, like for example appreciating things more, focusing on the things that really matter, or getting closer to certain people, were more likely to survive.

The most famous study on health benefits of optimism is the so-called "Nun Study" which showed that joy prolongs our life.

The study started in 1932 when 178 nuns, about the age of 22, were tested on numerous accounts. They had to write biographical sketches of themselves, and scientists looked at various factors. There was only one predictor for longevity: Positive feelings.

The researchers looked at the writings and categorized them into four categories. Most positive, least positive, and two categories in between.

After 85 years, 90% of the most-positive category and only 34% of the least-positive category were alive. After 90 years, 54% of the most-positive category and only 11% of the least-positive category were alive. Careful now, that doesn't mean that there weren't some "Fault Finders" who lived long, nor were there some "Benefit Finders" that died earlier. But on an average, "Benefit Finders" or optimists live longer.

Why aren't we all optimists?

We have a lot of proof that optimism makes you happier and healthier so we might ask ourselves "If optimism has such great benefits why isn't everyone optimistic?" Why does nobody teach us how to become more optimistic? Why does nobody tell us about these benefits in the first place? Why are optimists considered detached?

One reason for this is the media. We mostly see hatred, bloodshed, unhappiness, terrorism, corruption, and fraud. How can you be positive in a world like this? What most of us forget is that the media doesn't just report reality as it is. It's biased towards the negative. The news actually turns us into pessimists by magnifying the negative. We are shown terror when billions of people want to live in peace. We are shown fraud when there are billions of honest transactions going on every day. We are shown that one parent who abuses their child when there are millions of parents loving their children beyond measure.

The problem with that is that if our focus is on the negative all the time, if we hear and see this all the time, we'll end up seeing more of it. And then we start to believe that we have to commit fraud to become a CEO, or to be corrupt if we want to be politicians. Why? Because the millions of people who are succeeding honestly are not reported on.

I don't want you to ignore the negative, but focus on the positive. And yes, I turned off the box a long, long time ago. Try it. It's great. And don't worry, you won't become ignorant or detached from reality when you stop watching TV. It's actually the "Fault Finder" who is detached because there is much more good in the world than bad. Focus on the positive.

It's important, not just because it's healthier, but because FOCUS CREATES REALITY.

The same goes for your inner dialogue. For many people it's a constant negative chatter in our mind, why is it negative and not positive? You know the typical "Why didn't I do this, why didn't I do that," "What if this goes wrong," "What if they don't like me."

We are constantly dress-rehearsing drama in our life. Why? Because everything around us focuses on the negative. No worries, it can be fixed. You fix it by rewiring your brain to see more of the positive around you and the best exercise to do for this is practicing gratitude. If you are grateful for the things you have, more things to be grateful for will come into your life.

And yes, there is always something to be grateful for. Believe me. Even cancer patients and AIDS patients found reasons to be grateful for. When terminally-ill patients were interviewed, they said things like "For the first time in my life I feel that I'm alive" or "For the first time in my life I appreciate…

The Power of Gratitude

The sad thing is that a lot of times things have to get really bad before we appreciate what we have. It doesn't have to be that way if we learn the attitude of gratitude as a way of life. If I would have to name the single-most important ingredient of my success or why my life is so much better, and I, so much happier, than even some a short while ago, it would be because of gratitude.

A lot of times we just don't express gratitude enough. But that can be practiced. It means we should express gratitude over and over again until it becomes a habit.

In a study conducted by Robert Emmons and Michael McCullough from UC Davis, people who wrote down five things for which they were grateful every night before going to bed, were more optimistic, happier, healthier, more generous, benevolent, and much more likely to achieve their goals than the three other groups who didn't write down anything, wrote down 5 hassles, or wrote down 5 things they are better at than others.

You cultivate gratitude by doing it all the time. Write down the big things and the little things. When I started writing three to five things that I was grateful for every night on November 11, 2013, it was the little things that came to my mind:

- I'm grateful that I'm alive
- I'm grateful for my family
- I'm grateful for my friends
- I'm grateful for the cup of coffee I had on the beach
- I'm grateful for working hard
- I'm grateful for that good lunch that I had with a friend
- I'm grateful for that good presentation I attended.
- I'm grateful for a sunny day.

It's important that you FEEL the gratitude and that not do it mechanically. Feel the gratitude with your whole body. Visualize and make it as real as you can.

Tal Ben Shahar notes that it's better to do it once a week MINDFULLY than to do it every day automatically without caring for it. The important thing is the intensity of the emotion.

Apart from doing the three things daily I also have a gratitude list where I write down everything I'm grateful for in my life. This should be a long list. For me, it includes places I've visited, people I've met, vacations I took, and other such things. If you read this list once a day and add to it frequently, the gratitude effect gets bigger. Try it, it can make a lot of difference. Imagine how your days will start if you read your gratitude list first thing in the morning! And as they say, the start of the day determines how the rest of the day goes.

This exercise is the bomb. After a while, you start noticing things. It's so powerful because you are co-creating your reality with it focusing on all the things you can be grateful for in your life.

If you practice gratitude throughout a few weeks, you'll be happier, more optimistic, more socially connected; you'll sleep better and get fewer headaches; you'll have more energy, more emotional intelligence; and you'll be more forgiving, less likely to be depressed, anxious, or lonely.

In my class at the Geneva Business School, one of the homework assignments was writing down three things the students were grateful for every day. I saw exactly the benefits mentioned above when reading their assignments over the week.

You might say "Of course, these people are only grateful because they are happier", but it's the other way round: Gratitude has been proven to be a significant cause of positive outcomes.

I know it can be difficult to be grateful when you are in a bad place, and life is not going so well, but believe me, there is always something to be grateful for. The most essential thing: You are breathing, you are alive, and there is somebody who cares for you. Start there, you'd be surprised by how long the list can run.

Focus on the positive

The more you focus on happiness, gratitude, optimism, the more you pick up on all the positive things around you and the better you will feel.

But there is more to it. The more your brain picks up on the positive, the more you'll expect this trend to continue, which results in you being more optimistic. You are creating a self-fulfilling prophecy and an upward spiral.

Optimism is also one of the most powerful predictors of work performance:

Optimists set more goals and put more efforts into attaining these goals. They stay more committed in the face of difficulties and overcome obstacles more easily. They cope better with high-stress situations, and expecting positive outcomes makes them more possible to bounce back.

Are some people just lucky?

Richard Wiseman asks the question of questions "Why do some of us seem to be constantly lucky while others can't get a break?"

He adds: **"In science, there is no such thing as luck. The only difference is whether or not people think they are lucky or not. Whether they expect good things or bad things to happen to them."**

And he did a study on it: Subjects were to read through a newspaper and count how many photos are in it. Those who claimed to be lucky took mere seconds, while the unlucky ones took an average of two minutes. Why? Because on the second page of the newspaper, a very large message said "Stop counting. There are 43 photos in this newspaper".

The answer was plain as day, but people who considered themselves as unlucky were far more likely to miss it while the lucky people tended to see it.

But Wiseman didn't stop there. Half way through the newspaper there was another message that said: "Stop counting and help tell the experimenter you have seen this, and you win $150 USD". And once again the people who claimed to be unlucky in life looked right past this opportunity. Stuck in the negative focus, they were unable of seeing what was clear to others and their performance (and wallets) suffered because of it.
Another study found out that 69% of high school and college students' career decisions depend on chance encounters.

As we learned from the study explained above capitalizing or not on these meetings is purely a matter of focus! When we are stuck in negativity, our brain is literally incapable of seeing these opportunities. If we are positive, our brain stays open to seeing these opportunities and to seizing them.

The amazing thing is that if we expect a favorable outcome, our brain is actually programmed to notice the outcome when it actually arises

Train your brain on focusing on the positive

You can train your brain to focus on the positive, and as a result of that, see more opportunities with two very easy exercises:

1. Make a daily list of all the good things that have happened to you in your job, career, and life
2. At night, remember three good things that happened to you that day and relive them in your mind

Don't get fooled by the simplicity of these exercises. They are very powerful. I hold them primarily responsible for my success, for seeing opportunities everywhere now.

If you do this for just FIVE MINUTES a day, you are training your brain to become better at noticing and focusing on possibilities of personal and professional growth and also on seizing them and acting on them. At the same time, there is a great side effect: your brain can only concentrate on so much at once, so it will push out those little things that annoy you and the nagging negative voices at the back of your mind.

Doing this exercise for just one week will make you happier and less depressed, and you'll see a marked difference after one, three and six months. Even after stopping the exercise you'll remain significantly happier, and show higher levels of optimism. I highly recommend you to keep on doing this exercise as it will do miracles for you. You'll get better and better in scanning the world for good things and writing them down, and you'll see more and more opportunities – without even trying – wherever you look.

The things you write down don't need to be complicated or profound, only specific. A lot of times, it's the simple things like a child's smile, delicious food, acknowledgment at work, a moment of connection with Nature etc.

Make this a habit and ritualize it. Do it at the same time each day. Keep what you need for doing this exercise easily available and convenient. For example, a journal on your night stand. It's also enjoyable to do the exercise with children and spouses.

Will you be blind to the real problems if you only focus on the good?
This is a question that comes up often. It's something you have to find out for yourself. My suggestion is to let the really big problems into your field of vision, but stick to keeping your focus largely on the positive. I can't deny that there are times when it's good to be a pessimist. Pessimism can, for example, stop us from making a foolish investment, or a bad career move, or from gambling with our health. That's why we have to develop a realistic, healthy, and reasonable sense of optimism, but above all, always give priority to the good.

4. The Power of Choice

This is your incredible power. Free will and the power of choice. Even if you can't always control the things that happen to you, you can always control how they will affect you and how you react to them.

Choose your thoughts

First of all, it is about choosing the right thoughts. James Allen said, "You are today where your thoughts have brought you; you will be tomorrow where your thoughts take you." Your thoughts create your reality. You can actually improve your life by improving your thoughts. How is that done? Just like James Allen said: Observe your thoughts now and then. By controlling your thoughts, you ultimately control your life and destiny.

I know it sounds cheesy and easier than it is, but I'll still say it: Think positive! A person who thinks positively is not a dreamer, who thinks there are no problems in life. Instead, he or she recognizes that problems are opportunities to grow, and knows that they only have the meaning that they are given. Positive thinking is to see reality as it is, accept it, and make the best of it.

Train your mind to concentrate only on positive, creative, and inspiring thoughts. Remember what the power of focus does. If you train your mind like this for a while, you will see that the circumstances of your life change too.

You are the creator of your thoughts, but you are not your thoughts. Your thoughts are energy, and the energy follows the thought. Thoughts create emotions, which create behavior, which creates actions, and those actions have consequences in your daily life. Practice a thought often enough so that it becomes a belief, and your behavior and actions will follow its lead.

THOUGHT -> EMOTION -> BEHAVIOR -> ACTION

For example, if you constantly worry about not having enough money, you'll create behaviors based on fear. You'll play smaller. You'll try to hang on to the money you have versus playing to win.

Your thoughts depend on your beliefs about life. If you don't like what you are receiving then have a look at what you are sending! Remember that everything, or at least the vast majority of things, that you have in your life has been created by your thoughts, expectations, and beliefs. So analyze them, if you change your beliefs, you will get new results. Of course, there are horrible things in life that you haven't created, like for example being abused, or being exploited, or a close one dying. BUT you can still CHOOSE how these horrible things affect you. I guarantee you will find people, who went through the same, and still thrived. In fact, came out stronger. Take those people as role models.

Choose your emotions

Emotion is energy in motion, a physical reaction to a thought. Who is responsible for how you feel? YOU! Your emotions come from your thoughts, and you are in control of your thoughts. If you can control your thoughts, you are also capable of controlling your emotions.

Don't be scared by your emotions. They are a part of you, but they are not YOU. Accept them. They are part of human nature, and every emotion has its function. Fear protects you. Anger allows you to defend yourself, put limits on things, and show others what bothers you. Sadness allows you to mourn and identify a lack.

Be connected to your emotions, know how to express them, and do not neglect them.

Don't fool yourself and say "I'm happy" if you're not. Instead, analyze where the emotion comes from. Don't identify yourself with the feeling. I repeat, you are not your emotions!
Become an observer and watch where your emotions lead you. Observe them and watch them pass by like the clouds on a blue sky. Accept them like you accept rainy days. When you look out of the window, and it rains you don't think that it will rain all the time now, do you? You accept the rain as part of the Nature's plan, that doesn't mean that it will rain all the time.

You can do the same thing with anger, sadness, fear, etc. Just because they show up at one moment in time doesn't mean that they will be there forever. Remember, emotions are neither bad nor good. They just are. Sometimes, it helps to write about them to get them out of your system. Write the angry letter to a person that hurt you. Just writing will help you blow off some steam. I recommend you not to send it though.

For example, I write my angry e-mails and then let them rest for a day. If on the next day I read it and I still resonate with it, then only I send it...In 99% of the cases, it goes to the trash.

Emotions are messengers that we can feel in our body. Listen to them! If you are hooked to an emotion, you are hooked to the past, and you are losing the present. Ask yourself what it is that you really need and then stop searching in the outside and start searching inside of you.

The skill to perceive, use, understand, and manage emotions is also called "managing our emotions." So how does that work? And with whom?

You can use this skill on yourself or others. It works the following way:
1) Perceive and express emotions (Permit yourself to feel it).
2) Facilitation of feelings (How can I feel a different emotion).
3) Understanding (Why is this emotion coming up).
4) Emotional adjustment (Now I know why that emotion surfaced).

The first step is to identify your emotions and explore them, which means to permit their expression and then analyze the problems that provoked them. Connect and talk to the emotion, breathe, relax, and relive the situation.
Once again, everything is a question of attitude (acceptance or refusal).
YOU CHOOSE!

Advantages of managing of emotions:
• You recover better and faster from problems and setbacks.
• You achieve better, and make consistent professional performance.
• You can prevent build up of those tensions that destroy your relationships.
• You govern your impulses and conflicting emotions.
• You stay balanced and calm, even in critical moments.

Choose to take responsibility for your life

Sigmund Freud said, "Most people do not really want freedom because freedom involves responsibility, and most people are frightened of responsibility." I have bad news for you my friend: NO ONE IS COMING TO SAVE YOU! No guru, no prince, no millionaire, not even the lottery.

There is only one person that's responsible for the happiness in your life, and that is YOU! Not your boss, not your spouse, not your parents, not your friends, not your clients, not the economy, not the government. YOU!

Now that the elephant is out of the room, let's get to the good news:
The day we stop blaming others for everything that happens in our life and take full responsibility for our life and everything that happens to you, everything changes. Taking responsibility for your life is taking charge of your life and becoming the protagonist of it.

You go from being a victim of the circumstances to creating your own circumstances, or at least, you get the power to decide how you are going to act in the face of circumstances that life presents to you.

More good news:
It doesn't matter what happens to you in your life; it matters what attitude you adopt. And the attitude you adopt is your choice. If you are in a bad situation right now, I bet that there are hundreds or thousands of people in this world that have been in this situation and overcame it. That means that you can do it, too.

If you blame your life situation on others, what has to happen to make your life better? All of the others have to change! And that my friend – I assure you – is not going to happen.

On the other hand, if you are the protagonist, YOU have the power to change the things that you don't like in your life! And a lot of times, if you change, everything around you starts changing too.

Remember that it's you who is in control of your thoughts, actions, and feelings. You are in control of your words, the series you watch on TV, and the people you spend your time with.

Stop reacting to others and start responding. Reaction is automatic. Responding is consciously choosing your response. If you don't like your results, change your input, your thoughts, emotions, and expectations.

Let's look a little closer at the Victim and Protagonist archetypes:

The victim thinks that he or she depends on external factors; they feel powerless because the belief is that life happens to them and they can't change anything. Their focus is mostly outside of them and they are focused on excuses like crisis, age, "not a good time," etc.

The victim concentrates on problems, and most of the time, those are everybody else's fault. Because the victim is always right. Life is not fair to them, and everything is just a matter of luck, which you can't influence.

Every bad thing in a victim's life is the fault of others; the victim only reacts; is always innocent; and is constantly blaming others for his or her life situation.

The victim uses the past as justification for putting his or her hope always on a future that will miraculously bring solutions to problems or a change in others who are causing the troubles.

On the other hand, you have the protagonist, the person taking full responsibility for his or her life. Protagonists don't wait for change to come; they initiate it. People of this group are aware that life happens, but they are still free to choose their behavior in any given circumstances. Their focus is always inside of them.

They see themselves with options and the power of choice and know that success only depends on them. For example, if they are unhappy at work, instead of complaining, they start looking for alternatives. They are always focused on solutions; they fully understand that they have to act where they have control, and accept situations where they don't have control. Protagonists don't believe in luck, they believe in work. They make their own luck focusing on opportunities, creating them if necessary, and always hold themselves accountable.

Protagonists know that they are responsible for their life, and choose the adequate behavior; they use the past as a valuable experience from which to learn; live in the present where they see constant opportunities for change; and then decide and go after the future goals.

If you are not part of the problem, you also can't be part of the solution. If the problem is caused by the outside that you have no influence on, then the solution is also on the outside that you have no influence on. In that case, you are helpless. You have to hope that the solution magically comes through an outside force.

For example, if you go late to work because of "traffic," what has to happen so that you can get to work on time? Traffic has to disappear magically. Because as long as there is traffic, you will always be late. If you act like a protagonist, your being on time doesn't depend on the traffic. It depends on you leaving home early.

Another example: It rains a lot, and you get soaked. If you ask a victim "Why are you soaked?" they will tell you, "Because it rained." A protagonist's answer would be "Because I didn't take my umbrella." So once again, even if you don't have control over the stimuli that the environment sends to you continuously, you have the liberty to choose your behavior in facing the situation. This leads us to the most important question: "Who will you choose to be – by your actions – when life presents you with these circumstances?"

More choices...

Your life is the result of the decisions you take. How do you feel about that? Is this true for you? It's important that from now on, you are aware of the power you have over your life by making decisions!

Every decision, every choice has an important influence on your life. In fact, your life is a direct result of the choices and decisions you've made in the past, and every choice carries a consequence.

The most important thing is to make decisions. Whether the decision is right or wrong is secondary. You will soon receive feedback that will help you to progress. Once you have made a decision, go with it and face the consequences. If it was wrong, learn from it and forgive yourself knowing that at that point in time and with the knowledge you had, it was the best and the right decision to take.

Victor Frankl was a Jewish psychologist imprisoned in Germany's concentration camps during the Second World War. He lost his entire family, except for his sister. Under these terrible circumstances, he became aware of what he named "the ultimate human freedom", which not even the Nazi prison wards could take away from him; they could control his external circumstances, but in the last instance it was he who CHOSE HOW these circumstances were going to affect him!

He found that between STIMULUS and RESPONSE, there was a small space in time in which he had the freedom to CHOOSE his RESPONSE!

This means that even if you may not be able to control the circumstances that life presents to you, you can always choose your response to those circumstances, and by doing so, have a huge impact on your life.

In other words: What hurts us is not what happens to us, but our response to what happens to us.

The most important thing is HOW we RESPOND to what happens to us in our lives. And that my friend is a CHOICE!

Do you want to be healthier? Make better choices about food and exercise.

Do you want to be more successful? Make better decisions about who you surround yourself with, what you read, and what you watch. There are no excuses!

CHOOSING to do things even has health benefits!

The following experiment was conducted at an old age home:
Subjects were divided into two groups. Group 1 got everything. Group 2 had to do everything themselves. They had to water their plants, and they had to tell the employees if they needed something, which they then had to get themselves. They did their own thing independently.

After 18 months, the members of Group 2 were less likely to be depressed. They were healthier, happier, had more energy and…they were 50% more likely to be alive. The only difference between the groups was CHOICE!

Do you have to or do you choose to?

Are there many things in your life that you "should," but never do? Should you exercise more, go to the gym more, stop smoking, eat healthier, and spend more time with your family? How many of those "shoulds" do you have in your life? They don't help you to get anywhere; they only give you a bad conscience and open the gates to self-torture: "Why am I not going to the gym? I'm so bad! I will never lose weight", "I'm not good enough."

Make a list of all the "shoulds" that drain your energy and then forget it!

If you have had a goal since last year and didn't do anything about it, then you are better off forgetting about it. If your goal is going to the gym and you didn't go for a year, let it go. With the goal, you also let go of the bad conscience and the self-punishment for not accomplishing it. Throw out all your "shoulds" and set some new goals!

Try substituting "I should" and "I have to" with "I choose to," "I decide to," "I will" and "I prefer to" for a while and see how it makes you feel. Say things like "I choose to exercise more," "I will eat healthier," "I will read more." It's important that you enjoy your activities – if not, don't do them.

So get out a piece of paper now and make a list of your "shoulds." Once you're done, either let go of them or rephrase them to "I choose to" or "I decide to."

Stop these toxic habits

Stop making excuses. You don't have to agree with a lot of things with the "Wolf of Wall Street" Jordan Belfort, but with one thing he was surely spot on: "The only thing standing between you and your goal is the bullshit story you keep telling yourself as to why you can't achieve it." And you, my friend, are choosing what you are telling yourself. It might be a subconscious choice at first, but it's still a choice.

It's natural that once you start getting out of your comfort zone, excuses start popping up. It happens to all of us at some point in life. Fear and doubts make you come up with the "best" excuses: "It's not the right moment", "I'm too young", "I'm too old", "It's impossible", "I can't", and my favourite one, "I have no money". Guess what people with money say: "I have no time."

You can choose not to listen to these excuses. You can choose to move ahead in spite of fear and excuses. You can choose to feel uncomfortable and take actions or to make up an excuse. Try it. It's fun!

The second toxic habit is the habit of complaining. I share Lou Holtz' opinion: "Never tell your problems to anyone... 20% don't care and the other 80% are glad you have them." Complaining posions your attempts of becoming happier. It's an absolutely useless behavior that encourages self-pity and doesn't accomplish anything. It's not attractive at all. It's the mentality of a victim.

I was also a huge complainer till I learned the concept of the victim and the protagonist. I decided to give it a try. Instead of complaining about not having time, I got up an hour earlier. Instead of complaining about my weight, I started living a healthier lifestyle and eating cleaner. Instead of blaming my parents, my teachers, my boss, society, the government, or the economy, I took responsibility for my life. I worked hard in the last three years during the toughest crisis Spain saw in decades, and I prospered.

Take responsibility. It's really nobody's fault that you smoke so much, that you eat unhealthy food, or that you give up on your dreams, but your own. It's you who pushes the snooze button instead of getting up half an hour earlier and who chooses fear over risk. Don't blame others for not living a satisfying life. Don't even blame yourself. Blaming is useless too. Just use that energy and get to work or reflect on what you really, really want.

You own your life! You can do anything you want with it. The sooner you get this, the sooner you can move on in the direction of your dreams. Just remember where to focus! Complaining about your present circumstances will put your focus on them and attract more of what you don't like. You have to get out of this vicious circle and concentrate on what you want instead
This will make you will feel like you are in control of your life, and that will do miracles for you.

Take control
The belief that we have control, that our behavior matters, that we are the masters of our own destiny at home and work is one of the biggest drivers of well-being and success. And the best thing is, it doesn't even matter how much control we really have. It's more about how much control we think we have.

Shawn Achor shows us in his book "The Happiness Advantage" that students who feel in control have higher levels of happiness, higher grades, and more motivation to pursue careers they really want. So do employees who feel they have high levels of control at the office. They are better at their job and report more job satisfaction.

Another study Achor mentions showed that greater feelings of control at work predict greater satisfaction in nearly every aspect of our lives and lead to lower stress levels, lower conflict, and lower job turnover.

Remember: How we experience the world is shaped largely by our mindset. The most successful people believe that their actions have direct effect on their outcomes (internal locus of control), while people with a victim mentality think that their daily events are dictated by external forces (external locus of control).

For example, someone getting passed over for promotion, if they have an external locus, they would think that your employer doesn't recognize talent; that they never had a chance, which subsequently leads to a loss of motivation. The problem is that people with an external locus not only blame their failures on others, they also – and that's the real problem in the long run – don't give themselves credit for their success.

A person passed over for promotion with an internal locus will just ask themselves what he or she could have done better, and then work on improving that. Or, if they feel they are not valued, they will search for another job.

Believing that our actions determine our fate motivates us to work harder, and when we see this hard work pay off, our self-belief gets stronger. But there are even more advantages:

People who believe they are in control actually have higher academic achievements and better careers. They are much more motivated and happier at work, and experience less stress at the workplace. They also show a higher commitment to their company and better task performance. They build stronger relationships, are better communicators, problem solvers, and more attentive listeners.

Feeling in control is good for your health

In a study conducted on 7,400 employees, those who felt that they have little control over deadlines imposed by other people had a 50% higher risk of coronary heart disease. People who feel like they are not in control over pressure at work are at the same risk for heart disease as people with high blood pressure.

In a study of nursing home residents researchers found out that giving them control over simple tasks in their daily lives, like putting them in charge of their own house plants increased happiness levels and reduced the mortality rate by half!

Ask yourself the following questions:
Who are you blaming for your life's situation right now?
(Your partner? Your boss? Your parents? Your friends?)
What would happen if you stopped blaming others for what happens to you in life?
What would happen if you stopped being a victim of the circumstances?
Is it comfortable for you to be the victim?
What benefits does being a victim have?
What would happen if you stopped suffering in life and took the decision to change it?

5. Change is Possible

The way to happiness goes through change, chaos and through the constant state of feeling slightly uncomfortable. Get into the habit of doing things that others don't want to do, and do what needs to be done regardless of the inconvenience! Most of us think that to change our lives we have to make huge changes, and then we get overwhelmed by the magnitude of the task and end up not doing anything, and therefore, getting stuck with our old habits.

The answer is small steps! Start changing small things that don't require a huge effort, and those small changes will eventually lead to more significant changes.

Be prepared to have fear and doubts as your constant companions on the journey. You might never get rid of them, but you can become better at dealing with them.

Face your fears and do it anyway
According to Paolo Coelho "The fear of suffering is worse than the suffering itself", and Eleanor Roosevelt adds "You gain strength, courage, and confidence by every experience in which you really stop to look fear in the face. You must do the thing which you think you cannot do".

Don't let your fears frustrate you, limit you, or – even worse – paralyze you. See fear as a warning light, not as a red light. I see it over and over again with my clients: Once they start doing what they fear, their fear goes away. Mark Twain knew this already a hundred years ago when he said: "Twenty years from now, you will be more disappointed by the things you didn't do than with the ones that you did."

Face your fears. Ninety percent of them are pure imagination anyway. Illusions! Incredible stories of drama and disaster that will probably never happen and are made up by your mind – "the world's greatest director of soap operas," as T. Harv Eker calls it, to keep you in your comfort zone. The only problem is that great things like development, growth, and success happen outside of the comfort zone.

Fear is your mind's survival mechanism. It wants to keep you safe, and anything that it doesn't know, scares it. This was good thousands of years ago when you head to run from big predators to avoid getting eaten, but nowadays, most of the time it hurts us. Most of the time, behind your fears, there will be great opportunities waiting for you so make it a habit to always ask yourself: "What's the worst thing that can happen to me if I do this?" and evaluate if the risk is worth taking or not.

Be careful. There is also a price for not taking a risk or stepping out of your comfort zone. Ask yourself "What price am I paying for staying the same or not doing this?" Is it a higher one than the price of taking the risk? This also includes intangible things like inner peace, happiness, health, etc.

Start changing your relationship with fear, one step at a time. Let it warn you and consult you – sometimes, you can even use it as motivation or fuel – but don't let it paralyze or limit you. For example, I used to be totally paralyzed by fear and stayed stuck in my job for five years because of the fear of change or the unknown.

Nowadays, when my mind is invaded by fear and doubts, I think to myself, "Hm, if there are so many doubts and fears, I must be on the right track. I better take action."

Do the things you fear: make that call you don't want to make, send that e-mail you don't want to send, ask that person you're afraid to ask, and see what happens. When you notice fear, have a look at it, observe it, analyze it, but don't believe it. Instead ask it, "Fear, my old friend! What are you doing here again? What's your game? Are you here to warn me or do you want to paralyze me?"

What are you afraid of? Failure? Success? Making mistakes? Taking the wrong decisions? Do as Susan Jeffers says: "Feel the fear and do it anyway"! If you want to reach new territories, you have to take some risks and continuously do things that you are afraid of. Mistakes don't matter as long as you learn from them and don't make the same mistakes over and over again. The same goes for decisions – by the way not taking a decision or procrastinating is also a decision!

Be the change

One of my favorite quotes is "Be the change you want to see in the world" by Mahatma Gandhi. It reminds me not to try to change other people, but to always look at myself first, and be an example. Are you trying to change other people? Stop right NOW.
It's impossible, you can't help people who don't want to be helped. So stop wasting precious energy and start concentrating on what *you* can do. And that is, to be an example.

Be the change you want to see in the world. Other people are like mirrors of us. Things we don't like about them are often things we have to work on ourselves and balance them out. Remember that you are only responsible for your own behavior. Be an example. That's all you have to do.

You cannot change others. The only thing you can do is accept them as they are and be the best example and person that you can be. Are you complaining about your partner, colleagues, or spouse? Be the best colleague or spouse possible! Are you complaining about your employees? Be the best boss possible! Do you want to be loved just as you are? Start with loving other people just the way they are.

Step out of your comfort zone

Yes. Everybody is talking about it. "If you want to change, you have to get out of your comfort zone" or "the magic happens outside of your comfort zone." Yes, I know. Only if it was that easy! It's just so nice and cozy in the comfort zone. By the way…What the heck is the comfort zone?

The best explanation I've heard until now is: If you put a frog into a pot of boiling water, it jumps out. But if you put it into a pot and start heating up the water gradually, it doesn't react and dies by being boiled. (I hope this is just a metaphor and nobody actually boiled some poor frog) Anyway, that's what happens to many people: They are trapped in their comfort zone without even realizing that they're living a life of "quiet desperation".

Your comfort zone is the limit of your current experience. It's what you are used to doing, thinking, or feeling based on your current level of knowledge. It's where we know, most of the time, exactly what is going to happen. It's where you live life on autopilot. It's also where change doesn't happen. So if you want to change jobs, start a company, be creative, get out of a destructive relationship, you have to step out of your comfort zone.

Unfortunately, it really is more comfortable to stay where you are, and your mind does everything to keep you there. If you are trapped in a job that you don't like anymore, you might tell yourself "Well it's not that bad, it could be worse. Who knows, maybe in another job I would be even worse off.

My relationship is not that bad. It's going to get better I just have to be patient". This could actually be true. Unfortunately It could also be fear trying to convince you to stay in a job or a relationship that doesn't make any sense anymore.

Steve Jobs had a great technique to get out of his comfort zone: Each day he looked in mirror and asked himself, "If this was my last day on earth, would I do what I'm about to do today?" and if he answered "No" to himself for too many days in a row, he changed. Be careful if you use that technique because once you start asking yourself this question, everything changes.

When you step out of your comfort zone, start taking risks, and start to venture towards the unknown, you start to grow. But it starts with the feeling of discomfort and awkwardness, and that's a great sign! That's actually a sign that you are growing and moving ahead. Act in spite of your fears.

Life is a miracle – it always works out in the end. But there is always a price you pay, and it's your decision if you want to pay it and live with the consequences.

The price you pay if you want to get in shape is that you have to exercise and eat healthier. The price you pay for not exercising is getting overweight. If you want more time, the price is getting up an hour earlier or watching less TV. The price you pay for procrastination is anxiety and feeling bad. Choose your suffering wisely!

How does change work? The Power of Habit

A lot of people in this world have made drastic changes, and if the question you're asking is "is change possible"? The answer is yes, change is difficult, but possible. We've established that change is possible, let's get into the 'how' and 'what' part of it.

"How is change possible?", "What works?" and "What does change even look like?"

Until 1998, neuroscientists thought that the brain is fixed and that it neither changes nor grows. Nada. You got what you got, and that's it. Thanks to London cab drivers and monkeys, they found out that neurons are plastic, which means they change and that neurons develop and grow. What a breakthrough! Once again I will not tell you how your brain works because I think I'm not qualified for it, and you don't need to know it to make the change. What you need to do is DO.

If you DO something over and over again, it becomes a habit. If you practice, for example, sports or music regularly, your brain changes. The taxi drivers of London had to study the map of London, and their brains actually changed. That was great news because that means everyone can change. There are two types of change: The gradual and the acute approach. The gradual approach is like water dripping on stone. This is the healthy kind of change, the real change, and the change that takes time. This is the fun change where you enjoy the journey and the process of getting there.

The acute approach would be the sledgehammer. This process doesn't take as much time as the gradual process, but it still takes time. Even the acute change is not a quick fix. And let me tell you one thing right now: There is no quick fix. If somebody is telling you that there is a quick fix…, take a step back, slowly turn around, and run in the other direction!
The founder of Positive Psychology and probably the biggest expert in the field, Martin Seligman brings it to the point dramatically: "The belief that we can rely on shortcuts to gratification and bypass the exercise of personal strengths and virtues is folly. It leads to legions of humanity who are depressed in the middle of great wealth and are starving to death spiritually."

So many people want to change their lives, but they don't want to do anything. They want the quick fix, but the quick fix doesn't exist, so they give up. If only they could have patience and work consistently and persistently to make that change, they would succeed. Like my client, Mary who lost 37 kg (74 lb.) in 15 months after I convinced her that losing 37 kg in 2 months is not only unrealistic but also unhealthy, or my client John who was totally stressed and on the edge of a serious health problem but within 6 months got his life under control, and now has more time than ever, or Petra who tripled her income in 9 months, working consistently like water dripping on stone. Change takes time.

When Stephen Covey looked at success literature of the last 200 years, he found that until the 1930s, self-help was about character change, slow change, changing who you are from the inside. It was about struggling, hard work, failing and getting up again, going through inevitable hardships, and changing step by step; slowly, gradually. Self-help from the 1930s onwards was only about the quick fix, "fast", "do it now", and "easy".

What we see now is what Seligman found. We see a decline in people's well-being, a lot more depression, and a lot more of anxiety. One of the reasons for this development is that people believe in the quick fix. The 5 steps to happiness, 7 steps to success. They try it. They do the steps. Things don't work out, and they think "What's wrong with me?
What am I doing wrong". They start to question themselves, and that could be the beginning of a downward spiral. And the worst is…they're doing nothing wrong because there is no quick fix!

It takes time to change.

Why is change so difficult?

Why are 44% of doctors overweight although they know how important a healthy lifestyle is? Why is change so difficult? We all know what we should do, but this common knowledge doesn't make things easier. We all know that exercise is good for us and yet we don't do it.

Without action, knowledge is often meaningless. Another reason why change is difficult is that sometimes you think you want to change, but you don't really want to pay the price for it. For example, you want to lose weight, but you don't want to change your diet, or you want to exercise, but you don't want to get up earlier. So you really have to get clarity on that, and you can get clarity by asking yourself the following questions:

Do I REALLY want to change?
Do I want to improve?
Do I want to change things or character or behavior that I don't like?

Another obstacle is that, sometimes we want to change consciously, but subconsciously something stops us: This could be, for example, that subconsciously you think you don't deserve to have a better life. Or sometimes, you associate a positive trait with the trait you want to change, and then you get blocked because you think that if you get rid of the negative one, you'll also lose the positive one, which of course, is nonsense.
For example:
You think if you are saying no, you are not a nice guy anymore
If you're not grim, you lose your seriousness
If you lose your rigidity, you'll also lose your consistency
If you let go of your perfectionism, you'll lose your drive and ambition

- What are you tying in your mind to the characteristic that you want to get rid of?
- You can lose your fear of failure and still have drive and ambition.
- You can say NO and still be a nice guy.
- You can stop worrying and still be a responsible person.
- You can stop feeling guilty and still be an empathetic and sensitive person.
- You have learned by now that fault-finding has nothing to do with realism.

Changing emotions

Mindful meditation, which means putting your attention to the present moment, is an example of a gradual change. It's also probably the most powerful intervention for bringing about calm and equanimity. It's literally like transforming the brain. Studies show that eight weeks of regular meditation can transform the brain. We will discuss this in more detail in the chapter on mind-body connection.

Tara Bennett Goldman, in her book, "Emotional Alchemy", defines mindful meditation – or mindfulness – as "Mindfulness means seeing things as they are, without trying to change them. The point is to dissolve our reactions to disturbing emotions but being careful about not rejecting the emotion itself." This is what "Permission to be human" is all about. You experience the emotion, you breathe through it. Very often, not always, it dissolves and with the emotional dissolution comes the psychological dissolution of this painful emotion.

An example of an acute change in emotions would be trauma. Trauma changes our brain through chemicals and our neural pathways. An example is PTSD. After Vietnam, 30% of veterans suffered from PTSD, after the first Gulf War; 80%.
The acute positive change would be Post Traumatic Growth (PTG). Yes, this actually exists. PTG happens when you focus on the benefits of the trauma, and, for example, subsequently become closer to your family, appreciate every breath,

appreciate flowers, enjoy your friends' company more, and overall, learn from it and grow. It's about benefit finding and sharing. Surprisingly, a lot more people experience Post Traumatic Growth. But most of us don't know about it. If people knew about PTG and that it was common, there would be more of it! Because it would turn into a self-fulfilling prophecy.

Changing behavior

Let's talk about the most important ingredient of change. Changing behavior. Most of the people who take a workshop, training, or seminar become happy, motivated, and leave the seminar with great goals and plans just to become 'the same old' on the following Wednesday. Why? How can we make that change last? There is only one way; by introducing immediate behavioral change. Doing some of the exercises we learned, writing down our goals, taking risks we haven't taken before, and so on. This is the real and only secret to change: Behavioral change.

A class, a book or a workshop can introduce a change in your attitude. BUT IF YOU DON'T FOLLOW UP WITH BEHAVIOR, YOU WILL GO BACK TO WHERE YOU WERE BEFORE. If you only go to a workshop, you can have an "Aha" moment, but if you don't follow up with actions afterward, nothing will happen.

Attitudes influence behavior, but behavior also influences attitude. And not only that, behavior is actually more powerful; actions are always more powerful than words
If you have a certain behavior before a class or a workshop, all the class/workshop can do is change your attitude towards a certain thing, but if it doesn't match with your behavior after the class, the attitude is going to be pulled down to where it was before, and that's why on the following Wednesday, you are the 'same old' you were before.

The impact of behavioral change is so strong that prisoners of war writing about the good things of communism to their prison mates and friends actually changed their attitude towards communism.

That's why you can "Fake it till you become it." You can fake a smile to get a happiness boost; you can fake your body posture and body language to become more self-confident with time. Your behavior WILL affect your attitude. Walk with your head up, walk straight, walk like a self-confident person, and you will become more self-confident. Very often, behavioral change is gradual.

The acute change of behavior is about coping, taking risks, coming out of your comfort zone, and doing the uncomfortable.

We can talk about something all day long, we can think about something all day long, and nothing will happen UNLESS we bring about real actual behavioral change! Real actual behavioral ACTION

Tal Ben-Shahar mentions a fabulous study, which I wish I had taken part in thirty years ago:

Shy heterosexual men were told to take a test. They had to wait in a waiting room and were told that somebody would come and get them. In the waiting area, there was a woman waiting with them. These shy heterosexual men were sitting there for 12 minutes with a woman whose instructions were to start a conversation and to show a lot of interest about what the men were saying, listen intently, and ask questions. Then one woman left, and another woman came in. Same thing. Six times. In total there were six women and a total of 72 minutes of conversation. Then the man went to the experiment. And a day later, the same thing again. Of course – as so often happens in psychological studies – it wasn't about the test the men had to take. The researchers really wanted to see "What effect would the behavior of the women have on shyness".

When they followed up with the men six months later, they were far less anxious, especially around women, and less shy. A lot of times, they even initiated relationships and started to date for the first time in their lives. And all of this, after 144 minutes of intervention! Who still says that change is not possible?
The only problem was that they had to be debriefed six months after the study was over. Researchers told them that it was only a study and that these women were not really interested in them, but that they were told to pretend.

The fun thing is…IT MADE NO DIFFERENCE TO THESE MEN. By then, they were much more outgoing; they were doing well with women; they were going on dates; and they had started a positive spiral. Nothing breeds success like success. When they started to do well, it turned into an upward spiral. That those women were told to 'seem' interested didn't matter at all. 144 minutes changed their lives.

Self-discipline is overrated

Do you believe that you could be happier and more successful if you had more self-discipline? No matter if you do or if you don't. I have good news and bad news for you. The bad news first: You can't get any more self-discipline. What you have is what you have and you won't get a lot more of it. Self-discipline has a limit.

The good news is: It's actually not that important, neither for success nor happiness. Self-discipline is overrated. **Most efforts to change – organizational ones, as well as personal ones – fail because people rely too much on self-discipline.**

If you change your focus from relying on self-discipline for bringing about a change to introducing habits, you'll need a lot less self-discipline. You'll need it maybe in the first 5 to 10 days, but after that, things will come easier to you and before you know it, the habit is installed.

So how do we know that self-discipline doesn't work?
Roy Baumeister did the following experiment: He made two groups. The first group was in a waiting room. They were told the experiment would start in 10 minutes, and meanwhile they shouldn't touch the chocolate chip cookies on the table because they were for the following group. The second group got the same instructions, but there were red beetroots on the table.

The researchers gave both groups the same, very difficult test. What they really wanted to see is how long the groups persevered before giving up. The results were astounding:
There was significantly more perseverance in the group that had the beetroots. The researchers concluded that this happened because the "Chocolate Chip group" had used most of their self-discipline in order to not touch the cookies and that proved that we have a limited amount of self-discipline. The question is what do we do with it?

Take for example your New Year's resolutions! Are you keeping your resolutions? Then you are part of the 20% who do so, because a whopping 80% of New Year's resolutions die before the end of January! On the other hand, did you brush your teeth this morning? Did you have to get hyped up, set a goal, get motivated to brush your teeth? I'm sure it happened automatically, right? The reason is that New Year's resolutions rely on self-discipline, while brushing your teeth has developed into a habit. A lot of times, what seems like discipline – for example in athletes – in reality, are habits or rituals.

The only way of lasting change is habits or rituals.
Create the rituals of running, 3 hours of not checking e-mails, writing down three things you are grateful for, date night, family dinners, etc. If you don't create the habit, the ritual, time – days, weeks, and years will fly by, and you'll never do the things that you want to do. Remember that this doesn't happen in a day. Give yourself the TIME to create the ritual. How much time? Well…as much as you need.

A lot of experts say it takes between 16 and 188 days to create a habit. It depends on the person and the habit. For example getting into the habit of drinking a glass of water every morning after getting up will probably go quite fast. While getting up in the morning to go running for 45 minutes might take a lot longer. Give yourself at least 30 days and try to introduce one or two new habits each 30 days. That should be it. Go for small successes, they will add up to incredible results over time.

Even the Eureka or "Aha" moment takes time, although it seems like instant change, it goes through various stages:
- Preparation (Working a lot, immersion in your work)
- Incubation (Doing nothing. Relaxing.)
- The "Aha" moment (Under the shower. On the bus etc.)

You relaxed your brain and the idea comes. So afterwards, you evaluate and elaborate the idea. It's of utmost importance to take time for creativity. That's why taking time off sometimes is more valuable than working ten-hour days.

How to create habits?

There are various ways to create new habits. The easiest way to break a bad habit is to substitute it with a good habit. You can, for example, substitute a soft drink with green tea or the sandwich for breakfast with a banana. Another way is putting the new habit in a ritual that already exists. Drink the glass of water or fruit juice before making coffee. Make it as easy as possible for you to do the habit and eliminate all the excuses.

For example:
I always wanted to drink freshly-pressed fruit and vegetable juice in the morning.
First problem: No fruit and veggies in the house.
Solution: Buy fruits and veggies.
I started buying fruits, but it got bad in the fridge because I wasn't up for washing them in the morning.
Solution: Wash the fruit right after buying. Great. Still didn't make the juice. Problem: Making juice and then leaving the juicer without cleaning until the next day made it messy and time-intensive to wash the juicer.
Solution: Clean juicer BEFORE drinking the juice.
And that's when I started having freshly-pressed juice every morning.

Lower the activation energy for habits you want to adopt, and raise it for those habits you want to avoid.
If you want to exercise in the morning, prepare your clothes, have your shoes next to your bed and if that isn't enough… sleep in your gym clothes (Yes I've done that.)
Plan where you will exercise, when, and what…

Prepare fruits and vegetables in advance and have them in your fridge, so that when hunger strikes, it's easier to grab the fresh fruit than to go for junk food.If you want to break the bad habit of wasting your time watching TV, unplug your TV or take the batteries out of your remote control and have a book ready next to you on the sofa.

K.D. Vohs discovered in his study that too much choice saps our energy. And we make a lot of choices every day. With every additional choice people are asked to make, their physical stamina, ability to perform numeric calculations, persistence in the face of failure, and overall focus drop dramatically. That's why you see Mark Zuckerberg or Barrack Obama always in the same clothes. They are eliminating choices, so they take better decisions in important situations.

Another way to change your habits is making rules for yourself. For example to check your e-mail only once a morning, or taking only one coffee break.
But as I said before…you can know how your brain works, you can have all the knowledge of how to change your habits, but if you don't take actions, if you don't DO, nothing is going to happen. The key to creating these habits is repetition. Practice the habit over and over again, until the actions become ingrained in your brain's neural chemistry.

Shawn Achor tells us in his book "The Happiness Advantage" (one of the best books I've ever read):
"The key to daily practice is to put your desired actions as close to the path of least resistance as humanly possible. Identify the activation energy – the time, the choices, the mental and physical effort they require – and then reduce them." He adds: "If you can cut the activation energy for those habits that lead to success, even by as little as 20 seconds at a time, it won't be long before you'll be reaping the benefits."

6. The Power of Goal-setting

Until just some years ago, I didn't believe what Brian Tracy said: "People with clear written goals accomplish far more in a shorter period of time than people without them can ever imagine." I was not a goal setter; I just wanted to float.

My only goal was to be happy, which I was…until I wasn't anymore. Since I'm setting goals and writing them down, everything has changed in my life. I have become incredibly productive and a lot more successful than I ever was. I'm calmer and experience a lot less stress. Goals have turned my life upside down. The same will happen to you if you give it a shot. And the best part is that you don't even have to reach all your goals to have a great life, but more on that later.

The problem with goals is that most people overestimate what they can do in a month and under-estimate what they can do in a year. So they set huge goals for a month and then give up, because they couldn't reach them, instead of setting a series of achievable smaller goals during a year that would drive them to success.

In this chapter, we will talk about the importance of goals. From the point of theory and practice, but also how they help us deal with stress. I want to convince you to set goals as a way of life in your personal life as well in your professional life. The mere setting of goals and reflecting on them will catapult you into the 5% group that sets goals, and give you an advantage over the other 95%. Yes, 95% of people do not set goals!

Why set goals?

Science has proven that people who set goals are generally more successful and the main reason for that is because goals make us focus.

You surely know the old saying that goes "if you don't know where you are going, you're unlikely to arrive." Or as Nietzsche puts it "If you have a 'what for', every 'how' becomes possible." We are much more likely to overcome difficulties when we have something to attain.

We've already talked about the power of focus and how it gives us direction. Focusing on a goal brings forth internal and external resources that are necessary to get there, and then things begin to happen inside us, as well as around us. Countless studies show that goals contribute to performance and well-being, and strengthen our resilience (because we focus on the future).

When we set goals, we declare that we 'believe' we are going to get something and this turns into a self-fulfilling prophecy. If you write down a goal, if you believe in a goal, the external circumstances is likely to match that, making it much more likely to happen.

I like the following example that Tal Ben Shahar gives in his classes and courses:

When you go on a trip with your backpack, and you come to a wall. What do you do? You can turn around, or you can take a sledgehammer and try to take it down, but usually, you don't take a sledgehammer with you on a trip, do you? So there is this third option: You can take your backpack and throw it over the wall. What? Why would you do that in God's great name?! Because necessity is the mother of all inventions.

You need your backpack to continue. And now that it's on the other side of the wall, you have no other choice but to get over that wall, whether you have to break it down, find a way around it, under it, or over it. You changed your questions, and suddenly you will come up with solutions that you have not seen before.

When you declare a goal "I want to buy a computer" suddenly you see computer ads all around you, in newspapers, journals, etc. Why? Because you are now focused on it, and that's why you see it everywhere. The same happens when you want to buy a particular car; suddenly you see it all around. When you come up with the goal of "Buying a new car, let's say, a red BMW. Suddenly you see red BMWs everywhere. They were always there, right in front of your eyes, but before focusing on buying a new car, they didn't exist for you.

Back to our wall…
If I declare and decide that I have to get over the wall, my question changes from "Is it possible to get over the wall?" to "How do I get over this wall?" and this makes all the difference! Asking "How?" opens up opportunities, many of which we might not have seen before. Suddenly solutions are right in front of us. If you want to become happier make the question "How can I become happier" the central question in your life.

Another factor that comes in to play with goals is the power of the word. When we declare something, when we say something out loud, it's more likely to become a reality. Add to this that your goals are really meaningful for you and they are much more likely to become true. Words create an image in your mind, and when you create an image of the goal in your mind, the mind wants consistency. Scientists are not really sure how and why it works, but it works.

So what have goals to do with happiness? Here it comes: Goals that are properly understood lead to happiness.

It's not the goal itself that will lead to happiness – we know that now – but the understanding of the proper role of goals leads to happiness:
In other words, it's not the attaining of the goal that leads to happiness; it's the *having* of the goal that leads to happiness.

Goals and focusing on the present

The role of goals is to liberate us to enjoy the present. If you go on a road trip and don't know where to go, you don't have a destination; you are less likely to enjoy the present because every minute you look around, every crossroads or turn you reach, becomes an important decision. This is stress.

If you know where you are going and you have a sense of direction, then you are liberated. You are much more likely to enjoy the process, the environment, the landscape or the proverbial "flowers on the side of the way". No only that, if you have a clear sense of direction, you are much more likely to be happy.

This also explains why a lot of people become less happy after retirement. They might have been dreaming about retiring for years and then, when they finally retire, they get less happy. Bummer! But why does this happen? Because they don't have goals, they don't have a purpose anymore. The ones who do become happier when they retire are the ones who set goals, like learning something new, taking a class, spending time with friends, taking up a hobby.

The truth is that we need a goal for future orientation so that we can enjoy the present more.

Learn to enjoy the progress

Why are there so many high achievers who are unhappy and even turn to drugs and alcohol? How can it be that people who seemingly have everything – fame, fortune, anyone they want, living a life that most people can only dream about – are sometimes so unhappy? How come they end up in a rehab center?

Here's one explanation:
For years on their way to success, they kept telling themselves "I'll be happy when I get to the top," and when they get to the top, they realize that they are at the top and they are not happy. That's when the problems begin. Everyone, including themselves, has probably told them "Once you make it to the top, you'll be happy" but they are not happy. Initially, when they start acquiring fame, they are happier, but then they go back to the base level, and they are surprised, scared, and even upset. They have no idea what to do.

We've already learned that happiness doesn't depend on your bank account or status, but on your state of mind. It depends on how you interpret your reality and on what you choose to focus on. It's about having a goal; it's about having a destination in mind, and then letting go, and enjoying the process. The present is your point of power.

A great and very comforting thing I learned while studying happiness through Seligman's, Ben Shahar's, and Achor's work is that it doesn't even matter if you choose a certain path and then you regret it – you can be equally happy on both paths – as long as you have a goal, as long as you are committed, as long you are working on your base level of happiness.

It is important though to choose your goals freely. They have to be your goals – not your parents', friends', spouse's, or neighbors' – they have to be meaningful; and they have to be "want-tos," not "have-tos" or "shoulds."

The best goals are aligned with your personal interests and values, with things you care about, and with your passion. Goals that are not imposed from the outside, by someone specific, by society in general, and nor by your own sense of obligation and duty. It's things that you really, really want to do or achieve and not things that you have to achieve. They come from questions like "what are my goals?", "What am I interested in?", and "What am I passionate about?".

Ask yourself these easy questions over and over again, although sometimes the answers are not easy answers. Sometimes, they are not what you want to hear. Sometimes they are not pleasant. Sometimes you might have to go against the grain, choose difficult or least-chosen options. It might be scary, it might take courage, but these are the important questions. These are the questions that can change everything.

The benefits of these kinds of goals are that they are most likely to make you happier because when we pursue something we care about, it is likely to reinforce the enjoyment of the journey. They also resolve internal conflicts because they make you ask questions like, for example, "What am I doing?" and "Why am I here?", and mind you, these are always the first ones to pop up when we lack goals or directions.

Write down your goals
Writing down your goals makes a difference. Writing down shows your commitment to your goals and those goals will drive you to take action!

They are like the GPS system leading the way. But to be led, first of all, you have to know where you want to go.

When you write down your goals, you declare to your mind that out of the 50,000 to 60,000 thoughts you have per day, THE ONES that are written are the most important.

Writing down your goals helps you to start concentrating and focusing on the activities that bring you closer to your goal, and you start taking better decisions. While you are focused on where you want to go, you are also keeping in mind whether what you are doing at this moment is really the best use of your time or not.

When you look at your written goals every day, you are forced to act, and it helps you to prioritize your actions for the day by asking yourself questions such as "At this moment, is doing what I'm doing bringing me closer to my goals?" It's much more difficult to cheat on yourself if you have it written down than if you only have it in your head. For example, you can tell yourself "I've worked so well on my web page today", but if in your agenda it's written down that you only worked one hour instead of five hours, the story changes.

It's important that you are clear about your goals like "I'm going to increase sales by 5% by December 2017", "I'm going to run 5 miles four times a week by November 30, 2017".

Then break them down into small achievable action steps and make a list of all the steps that you will take to get there. Calculate how long it will take you, and don't forget to set a deadline for each action step and goal.

Don't worry if you don't reach the goal by the exact date you've set; it's just a way of focusing on the goal and creating a sense of urgency. Personally, in the last years, I reached only half of the goals I had set. Still, it has been the best two years of my life, and now I'm working on the goals I didn't achieve last year.

In the exercise at the end of this part, I want you to write down what you want your life to look like in 10 years. When you write it down, I want you to write down what you want, not what you think is possible. So GO BIG! There are no limits to your imagination.

The answers you write are indicative of the direction in which your life is headed. Create a clear vision of your goals in your mind. See yourself as already having achieved the goal: How does it feel? How does it look? How does it sound? How does it smell?

Remember the goals have to be yours, specific, stated positively, and you have to commit to them.

It's also very important that when pursuing your goals, you reward yourself for the effort put in, and not just for the results. Self-punishment is strictly not allowed! Keep in mind that you are much further than you were a week or a month ago.

And above all, remember: The most important thing about goals is not achieving them. It's not going to make you happier or unhappier if you do or don't achieve them. I know it's crazy, isn't it? The most important thing is that goals energize us, motivate us, liberate us, and contribute as a means to the end.
Goals will not save you from failures on the way to success, from hardships, from insecurity, or from disappointments – I repeat, those are normal and inevitable. Meaningful goals will help you overcome these obstacles and keep you going and persisting on your way to success and happiness.

Other useful tips that enhance your goal-setting journey are:
- Put a little card with your goals written on it in your wallet and re-connect 4-5 times daily.
- It's extremely beneficial to have a to-do list. Put your action steps on it, as well as the time it takes to do the task as and put deadlines for each task.
- Balance your goals (physical, economic, social, professional, family, and spiritual).

Goal-setting exercise:
1) What do you want your life to look like in 10 years? There are no limits! Go big!
2) What do you have to achieve in 5 years to get closer to your goal in 10 years?
3) What do you have to achieve in 1 year to get closer to your goal in 5 years?
4) What do you have to achieve in 3 months to get closer to your one-year goal?
5) What are the things that can you do NOW to reach your three-month goal?
6) Write down at least three things and TAKE ACTION!

Examine your values

It's impossible to talk about goals without talking about values. Not in a moral or ethical way, but looking at what fuels you and what motivates you. Being clear about and knowing your values is one of the most important steps to getting to know yourself better. By knowing your values, you will meet less resistance on the way to your goals if those are in line with your values. Build your goals around those values and make sure your profession – whether it's a day job or a business – is according to your values. You don't have to rush into something new, but you can start doing more of the things you love.

If there is a big difference between the life you are living and your values, this might create suffering and tension. Once you find out what your values are, you will be able to understand yourself and your actions a lot better.

So, one of your most important tasks is to find out what your most important values are. Those that bring you joy, peace, and fulfillment. From the list of values (you can download it on my web page www.marcreklau.com for free), choose 10. You may find that you can group values. Then narrow them down to your top four values.

The following questions will lead you to know more about your values:
When do I feel authentic?
When do I feel like myself the most?
When does the real me come out?
When do I feel the most alive?
What is very important in my life?
What gives purpose to my life?
What am I usually doing when I experience that feeling of inner peace?
What am I doing that is so much fun that I usually lose track of time?
What activities do I enjoy the most?
What kinds of moments bring me joy and fulfillment?
What can't I put up with?

Think of some people that you admire. Why do you admire them? What kind of qualities do you admire in them?

Find your Purpose

"The two most important days in your life are the day you are born and the day you find out why." I love this phrase by Mark Twain, maybe because I took so long to find my purpose in life. One of the most important things along your life's journey and one of the key ingredients to your happiness is the discovery of your purpose, which means doing what you love to do.

If you feel like you are driving without a roadmap or a GPS and don't really know where to go or if you never quite know what you are doing here and why, and you feel kind of lost and empty, then that's a sign that you have not found your purpose yet. And of what I hear and read, we have a whole generation facing this problem, but don't worry, it can be fixed. You can find clues to your purpose by examining your values, skills, passions, and ambitions and by taking a look at what you are good at.

I always tell my students "You cannot hide from your purpose, or at least, not forever. You can deny accepting the "wake up call" when it first comes, you can run away, you can hide for a while, you can distract yourself, but sooner or later you will have to accept your calling and the moment you find the courage to do that, everything changes."

Your answers to the questions "What would you do if success was guaranteed?" or "What would you do if you had ten million dollars, seven houses, and have traveled to all of your favorite destinations?" will lead you to your purpose.

I avoided answering these questions for 17 years. In my case, the answers were the same at age 23 as they were at 40: I wanted to write books, inspire people, and show them that a happy life is possible even if you had to overcome the direst of circumstances. I wanted to travel the world and speak about how we can become happier. When I was twenty-three years old, I didn't dare to assume this role, and I had to take a "detour" of seventeen years full of great experiences, which made me the person I am today. And to be honest, I don't know if I would have finally answered to my calling, had I not been fired from my job. Three years ago, I assumed the role, and since then, things have started falling into place. It sounds jargon, but it's true: once you find your purpose, things will start to fall into place. You will start to attract people, opportunities, and resources naturally, and incredible things will start to happen. Nothing attracts success more than somebody who is doing what they love to do.

Here are some more questions that should help you. Have the courage to answer them, better still write down those answers. And, if you're uncomfortable then nobody else but you can see the answers. Don't skip them. I did that for over 20 years, but when I finally answered them, everything changed! Did you ever ask yourself what your mission, your calling, your vocation is? I'm asking because the big problem of our times is that we don't take the time to think about these questions, maybe because sometimes we are afraid of the answer. I highly recommend you to start asking the following questions NOW.

Who am I?
Why am I here?
Why do I exist?
What do I really want to do with my life?
When do I feel fully alive?
What were the highlights of my life?
What am I doing when time flies by?
What inspires me?
What are my greatest strengths?
What would I do if success was guaranteed?

What would I do if I had ten million dollars, seven houses, and had traveled all around the world?

Purpose at the workplace

What does purpose at the workplace look like? How many people who are following their calling and working jobs they really love, do you know? I don't know many. But it's possible.

When it comes to work, everyone falls into one of these three categories:
1) You have a JOB. Your motivation is your paycheck or your monthly salary.

It's a chore. Most of the time you're not enjoying your job, but you have to do it. You don't expect too much from it and you keep looking forward to the next paycheck, to the weekend, or to the next holidays.

2) Maybe you have a CAREER. Your motivations are money, advancement, and getting to the next stage. It's a race to the top, and you are in it to win it. You want more prestige, more power, more money and you are always looking forward to the next promotion.
This is also the typical life of the "Rat-Racer."

3) The lucky ones are in the third group, where work aligns with CALLING:
You have goals that inspire you and a mission at their workplace. For you, work is a privilege. You want to do what you do, and actually look forward to more work. You are sad when Friday comes and get excited on Sunday afternoons because finally you can get back to work again the next day.

Now comes the big news:
The interesting development here is that your happiness doesn't depend so much on the work you do but on your per-

ception of the work. There are countless studies on this subject. A study done on the cleaning staff in a hospital showed that some cleaners saw their work as a calling. They perceived their work as very important for the functioning of the hospital. Talking to patients, nurses, and doctors, they felt they were bettering life at the hospital.

In the same clinic, there were doctors who saw their work as a job. And of course, there were doctors who saw their work as a calling and cleaners who saw their work as a chore.

What I want to say is that there are always positive components of a job and the people who burn out don't see them. In the end, once more, it's you who decides how you interpret your work. What is positive about your work?

So what if you feel burnt out at your job and/or your job makes no sense to you anymore?

You have three options, actually no, when you look closer, you have much more than three options, but for the sake of simplicity of the example let's look at the extremes:

So you hate your job, you're tired of it, it makes you sick, but you hang on because you don't have or see any alternatives. Once you reach this point, you can either leave your job – that's option A; you can stay and become bitter and frustrated – that's option B; or option C – you can change the interpretation of your job, and see if you can find purpose in the current job you are doing. You can choose to perceive your work differently. You can change your expectations towards your job, and also reflect on what you are looking for at your job – whether it's the current one, or your next one.

I was at this place once. Burnt out, tired of my job, seeing no more sense in it, but because of fear and lack of courage, I stayed with the company. One day I had a horrible fight with my boss, which resulted in him wanting to fire me right away – until he saw the worth of my severance package – then he quickly changed his mind and tried to fix things, and I agreed, which financially was an idiotic move and cost me a lot of money.

On the other hand, that day I also found a new purpose in my job. I knew that my days at that company were numbered. I decided to save as much money as I could every month to have savings that equal 12 to 18 months of my salary. Having this amount of savings would mean that I could leave the job and start my own business or have more than enough time to find a new job. Suddenly going to work became comfortable again. I had a new goal and purpose: Saving money.

7. The Ugly Twins – Perfectionism & Failure

Remember the question that this book is all about? "How can I become happier?"

Another step on the way to becoming happier is by being less and less of a perfectionist. Now, if you are a perfectionist, you might think "No way, I can't let go of my perfectionism! This would mean I have to give up my ambition". Think again. It's not. You will probably become even more ambitious.

This chapter is about having a different approach toward the journey of your life, towards each step of the way, and especially towards failure. We will talk about perfectionism. The characteristics of a perfectionist, the consequences, and about how it is possible to be both successful and happy. We will investigate where perfectionism comes from, how to overcome it, and how to help other people overcome it. Paulo Coelho hits the spot when he says "There is only one thing that makes a dream impossible to achieve: the fear of failure." The fear of failure is the number one dream killer because most people are so afraid of failure.

Unfortunately, there's no skipping the pain of failure, because that's inevitable, but we can learn to have a more rational, helpful, and empowering approach towards it. Maybe like Napoleon Hill, who indicated that "Every adversity, every failure, every heartache carries with it the seed of an equal or greater benefit." I want you to come to see failure as a learning experience that is necessary for growth and for providing us with information and motivation, instead of something terrible.

What would happen if you could fully embrace the idea that in reality, failure is a sign that points towards progress?

Why not adopt the "Edison Mentality." Edison said things like "I failed myself to success" or "I have not failed. I've just found 10,000 ways that won't work." This is what enabled him to bring many of his inventions to us. The man just didn't give up!

If you have the need, the urge that everything has to be perfect, you are doomed to encounter unhappiness, because, guess what, perfection does not exist. You can come close to it, and that should be the goal, but at the same time, you have to accept that it doesn't exist. The good news is that you don't have to be perfect.

"The important work of moving the world forward does not wait to be done by perfect men" George Elliot

Take a minute and remember. How did you learn to walk? How did you learn to eat? How did you learn to draw? Right. By trying over and over again. Could you have walked without falling hundreds of times? Remember how you ate when you were a toddler? It took some practice to eat as you eat today. As kids, we enjoy the joy of learning; enjoy falling and getting up again. And then it goes away...When does it go away? Where does it go?

It goes away when we get to a certain age and notice that people are watching us. Suddenly, we want to maintain a certain image. Suddenly, we avoid things instead of trying it, because "What if I fail," "What if she says no?", "What if my classmates don't like what I say?" and so on.

And we pay the high price for not coping, and it affects a lot of things: our self-esteem, our confidence, our resilience, and finally, our happiness levels in the long term.

Learn to fail or fail to learn

Remember how you learn. You fall, and then you get up again. You miss and then you hit. That's the way. This is how you grow; this is how you learn; how you become resilient, happier, and more successful. It's trying and failing, trying and failing and succeeding, and trying and failing again. Accepting your mistakes as feedback and learning from them.
As Tal Ben Shahar says: "Learn to fail or fail to learn."

You MUST accept that you will fail now and then. I hope you fail many times, because the more often you fail, the more often you will succeed. It's a numbers game. Edward Hubbard was absolutely right when he said: "The greatest mistake a man can make is being afraid of making one."

Be prepared for failure. Be prepared for the worst-case scenario. "What happens if...?" Careful though, I said "be prepared" and not "expect", as by now you know about the power of our beliefs and expectancies. So in the worst case, you fail. What happens then? You learn. It's not comfortable. It hurts, but you will bounce back again, as you did before. That's it.

I failed more times in the last three years than ever before in my life. I was also much more successful than ever before in my life. It was all worth it. And you know what. You get better and better at failure with every time you fail! It hurts less and less every time. If you want to succeed more, fail even more.

If you've read my book "30 Days" you have come across the following examples. Still - in our fight against the fear of failure, they can't be mentioned often enough.

Here is a story of a famous "failure" who literally failed his way to success:
- Lost job, 1832
- Defeated for legislature, 1832
- Failed in business, 1833
- Elected to legislature, 1834
- Sweetheart (Ann Rutledge) died, 1835
- Had a nervous breakdown, 1836
- Defeated for Speaker, 1838
- Defeated for nomination for Congress, 1843
- Lost re-nomination, 1848
- Rejected for Land Officer, 1849
- Defeated for Senate, 1854
- Defeated for nomination for Vice-President, 1856
- Again defeated for Senate, 1858
- Elected President, 1860

This is the story of Abraham Lincoln, a man we would not exactly characterize as a failure, would we?

Here are some more famous failures:

Michael Jordan: cut from his high school basketball team.
Steven Spielberg: rejected from film school thrice.
Walt Disney: fired by the editor of a newspaper for lacking ideas and imagination.
Albert Einstein: learned to speak at a late age and performed poorly in school.
John Grisham: first novel rejected by sixteen agents and twelve publishing houses.
J.K. Rowling: a divorced and single mother on welfare while writing Harry Potter.

Stephen King: first book "Carrie" rejected 30 times. He threw it in the trash. His wife retrieved it and encouraged him to try again.

Oprah Winfrey: fired from her television-reporting job as "not suitable for television".

The Beatles: told by a record company that they have "no future in show business".

So just do it. Just act. Be prepared to fail. Fail and then learn from it. Remember that, in most cases, the most successful athletes are also the ones that have failed the most, like Babe Ruth or Michael Jordan.

Perseverance is more important than talent, intelligence, and strategy. There is great virtue in never giving up. When life doesn't go according to plans, keep moving forward, no matter how small your steps are. The top two habits that will decide between success and failure, between the real change and staying in the same place, are patience and perseverance.

It's highly possible that before success comes, there may be some obstacles in your path. If your plans don't work out, see it as a temporary defeat, and not as a permanent failure. Come up with a new plan and try again, and try, and try, and try, and try some more. If it still doesn't work, adapt until it works. Most people give up because they lack patience and persistence in working out new plans! Just one thing: Don't confuse this with persistently pursuing a plan that doesn't work! If something doesn't work for long, if you've tried every other option and it still doesn't, then change it!

Persistence means persistence toward achieving your goal. When you encounter obstacles, have patience. When you experience a setback, have patience. When things are not happening, have patience.

Personally, I follow Thomas Alva Edison's recipe for success, and I remember it always when I'm struggling and nearly giving up: "The most certain way to succeed is always to try just one more time."

On a business level that means that that organizations or groups that allow their employees to make mistakes, to fall without being afraid of the consequences are significantly more successful. These are learning organizations, where employees constantly learn and grow and are getting better and better.

There is this story – some attribute it to IBM; some attribute it to Southwest Airlines – of an employee made a strategic error. He cost the company a million dollars. So the next day he comes to see his boss and hands him his letter of resignation. And his boss asks "Why?" and the employee says; "I just made a mistake that cost the company a million dollars" And his boss answers: "No way will I accept your resignation. I just invested a million dollars in your education!"

In his book, Geeks and Geezers, Warren Bennis compared very successful leaders who were very young (in their early 30s) and an older generation leaders (in their 70s – 90s).

There were a number of meaningful and interesting differences between the generations, like for example work-life balance. While being very important for the younger ones, the older ones didn't even know what it meant.

But all of them had at least one thing in common: they all had had at least one significant failure, a real crisis, or a significant loss – losing their job, their identity being insulted, or the loss of a person. Both groups saw this point as a turning point in their life. They made the best of what happened to them.

They saw it as a learning opportunity, a learning experience, or a stepping stone.

The characteristics of perfectionism

Perfectionism is closely tied to the fear of failure. Its root is the setting of high, nearly-unreachable standards accompanied by an extremely critical self-evaluation and concerns about what other people might think of us. And while perfectionists desire success, mostly, they are focused on avoiding failure. There is a huge difference between demanding perfection and being a person committed to excellence. It's about your approach towards life, towards the journey, towards the process of getting from point A to point B. It has nothing to do with ambition.

1) Perfectionist   **2)** Person committed to excellence

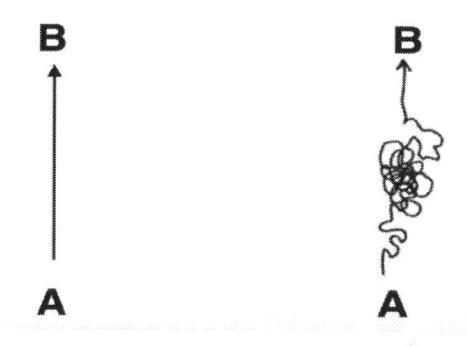

Which one of the two approaches is realistic? I know nobody who has succeeded with method number 1 because it doesn't exist. There is just no straight line from A to B, it's not realistic. It's a fantasy. And people who have this "plan" are doomed to be unhappy and frustrated in life. It's like not accepting the law of gravity. Many people who think approach 1 is possible are constantly frustrated.

Let me make one thing clear: the second option doesn't mean that we enjoy failure. But the first solution provides us – in addition to not enjoying failure – with the frustration of not accepting reality. In the following table, you'll see the major differences between a perfectionist and a person committed to excellence.

PERFECTIONIST	PERSON COMMITTED TO EXCELLENCE
Defensive (in arguments). Doesn't like criticism. There is something that I'm not doing perfectly well.	Open. Welcoming suggestions and criticism - that doesn't mean he or she enjoys it, but it's an important part of growth and development.
Constantly focused on what's not working (half empty glass). Obsessed with failure.	Glass is half full. Enjoys every step of the way. Even failure is an opportunity.
Overgeneralizes. It's all or nothing. Either I'm perfect or I'm a failure	Realistic: Progress.
No self-acceptance	Acceptance of reality, acceptance of personal failure, and acceptance of self.
There is only one way. There is no room for improvisation or deviation. No trial and error.	Flexibility, spontaneity.
Terrified of failure. From within, but also that others see him/her as a failure.	Failure as feedback, growth opportunity.
It's all about getting to B.	The journey is as much part of the success as the destination.

The consequences of the mindset of the perfectionist are that they only experience, at best, a temporary relief, while a person committed to excellence enjoys the journey and much higher levels of happiness. A person committed to excellence is not just about temporary relief, but about lasting satisfaction.

They go through the ups and downs that we all do, but they are also able to enjoy the present day and its small everyday blessings like dinners, free time, reading time, etc.

So the question you have to ask yourself is: "What kind of life do I want for myself?"

The consequences of perfectionism

Perfectionists often waste time. Their mentality is ALL or NOTHING. Either I turn in a perfect paper or none, either I get an A or an F, either no cake or the whole cake, either I write a perfect book, or I write no book at all. Supermodel or overweight. This is a very destructive point of view and hurtful on many levels. Don't get me wrong, there are places and professions where you want perfectionism, for example in an E.R. or surgery, but in many other areas of our life it's not necessary, and when it comes to happiness, perfectionism hurts us. The constant feeling of failure and lack of self-acceptance hurts our self-esteem. If you constantly perceive yourself as a failure, it's nearly impossible to have a high self-esteem.

Because of their fear of failure, perfectionists are less likely to try, less likely to put themselves on the line. Unfortunately, those are two of the main ingredients to personal success and happiness. Further, this constant fear of failure also leads to anxiety and stress.

Perfectionism also harms relationships, because perfectionists, many times, are extremely sensitive to criticism and are on the defensive, or, even worse, expecting perfectionism from their partner. If you expect your partner to be perfect, you'll inevitably get disappointed. This leads to frustration and lack of acceptance of the partner, which usually harms the relationship. Perfectionism is also the enemy of creativity. When you are obsessed with perfectionism, you are also much less likely to act. That's what makes it also one of the primary causes of procrastination because if we don't act, we don't fail. So in the end, we don't act. Or we never cease to act, to rewrite the book or the paper, because it's not perfect yet. And so time goes by. That's why many people start a book and never finish it.

The sources of perfectionism

We are more likely to get over perfectionism if we knew where it came from.

We are not born perfectionists. As children, we actually enjoy the learning process much more than we do after growing up and start being afraid of failing. Children fall, and they get up again. The problem is the scheme we internalize constantly reinforce that the destination is the only thing that matters. It's the destination that gets rewarded, while the journey goes unrewarded. We believe we are accepted when we reach a certain destination.

Very few times we reward the journey, the enjoyment of the journey and failure. This is the kind of social environment we are born into, we are raised in, and it's tough to change. This massive, ongoing, constant pressure to be perfect is all over the media, we can see it on magazine covers, in movies. It's in the workplace. It's in the educational institutions. We are surrounded by unrealistic models and impossible standards.

How to overcome perfectionism

Well, first of all, and as most of the time, it's about self-awareness. Getting aware of what we want and what we don't want. For example, I don't want to be defensive. I want to deal better with criticism, with failure, etc. How can I do it?

Start focusing on and rewarding effort. Yes. Rewarding ourselves for failures, for even trying, and then try again.

A third stepping stone in overcoming perfectionism is acceptance. Acceptance of the outside as well as acceptance of ourselves. You don't have to be perfect. Take my word for it. So accept "stuff" and take action, cope with things, put yourself on the line, and last but not the least, look at your weak points and use them as a tool of growth. Change it by introducing behavior, like for example putting yourself on the line more, and also by visualization and imagining yourself, seeing yourself and behaving like a person committed to excellence

If your perfectionism blocks you from writing a paper, a book or starting a project, use the technique of the "first draft." Tell yourself that it's only a "rough draft," that you will improve it later (like software companies do with their versions 1.1, 1.2, 1.5, etc.) This will take the pressure away and help you to get things done.

Another suggestion is to apply the same rules you apply to others, to yourself, meaning "Do not unto yourself what you wouldn't do unto others", or better said, treat yourself as you would treat a friend in the same situation. What would you do if a friend fails terribly, or if they make a mistake? I'm sure you'd be much easier on them than you are on yourself, right? Start doing unto yourself what you do unto others. Accept failure in yourself the same way as you would accept it in others, in the people you love. Don't treat yourself differently than you treat others. Be nice to yourself.

Can we help others to overcome perfectionism?

This is a highly difficult task. The will to change has to come from within. Many of us learn it the hard way: you can't help people that don't want to be helped. They actually have to want to change. And always remember, change takes time and doesn't happen overnight.

What you can do is, be an example. If you can change, if you can become a person committed to excellence, a person who enjoys the journey, if you can celebrate even failures, even falling once in a while, then my friend you are leading by example.

People will always rather do what you do than do what you say. Share your experiences. Tell stories about it. Reward effort, reward the journey, reward the attempt saying "What a great attempt, we will get much better next time".

How to deal with perfectionism

Apart from the ways of dealing with perfectionism that we so far talked about, here are some more possible solutions:

Acceptance or what Tal Ben Shahar calls the 'Permission to be human': Accepting emotions; accepting that it's difficult; and accepting reality. Something has just happened, and I can't change it, but what I can change is my interpretation of what has happened.

Reframing: What's the growth opportunity here? What can I learn?

Distraction. Sometimes it's better to distract ourselves when a negative thought comes up. Analysing too much is not always the solution. Go for a run, listen to music, take a break, and then get back to the subject in question at a later time.

Get perspective: Is this really going to matter in ten years? In a year? Is it worth my worrying and being upset? Hint: Most of the time it won't matter.

Will you be nicer to yourself? Yes? OK then. On to the next chapter!

8. Overcoming the Silent Killer

Overcoming stress

Stress has become a global epidemic. Nationwide polls show that 45% of the students experience at the best US Universities suffer from depression until not functioning, and 94% of the students are overwhelmed, which is the result of trying to deal with too much in too little time.

Feeling overwhelmed leads to stress and anxiety, which leads to a higher likelihood of depression. Doctors estimate that about 80% of our physical illnesses are a result of stress, because stress weakens the immune system. The number one cause for loss of days at work globally is something related to our psychology, whether it's stress or related emotions, feelings, experiences

While conventional psychology didn't make a lot of progress asking the question "Why are so many people stressed?", positive psychology researchers were asking "What are those who are successful and able to lead a healthy and happy life doing?" True. Most people are stressed, but not all of them. Some people succeed and at the same time lead a healthy and happy life. What do those people do? How do they deal with stress?

They set rituals/habits for themselves.
They set rituals/habits for work and recovery.

When researchers studied more, they even found out that stress is not the problem and that it's actually GOOD for us! Stress cultivates resilience, strength, and helps to be happier in the long run! Now that's something you didn't expect, did you? But there is more: High level stress turns our immune system to its highest posible level, speeds up our processing, improves our memory and deepens our social connections.

Once again it's extremely important how we look at stress.
Shawn Achor speaks of one experiment with two groups. Group one was told "stress is bad for you", group 2 was told "stress is good for you".

Both groups had a high level of stress, but the group that saw stress as a challenge saw a 23% decrease of the negative effects of stress like anxiety, back aches, headaches, fatigue, burnout.

When you go to the gym and lift weights, you are stressing your muscle, and that's a good thing for your muscle. You lift weights, and two days later, you lift weights again and on and on, and after a year of lifting weights, you probably look like Arnold Schwarzenegger during his best days, and you also get stronger.

So stress is not the problem
The problem begins when you don't take breaks, when you don't give yourself the time to recover, when you go to the gym every day. That's when you tear or pull a muscle on a physical level. That's when you become overworked, and that has psychological, as well as physical effects. The problem is a lack of recovery.

If you want to deal with stress effectively, you need to take breaks now and then. If you don't, you will pay the price for it. On a physical level that means you will get injured. On the psychological level that means you will experience anxiety and eventually burnout and depression.

If you give yourself time for recovery, stress is good for you; it might even be exciting at times. Just now I'm reminded of my crazy, very stressful days at work. The stress was nearly unbearable.

I think my gift of totally disconnecting after walking out of the office and re-connecting the next day just 5 minutes before entering the office might have saved me a lot of trouble.

A good trick is to change the way you work. One of the most effective and efficient methods is working in time blocks, meaning work hard and focused for 60 to 90 minutes and then take at least 15 minutes for recovery. You could meditate, listen to your favorite music, have lunch mindfully, or do a bit of yoga. Try it. Experiment with it. If you organize your day like this, you'll have more energy, become more creative, more productive, and a lot happier

Of course, you should also maintain flexibility. You can work for two hours straight and then take a one-hour break. When I'm in the flow, I sometimes manage to work with full concentration for four hours, and then I'll take a two to three hours break for lunch, a walk on the beach, and a power nap, and sometimes, maybe, I even treat myself to a chapter of A Song of Ice and Fire.

Organize your day similar to what I just described, take at least one day off per week and always get a good night of sleep, and last, but not the least, take vacations regularly. The problem is that we are constantly on the run, which makes us miss the beauty that is all around us. That is why we take things for granted and don't take the time to appreciate things anymore.

Stop multitasking

The solution: Simplify. Cut activities. Do less. Fewer commitments. It affects every area of your life. If you have lunch as recovery and you use that time for e-mails and phone calls, then you are not recovering. You are adding more stress. Recovery is just focusing on your lunch or focusing on spending time with people.

Sometimes, as leaders, it's not possible to eliminate multitasking, but it's possible to reduce it.
And after reading the next study, you should seriously consider whether you should go on working with your e-mails popping all the time.

The University of London found in a study that when you have your e-mail on while doing concentrated work, it's like taking off 10 IQ points from you IQ, which is the same effect as going 36 hours without sleep. On a side note: Smoking marijuana only reduces the IQ by 4 points.

Nothing will happen if you turn your e-mail off for two to three hours, nothing will happen if your phone is off for two to three hours (unless you are an ambulance driver or a doctor).

Do less and get much more done. Applying this little trick will drastically raise your productivity and work satisfaction. Another way to gain a lot of time is by saying "NO"; to people; to opportunities; and to offers. Simplify, simplify, simplify.

Ask yourself the following questions:
What do I really, really, really want to do?
Where do I need to simplify?
Where do I need to do more?
Where do I procrastinate?

Procrastination
Procrastination is associated with lower levels of happiness, a weakened physical immune system, higher levels of stress and anxiety, and could also lead to depression.

So how can we get rid of it? There are thousand of books written on it. To simplify, here are six ways to overcome procrastination:

1. Push: Tell yourself you are going to stay at least 10 minutes on the task at hand. A lot of times we think that we have to be inspired to start working. That's not true. Most of the times we first need to start working to become inspired and "Just do it".
2. Reward yourself for a task done: Watch your favorite series. Go for a walk.
3. Go public: Set dates, deadlines, and tell it to your friends or on social network sites.
4. Have a team approach: Work with other people. (It's not right for everyone, but it helps most people).
5. Write: Write down your goals, plans, lists, and start working on them.
6. Permit yourself to recover: Procrastinate on purpose, you are not a machine.

If you want more tricks on time management or productivity, you can find an entire collection of them in my book "The Productivity Revolution" which is available on Amazon.

9. Raising Your Self-Esteem

Self-esteem. I actually wanted to write an entire book about it, and I probably will. Nathaniel Branden says that "of all the judgments we pass in our life, none is as important as the one we pass on ourselves."

When I analyzed the challenges my clients had when they come to me, the origin, most of the time, is a lack of self-esteem. Many of the things we talked about in this book like healthy relationships, happiness, benefit finding, benefit creating, depend directly on your self-esteem. And so does not getting the raise you're waiting for, the limits you set for others, how much you value your time, and much more. Once again, it's not about asking "Do I have high or low self-esteem?" but "How can I enhance my self-esteem?" And this is where it gets interesting: Sometimes, people associate too much self-esteem with arrogance, conceit, and narcissism. That's totally wrong. Arrogance or narcissism are not signs of too much self-esteem, on the contrary, they are signs of a lack thereof.

Definitions of self-esteem:

Albert Bandura, one of the experts on self-esteem, defines it as how people evaluate themselves. "Those who express a sense of unworthiness are said to have low self-esteem or the person who is to express self-pride are said to hold themselves in highest esteem." Self-esteem is "The judgment and feelings about the self".

Stanley Coopersmith defines self-esteem as "an evaluation that an individual makes and customarily maintains about himself. It expresses an attitude of approval or disapproval and states the extent to which an individual believes himself to be capable, significant, successful, and of worth. In short, self-esteem is a personal judgment of worthiness that is expressed in the attitudes an individual hold towards himself".

Self-esteem is about the attitude you have towards yourself. It's your evaluation of yourself. "The disposition to experience oneself as competent to cope with the challenges of life and as worthy of happiness." as Nathaniel Branden states.

Feeling competent and worthy. Both are important. You need both to have a healthy self-esteem. If you lack one of them, your self-esteem will be low. The evaluation or judgment about ourselves affects every area of our life. Self-esteem is essential, yet when we look around us or inside of us, there is room for improvement, isn't it? It's constant work, same like working on gratitude, goals, and so on. When I work with my coaching clients I always also automatically work on self-esteem, because when the self-esteem is high, problems and obstacles tend to disappear.

The benefits of self-esteem:
High self-esteem means high levels of resilience. You'll be better at dealing with difficulties, anxiety, depression, and with the inevitable hardships that accompanies it all.

All your relationships will improve, no matter if it's romantic relationships, friendships, or blood relationships. People with high self-esteem also show higher emotional intelligence. And last but not the least, there is a very high correlation between self-esteem and happiness. Self-esteem is one of the most important determinants of happiness.

Low self-esteem, on the other hand, causes an unhealthy anxiety. The one that appears for no apparent reason which is also known as self-esteem anxiety. But that's not all… low self-esteem can also cause depression and many psychosomatic symptoms including insomnia, or getting sick because the immune system is weaker.

Nathaniel Branden considers self-esteem as "the immune system of consciousness" because when we have high self-esteem, we are more resilient psychologically. Remember, a strong immune system does not mean we never get sick. It means we get sick less often and when we get sick, we recover quicker.

When Bednar and Petersen studied if there was an underlying cause for most psychological disorders and what it was, they came up with one single thing: Self-esteem. Further, they found out that self-esteem is critical in understanding many of the behavioral and emotional problems and also in treating most – not all – of them. And that doesn't just apply on an individual level, but also on the societal level.

As a matter of fact, in the nineties, there was a California task force by the government that coined self-esteem as a social vaccine, because they found that low self-esteem is associated with substance abuse, teen pregnancy, school dropouts, violence and crime, while high self-esteem, on the other hand, helps to overcome these social ailments.

Critics

But there are also critics: Often, self-esteem is equated with arrogance and conceit. If you take a questionnaire on narcissism, for example, a lot of times, those who are high on narcissism will also score very high on self-esteem. Now, wait a minute, a person who is a narcissist, who is arrogant doesn't have high self-esteem, do they? We all know that. It's common sense. Someone who walks into a room showing off, bragging, looking like a peacock, probably doesn't have high self-esteem.

In fact, this behavior is the exact opposite of a healthy self-esteem. People with higher levels of self-esteem are mostly humble and don't need to constantly show off.

Unfortunately, when we measure self-esteem today, we still depend on questionnaires and if you ask a narcissist "Do you have high self-esteem? " The answer will, of course, be yes.

Most questionnaires are just not sophisticated enough to differentiate between true self-esteem and pseudo self-esteem (the pretense of self-belief and self-respect).

Another critic is that high self-esteem leads to unrealistic evaluation of reality, and that ultimately hurts us. Tal Ben Sahar tells us about an article published in TIME Magazine about a standardized math test that was given to 13-year-olds in six countries. Koreans did the best, Americans did the worst, just after Spain, Ireland, and Canada. But that's not the bad news. The bad news is that the kids were shown the statement "I'm good at mathematics".

68% of Americans agreed to that statement. So while they are bad at maths, they obviously have learned the lessons of the newly-fashionable self-esteem curriculum, wherein kids are told to feel good about themselves

For the longest time, it was "fashion" for teachers to give indiscriminate praise. They thought they were raising the self-esteem of their students by telling them how terrific, how wonderful, how great they were.

The problem is that indiscriminate praise doesn't help in the long run. It reduces the student's motivation to work, makes them unrealistic, and actually makes them less happy than they potentially could have been.

To build self-esteem, we have to understand its true nature.

It's NOT a product of empty reinforcements like "Oh you are wonderful. You are terrific".

Self-esteem has to be distinguished from pseudo self-esteem, from the pretense of self-efficacy and self-respect without the reality. Pseudo self-esteem is not self-esteem; it's narcissism and detachment from reality.

Real self-esteem is founded in reality, in actual performance, in actual success, and in actual practices. And yes, you probably saw it coming, it's the product of effort and hard work.

More criticism:

A lot of research shows that people with high self-esteem are more generous, more benevolent towards others, and they are generally good. That's good news!

However, there is also a lot of research that shows exactly the opposite: People with high self-esteem show antisocial behavior, especially toward people close to them. Self-esteem has been associated with being aggressive and uncooperative.

What's going on here?

How to cultivate self-esteem

Nathaniel Branden shows us six practices that are essential for cultivating self-esteem:

1. Integrity: There has to be a match between what we say and what we do, the little things and the big things. When we communicate but don't follow up on what we say, we are mainly communicating to ourselves: "What I say is not important. It doesn't matter". Every time we do this, our self-esteem takes a hit. So if we do it very often, our self-esteem suffers a lot.

2. Self-awareness: Know yourself. Knowing yourself is the beginning of everything.

3. Having a purpose: Have a calling. Have self-concordant goals.

4. Taking responsibility: No one is coming. No excuses. No blaming. No complaining.

5. Self-acceptance: You don't have to be perfect. It's impossible. Give yourself the permission to be human on a daily basis

6. Self-assertiveness: Say no or yes when it's appropriate, stand up for what you believe in. Draw a line in the sand that can't be crossed.

Based on the work of Lovinger, Maslow, Carl Rogers, and Nathaniel Branden, Tal Ben Shahar divided self-esteem into three parts, examining it under the viewpoints of worthiness and competence.
1) High dependent self-esteem (everybody has a bit of it. The question is the degree)
2) Independent self-esteem
3) Unconditional self-esteem

	Worthiness	Competence
High dependent self-esteem	They enjoy and need appraisal. Their life is constantly affected of what other people think and say. They take other people's evaluation as the sense of self they have. They are primarily motivated by what other people say. They choose the job with the highest social status, the highest prestige. They choose a partner that they think most people would approve of. They make important decisions based on other people's approval or disapproval. They are afraid of criticism.	Their feeling of competence comes through comparison. (How am I doing relative to other people?). If they do better than others on a test or in a job, they feel great. If others do better than them, they feel bad.
Independent self-esteem	They value themselves according to their own standards. They are self-determined. (They determine how good a book they wrote is). They take into consideration what other people are saying, but at the end of the day, they are the ones who decide. They look for criticism as feedback.	Their feeling of competence doesn't come from comparison to others but comparison to their past selves (Have I improved?). They are mostly focused on the self.

| Unconditional self-esteem | No evaluation. They are confident enough not to be engaged in evaluations. | Interdependent. They don't compare themselves. They are in the state of being. Comfortable in their own skin. |

Over time, your self-esteem evolves. It takes time to become a "third level," self-actualized individual. It doesn't happen overnight. It takes work: Self-Awareness, falling and getting up again, and learning from failure. It takes learning to accept oneself, being open, being vulnerable and making mistakes. It takes being human. It's a process. It takes time.

The importance of independent self-esteem?

Think about it. The worst atrocities throughout history were conducted by people who were conforming, obedient to authority, and racist or of ethnocentric beliefs and behaviors. A person with high dependent self-esteem is much more likely to be obedient to an authority figure because they are seeking approval. They need that kind of charismatic leader who tells them "you are the best, you are superior." The root of this is low self-esteem. The feeling of "I'm not good enough. I need to compare myself to others." People with a high, independent self-esteem have less need for comparison, as well as less need to conform.

When we cultivate self-love, we cultivate self-esteem. That's when we are most likely to be emphatic and love others. Love your neighbor like you love yourself or love yourself like you love your neighbor. You are the standard of how you evaluate others and very often, not always, your behavior towards others mirrors your behavior towards yourself.

Another reason is that people who have a strong dependent self-esteem will always follow the road that has already been taken, while individuals with a high independent self-esteem follow the road less traveled and think outside the box. They think "What do I really, really want in my life?"

People with independent self-esteem are committed to continuous learning, have higher happiness levels, and a calmer sense of being. They don't have to constantly prove themselves to others. Instead of looking for approval, they say "Let me express myself. Maybe they won't like me, and that hurts. But that's ok. I'm resilient. I'm strong. I can deal with it."

Melissa Christino found a connection between independent self-esteem and happiness and flow: People with high independent self-esteem were more likely to experience flow. While Tal Ben Shahar found that narcissism is connected to high dependent self-esteem.

People with high independent self-esteem are generally much more open, cooperative, generous, and less likely to be perfectionistic

Michael Kernis examined the concept of self-esteem stability and found the following:
"We can predict whether a person will be hostile or generous, whether their self-esteem over time will be higher or lower. It's not self-esteem per se. It's the stability of their self-esteem."

People with unstable self-esteem were more likely to be hostile. People with stable self-esteem were more likely to be generous and benevolent. Dependent self-esteem was associated with instability; independent self-esteem was associated with stability.

Remember that behavior changes attitude!

We pay a high psychological and emotional price whenever we lie, cheat, or are dishonest. Be very cautious about your conversations. Are you just saying things to impress? Things that are not authentic? When we tell the truth, the message we communicate to ourselves is that our words are worthy, our words are important. We matter. When we tell lies or when we are about impressing constantly we are saying I'M NOT GOOD ENOUGH AS I AM. I need to be someone else so that the other person likes me", and our self-esteem and self-confidence take a hit.

How do we enhance our self-esteem?

So how do you improve your self-esteem? Most of the things we already talked about automatically increase self-esteem. For example physical exercise, or finding out what you really, really want in life. Following your passions, your purpose. Answering questions like "What would you do in a world where no one would know what you are doing?" "Where do you see yourself in 10 years from now?" "What's important for you that you would do regardless of other people's approval?" Do you notice that it's always the same questions that come up? The earlier you respond to them, the better.

Another important thing that will enhance your self-esteem is moments of reflection.

If you want high self-esteem, then you have to behave like a person with high self-esteem! Self-esteem, as so many other things, is simply an attitude. It's the attitude you have towards the self. So look for role models and learn from them. Walk like a person with high independent self-esteem, talk like a person with high independent self-esteem, feel like a person with high independent self-esteem. Practicing mindfulness or meditation will also enhance your self-esteem

10. Habits to Boost Your Self-esteem

Stop being so hard on yourself

Don't fall into the habit of self-criticism because of past mistakes or because things didn't work out as you wanted them to. Why? Because it doesn't serve you at all. It's time that you accept that you are not perfect! You never will be, and the best thing is YOU DON'T HAVE TO BE! Stop being so hard on yourself! This is one of the top reasons that prevent people from living a happy and fulfilled life.

A lot of the misery we have in our life is because we subconsciously think we have to punish ourselves for something. It's time to leave the habit of exaggerated self-criticism and self-punishment behind.

You're doing the best you can. This doesn't mean you should stop analyzing your mistakes. It means, you should correct them if you can; and if you can't; accept them, let go, and promise yourself not to repeat them. It only becomes a problem if you keep repeating the same mistakes over and over again.

So here is the magic recipe. It's not for sale at any pharmacy, and it's free! Ready?

1) Accept yourself as you are.
2) Forgive yourself and love yourself.
3) Take extremely good care of yourself.

That's it! Easy, isn't it?

Raise your standards

You teach people how to treat you by what you allow. Expect and demand a lot from yourself, but also from those around you. If you really want to make a change in your life, you have to raise your standards.

Have a zero tolerance policy for mediocrity, procrastination, and behavior that impedes your best performance!

Your standards could be, for example, to always tell the truth, to always be punctual, to really listen to people until they are finished, and so on. Hold yourself to high standards and – what is of the same or even more importance – set boundaries for those around you! Boundaries are things that people simply can't do to you, such as yelling at you, making stupid jokes around you, or disrespecting you.

Communicate clearly and make it a habit to address anything that bothers you on the spot. Remember what the proverb says: "In the right tone, you can say everything, in the wrong tone; nothing. The key is to find the right tone". Practice saying things in a neutral tone of voice like you'd say "The sun is shining."

If somebody oversteps your boundaries, inform them: "I didn't like that comment" or "I don't like you talking to me in that tone." If they go on, request them to stop: "I ask you to stop talking to me like this." By now, most people should get it, but there are always one or two that don't. If that happens, then insist: "I insist that you stop talking to me in that way." If all three steps don't help, then leave! Walk away neutrally stating "I can't have this conversation, while you are _____. Let's talk later".

Self-love is #1

I said it before: Love yourself like your neighbor! A lot of times you see the good in others and fail to see it in yourself! That stops NOW. From now on, when you make a mistake – before beating yourself up – think of how you'd react if a friend or a loved one would have made that mistake. I'm sure in most cases you are much more understanding and forgiving to them than to yourself.

The most important relationship that you have in this life is the one you have with yourself!

If you don't like yourself, how can you expect others to like you? How can you expect to love others if you don't love yourself first?

Accept yourself as you are. You don't have to be perfect to be great. Learn to spend time with the most important person in your life – YOU. Enjoy going to the movies with the best company you can imagine: YOU! French writer and philosopher Blaise Pascal says "All of humanity's problems stem from man's inability to sit quietly in a room alone." Get comfortable with spending some alone time. Find a place where you can disconnect from the fast-paced everyday life. It can't be mentioned often enough: Accepting yourself is the key element of your well-being.

Recognize your value as a person. Know that you earn respect. If you make a mistake, don't beat yourself up over it, accept it, and promise yourself to do your best and not repeat it. That's it. There is absolutely no use in beating yourself up about something that you can't change.

Be selfish! What? What am I saying? Yes, you read right: Be selfish! I don't mean in an egocentric way, but by being well within yourself so that you can transmit this wellness to your whole environment. If you are not well within yourself, you can't be a good husband, wife, son, daughter, or friend. But if you feel great, you can transmit these feelings to your whole environment and everybody benefits.

Live your own life

"Your time is limited, so don't waste it living someone else's life. Don't be trapped by dogma, which is living with the results of other people's thinking. Don't let the noise of other's opinions drown out your own inner voice. And most importantly, have the courage to follow your heart and intuition. They somehow already know what you truly want to become. Everything else is secondary." This Steve Jobs quote already says everything. It's difficult to add something to his wise words. Live the life you want and not the life other people expect of you. Don't worry about what your neighbors or other people think of you, because if you care too much about what they say, there will be a moment when you don't live your own life anymore, but the life of other people. Listen to your heart. Do the things you want to do, and not necessarily those things that everybody else does. Have the courage to be different!

Become a receiver

Accept compliments, gifts, and things with joy, this is also the secret to getting more of what you want. If you get a present and you say "Oh, that's not necessary", you are taking away the joy of gifting from the other person, and the same thing goes for compliments.

Take a closer look at this behavior. Is there a hidden feeling of "I don't deserve this," or "I'm not worth it" behind the "That's not necessary?"

There is no need for justification. Don't diminish other people's pleasure of giving. Just say "Thank you!" Practice your "receiving skills." If somebody compliments you, accept it graciously with a "Thank you." Own it. Don't return it.

You may say: "Thank you! I'm happy you feel that way!", and let the other person enjoy the experience. It will help you a lot and take your self-esteem to a whole new level if you manage to eradicate the following behaviors:
- Rejecting compliments.
- Making yourself small.
- Giving credit to others although you have earned it.
- Not buying something nice because you think you don't deserve it.
- Looking for the negative if someone does something good for you.

Invest in yourself

The best thing you can do for your further personal and professional growth is to invest in yourself. Commit yourself to becoming the best person you can be. Invest in training, books, CDs, and other ways of personal development. Stay curious and eager to learn new things and better yourself.

There are so many possibilities: you could partake in some sort of training that improves your negotiation skills, time management, financial planning, and much more. In a two or four-hour workshop you can learn powerful strategies or tools that can transform your life.

My best investments in myself ever was hiring coaches and mentors. They helped me to get unstuck, get clear about what I really want from my life, and change my relationship with fear completely.

You can also start in a less-expensive way by reading more or listening to a learning CD or a course. I made it a habit to read at least one book a week, buy a new course every two months, and sign up for at least two seminars a year. What are you going to do? Remember that baby steps count too.

Be authentic

Did you notice that some of the most successful people are the ones who are authentic? They are not playing any roles. They are who they are. They know their strengths and their weaknesses. They have no problem with being vulnerable and taking responsibilities for their mistakes. Neither do they fear the judgment of others. They put themselves on the line. They cope instead of avoiding. They are incredibly humble and show a great deal of integrity

Don't let the world tell you who you are supposed to be, and don't play any roles. Stop thinking about what others want from you, or might think of you, and permit yourself to be your authentic self. The rewards are awesome! Funnily enough, you will notice that the more you are yourself, the more people will be attracted to you. Try it out!

Honor your past achievements

Oprah Winfrey is totally right. "The more you praise and celebrate your life, the more there is in life to celebrate." This is one of my favorite exercises to boost my clients' self-confidence (and my own).

We are always so centered on the things that don't work so well that we forget what we have already achieved. I'm sure that you have fantastic achievements in your life, and in this chapter you will become aware of those past successes, and use them as fuel to achieving your goals and future successes.

So the big question is: What great things have you accomplished in your life so far?

You put yourself through college, traveled the world, have a great career, have lots of great friends. Maybe you lived abroad for a while all on your own. Or maybe you have overcome a terrible childhood or major personal setbacks. Maybe you raised wonderful children. Whatever challenges you've overcome or successes you have achieved—now is the time to look back and celebrate them.

Remember the chapter on focus? In this case, it means that the more you recognize and acknowledge your past successes, the more confident you'll become. And because you are concentrating on achievements, you will see more opportunities for success.

Make your list. Remind yourself of your past successes. Pat yourself on the shoulder and say to yourself "Well done!". Get into the same state that you were in, see the success once again in your mind, and feel the same feeling you had then.

Stop for a moment now. Take five minutes, take a pen and a piece of paper and list down all the biggest successes you've achieved in your life. Come on. Do it NOW.

Are you done? Then read them out loud and allow yourself to feel fantastic for what you have accomplished. Do this various times a day. It will do wonders for your self-esteem. It did for mine.

Listen to great music (Yes, it's important)
A straightforward way to feel happy instantly is to listen to your favorite music. Make a soundtrack of your all-time favorites and listen to them, dance, sing. It might feel stupid at

first, but doing this every day will be very beneficial! What are your top 5 favorite songs of all time? Make a playlist on your iPod, phone, or PC and listen to them right now! Do it NOW, and also make it a daily habit.

Celebrate your wins

On your way forward to changing your life and reaching your goals, it's also important to be aware of your progress. Stop now and then to celebrate your wins. Celebrate that you are better than you were last week. Don't let your small victories go unnoticed; celebrate the small wins. Reward yourself: buy yourself something you always wanted, go to the movies, do whatever feels right for you. If you learned new habits and saw great improvement, go on a short trip. You earned it. What will you reward yourself with for your progress so far? Will you have a spa day or a nice dinner? Will you go for a walk?

Have a highlight every day

Don't let routine and boredom crawl into your life. Create things you look forward to after a hard day at work instead of just ending up in front of the TV every evening. Here are some examples:
- Take some "alone time."
- Go for a walk amidst nature with your spouse.
- Take a bubble bath or have a spa day.
- Celebrate something: a good job, family, life!
- Call a friend.
- Take somebody out for lunch.
- Get a massage.
- Go for a drink.
- Go to the movies/theater/a concert.
- Get a manicure/pedicure.
- Movie night at home.
- Watch the sunrise.

Remember to reserve some time for your special moments in your schedule.

Pamper yourself

Self-esteem goes hand in hand with self-worth. Do you value yourself? Do you think you deserve things? Write down a list of 15 things that you can do to pamper yourself and then do one of them every other day for the next two weeks. This exercise is truly miraculous! (Examples: read a good book, go to the movies, get a massage, watch the sunrise, sit by the water, etc.) Once you start treating yourself better, it will do miracles for your self-confidence and self-esteem. These little things will make you feel better, and feeling better will raise your mood and self-esteem. You're sending your subconscious mind little messages like "I deserve this" and this starts an upward spiral.

Unfortunately, this also works the other way round. You don't just lose your self-esteem. It's a slow process. You start denying yourself little pleasures, you stop taking care of yourself, and this leads to a downwards spiral that ends up in a complete lack of self-esteem. Pamper yourself. It will change your life!

Forgive everyone

Mahatma Gandhi said "The weak can never forgive. Forgiveness is the attribute of the strong." Forgiveness is crucial on your way towards success, fulfillment, and happiness. Personally I needed a long, long time to learn this. Why forgive someone if the person did me wrong and it's only their fault? The short answer: It's a selfish act. You're doing it for yourself, not for the other person! This is not about being right or wrong!

This is about you being well and not losing a lot of energy. Anger and resentment and – even worse – reliving hate over and over again are huge energy drainers. Who have sleepless nights? Who is full of anger and doesn't enjoy the present moment? You or the person you're not forgiving? They say cultivating anger and resentment is like drinking poison and hoping the other person dies.

Do yourself a favor and let go. When a journalist asked the Dalai Lama whether he is angry at the Chinese for occupying his country, he answered: "Not at all. I send them love and forgiveness. It's of no benefit at all to be angry at them. It will not change them, but I could get an ulcer from my anger, and that would actually benefit THEM."

Adopt Dalai Lama's attitude towards people who have done you wrong and see what happens. Let go, forgive the people that hurt you, forget them and move on. This doesn't mean you can't put limits on others' behavior or call them out on the spot. But afterward, understand the consequences and let go. Call up people that you have wronged or hurt, and apologize, and if that's too uncomfortable, write them a letter.

Above all: Forgive yourself. When you learn to forgive yourself, it will be easier to forgive others. Just do it. The changes you will see when you manage to forgive others and yourself are amazing.

How to work on this? Here is one suggestion:
First make a list of everybody that you haven't forgiven. Then make a list of everything that you haven't forgiven yourself for. And then – the most important thing – start working on the list.

11. The #1 Predictor of Happiness: Relationships

Let's talk about love. No other topic is talked about so much and also so misunderstood. Scientists found out that close intimate relationships – whether it's with family members, lovers, friends, soul mates – are the number one predictor of happiness. Science has proven that relationships make us happier, more productive, more engaged, energetic, and resilient, and when we have a network of people we can count on, we bounce back faster from setbacks. Thanks to relationships, we achieve more and feel a greater sense of purpose.

Relationships are a natural need. No one can survive and thrive without functioning relationships.

In their research on extremely happy people, Martin Seligman and Ed Diener chose the group of the happiest 10%, and studied them:
They experienced hardships, anxiety, stress, depression, and frustration like everybody else. The only difference between them and the rest was that they recovered faster. Why? Because they interpreted their experience differently because they have thriving personal and interpersonal relationships, either with romantic partners, family members, friends or all of the above.

David Myers says: "There are few stronger predictors of happiness than a close nurturing, equitable, intimate, lifelong companionship with one's best friend".

Relationships make a difference. When you are happy and you share, it enhances relationships. On the other hand, when you go through hardships and difficulty, a strong relationship helps you overcome it

Know yourself

Isn't it funny how we always come back to the same thing? The most important key to everything in our life seems to be knowing oneself. Know how many hours a day is good for you to spend time with other people, know exactly what your relationship needs are, and know how many relationships you need. All that depends on your personal and individual needs. The number of hours you want to spend with other people differ for everyone.

There's no right or wrong on this one, and it doesn't mean you love people any less if you spend less time with them (that's a trap I fell into so many times in my relationships).

If we look at relationships today, it's a pretty dire picture. Two-third of marriages end up in divorce, and the worst of all is that this doesn't mean that the other one-third is just peachy. Often, people stay in relationships out of comfort, out of habit, because of a lack of alternative, or because of a sense of duty. In our times, there's clearly a failure to sustain love over time.

How can we create relationships that thrive?

The first step for accepting reality is understanding what true love really means. Does it exist? It does in fiction and movies. Or better said, it only exists in fiction and movies. In real life, there is no perfect love, and a lot of times relationships fail because we expect perfect love. If your expectations are larger than life, if your expectation is perfect love, then, my dear, you are setting yourself up for failure.

The problem is that "perfect love" is all we read about and all we see in movies. I'm convinced that it's also the fault of the movie industry that some marriages fail.

They paint a picture of romantic relationships that have nothing to do with reality, and we internalize it and look for it, and no one can live up to our expectations. I'm sorry to be the one who tells you that Prince or Princess Charming never comes. But I have good news! While perfect love doesn't exist, true love does. True love exists.

Let positive psychology help us identify true love by once again asking different questions, focusing on what works best, and focusing on the few relationships that actually thrive. Traditional psychology counselors or researchers, over the years, have asked: "Why do so many long term relationships fail?" "Why do so many people, after a year or two or five together, end their relationship?" "Why do people stay together although they are no longer okay with it?"

By now you know what happens if we only ask these questions: We miss a critical part of reality, and unfortunately, it's the part of reality that can lead to lasting, thriving, and passionate relationships.

Positive psychologists changed the question to "What makes some relationships thrive and grow stronger over time?" These relationships exist. "What makes them successful?" And the most important question: "What can we learn from those and apply to our relationships?"

John Gottman, one of the leading researchers on relationships – who also can predict divorce with an accuracy level of 94% - says "When I figured out how to predict divorce, I thought I had found the key to saving marriages, but like so many experts before me, I was wrong. I was not able to crack the code to saving marriages until I started to analyze what went right in happy marriages."

David Schnarch showed in his research studying the best relationships that those couples not only enjoy spending time together over the years but that the best sex they have in their lives actually comes when they are 50 and 60 years old, and not when they are 18, 25, or 35.

Sorry that I have to be the killjoy here but I think you guessed it already. Unfortunately the majority of relationships are not like that. Mostly because a significant number of people today are in their second or third marriage or long-term relationship at the age of 50 and 60.

So what are the secrets to a thriving relationship?
It's hard work. You need to invest if you want to thrive in a relationship. Create high levels of intimacy. Maintain passion. Appreciate the good.

One of the key mistakes that I made for the longest time, and I actually was able to start changing it when I heard about this the first time from Tal Ben-Shahar, was that I had a so-called "Finding Mindset" for most of my life. Boy, was letting go of the "Finding Mindset" and learning the "Cultivating Mindset" a relief! It's like a huge weight off my shoulders.

When you have a "finding mindset" you focus on finding the right partner. Big mistake! Finding the right partner is important, but it's not the most important.

The problem with the "Finding Mindset" is that when you go through rough times with your partner, which by the way is totally normal, you start thinking "Wait a minute. Something is wrong here. I must not have found the right partner. I must have made a mistake." This happened to me every single time, and it made the situation worse. And sooner or later the relationship ended.

With a "Cultivating Mindset" that wouldn't have happened, because you rather think: "Okay. We are going through some difficulties, but we are working on our relationship. It's normal. We make an effort to understand each other. We grow together." It's this mindset that makes relationships last.

It's more important to cultivate the relationship than to find the right partner. Don't misunderstand me: It is important to find the right person, but it's even more important to then cultivate that relationship

So why in the world do people have the "Finding Mindset"? Here I am, once again, blaming the movies. They are beautiful, but there is one problem, they focus on finding the right partner. And the actual work starts when the movie ends and the curtain drops. Having a good relationship at the beginning is easy. The honeymoon phase usually lasts through the first year or two. But what happens then? What happens when we see that the partner is not perfect? That's where true love begins, and that's where true love is cultivated.

I always believed that there is more than one right person. Mostly after a relationship ended of course. And come on, we are nearly 7 billion people in the world, it's insane to think that there is only one person for us. It's also not important because true love is not about finding the right person. It's about cultivating the one chosen relationship.

It's working together, being together, spending time together, and dedicating one to another. That's how we create the one special relationship. It's a process, and it takes time. We cultivate a relationship not simply by putting on the ring or by reciting the vows, but by doing things together, by actually getting to know each other.

John Gottman found out that "in the strongest marriages, husband and wife share a deep sense of meaning. They don't just get along, they also support each other's hopes and aspirations and build a sense of purpose in their lives together."

How do we sustain love?

1) Create relationship rituals.
We've heard it often: "Love is in the details." Love is not in the three months around the world cruise or the diamond ring. These things are lovely, but they don't sustain a relationship.

It's the details, the habits, the day-to-day rituals that maintain relationships. The touch, the gaze, the meal together, remembering important dates, compliments, text messages, kisses, hugs, and appreciating our partner every day. These little details and day-to-day activities make a relationship extraordinary.

And you do this by demonstrating interest. Asking "How was your day honey?" "Tell me about…" "What have you just been thinking?", "You look a bit sad, anything I can do?", and listening with empathy. Are you really listening to your partner? Are you really looking at your partner? Do you really want to get to know them?

And of course, sex is also important for a long-term thriving relationship. A divorce lawyer once told me: "You know, I never divorced a couple that had great sex." And while this might be his exclusive opinion, it is very rare to have a romantic relationship without the physical component.

The most important thing also in this department is healthy communication. Very often there is a difference in expectations because there's no "right prescription" of how many times you should have sex to make your relationship work. Once a day? Five times a week?

This is a potential source of conflict so communicate with your partner. For you, sleeping with your partner three times a week could be a lot, but maybe for your partner it's not enough. Find out by talking to each other.

My relationships improved a lot when I started talking about my wishes openly with my partner instead of hoping they could read my mind about what I desired.

2) Shift from "to be desired/validated" to "to be known"
No matter what kind of relationship – romantic or friendship – the foundation of great relationships is to be KNOWN. You get to deeper levels of intimacy by getting to know each other more and more.

We do this by opening up, sharing meaningful things with our partner, opening up and also sharing our weaknesses, our insecurities, and our passions. As Tal Ben Shahar says "A healthy relationship is about expressing ourselves rather than constantly trying to impress".

This is risky because what happens if she doesn't like you? But it's worth the risk because if you express yourself and open up, you are more likely to have a thriving relationship. There is no guarantee, but one thing is for sure: If you just try to impress, failure is guaranteed.

Did you notice that people who take the risk, who authentically express themselves over time attract more and more people? Genuine people are more attractive. It doesn't matter if it's friends or leaders. There is nothing like being authentic. Integrity attracts.

If you only impress, you'll always be asking yourself "Who do they really like? Me or the image?" and this will soon become a self-inflicted torture.

Make an active effort to get to know your partner. This takes time and doesn't happen on the first date.

3) Allowing conflicts in the relationship.
There will always be conflicts in relationships. It's okay. It's normal. All relationships face it. Instead of asking "What's wrong" in the relationship we can shift to "Ok. It's normal. It's natural. Let's see how we can learn from it and grow as a couple". Once again, everything is about concentrating on and strengthening the positive.

By the way, people who have a 1:5 conflict ratio usually have a thriving relationship. 1:5 means one conflict every five positive interactions. People who have a lot less or a lot more conflict usually don't have a relationship that thrives in the long term. At 1:100, for example, it could mean there are some oppressed things. And if you fight all the time it really might be time to part ways.

For a long time, it was thought that you only have to bring the conflicting parties together and talk to solve the problems. That was wrong and frequently made things worse.

The important thing in resolving conflicts is that both parties have a higher common goal together, working together, and supporting one another. We also have to be aware that there is positive as well as negative conflict. Healthy conflict focuses on a person's behavior, thoughts, ideas and challenge, for example, saying "You mind putting down the toilet seat when you are done?" or "It upsets me to return to a dirty home, we agreed you'd throw away the garbage".

Unhealthy conflict focuses on the person, on the emotions, on who they are, such as saying "You're so inconsiderate" or "You're such a slob, you promised to throw away the garbage. I can't trust you."

When you attack someone for who they are, the person, the emotion it's very unhealthy no matter if it's a group or a couple.

It's of utmost importance to avoid hostility, insult, and contempt.

John Gottman – the guy who can predict divorce with a 94% accuracy rate – talks a lot about it in his research. He predicts divorce based on whether he sees hostility or contempt when he asks couples about their conflicts.

When there are hostility and contempt, it's a very bad sign. It doesn't always lead to divorce, but it's a bad sign for the long-term likelihood of success of the relationship and regarding the current enjoyment of the relationship.

It's important to keep these insults away, to focus on the person, to validate/appreciate the person and disagree with their behavior or the ideas and their thinking. It goes without saying that the key is to keep the disputes private. It's difficult enough to fight in a relationship; it's extraordinary difficult when embarrassment is also associated with it.

Couples shouting at one another, or showing contempt in front of others are on a very destructive, and extremely unhelpful path.

We have to learn to fight better:
Improving the ability to disagree by being more positive, introducing more humor, more affection, more touching, and more

talking. This helps to dissolve tension. Stop taking negativity by personally telling yourself "I understand this is part of the growth. We may not be enjoying ourselves now. It's a serious fight. But what can I learn from it."

Show more attention to your partner's side. Calm down, understand, and be emphatic. Learn to treat those we love the same or even better than we treat others because a lot of times we treat others better than the ones we love.

4) Positive perception
We have to appreciate the other person and vice versa. I'm sure we've all seen and experienced it: Once we take a relationship for granted, it starts to worsen. Unfortunately, that happens to most relationships. The secret is to always focus on what works. Focus on your spouse's sense of humor, on their support, on how they are a good mother or father, etc. Become a "Benefit finder" in your relationships.

Sandra Murray conducted another one of these remarkable experiments that more people should know about. She asked couples to evaluate each other's strengths. Afterwards, she asked friends and family to do the same. The results were once again mind-boggling:

On an average, relationships of couples that evaluated their strengths on a lower level than friends and family didn't last very long, while couples that evaluated one another's strength on a higher level, who thought of their partner more than other people thought of them, were most likely to succeed over time.

The fact of thinking more of their partner than other people think of them is also called "positive illusions." Only that, it's not an illusion, it becomes a self-fulfilling prophecy! These thriving couples are actually "benefit creating".

They are seeing things that are not there or that other people have not seen, and then these things come into existence. It's the Pygmalion effect all over again, this time in relationships.

The importance of asking the right questions and open communication

You remember that when we ask certain questions, we start seeing things that we didn't see before, right? So here are the two most important questions that you should ask over and over again to create and maintain a thriving relationship:

1) What am I grateful for in my partner? There is always something to appreciate, especially in difficult times.
2) What's wonderful about our relationship? What's working? What do I love about him/her? What's good? When we ask what's good, then we perceive it. When we perceive it, we appreciate it. When we appreciate it, it grows.

We have to change our questions to the right ones, focus on the potential of our relationships, and communicate mostly about the positive events we are experiencing.

Which brings us to our next study about positive communication. Shelly Gable found out that the way couples communicate about positive events is a better predictor of long-term success in a relationship than how they talk about negative incidents.

So, when you come home and talk about something positive, a good thing that happened to you, and the way your partner responds is a predictor of the long-term success of your relationship.
There are four ways of responding: constructive vs. destructive and active vs. passive. Out of the four ways to respond, only one contributes positively to the relationship.

Active and constructive: Comprise of enthusiastic support, specific comments, and follow up questions:
"I just got a promotion!" "That's amazing! What happened? Tell me! We have to celebrate. Let's go out."

Harmful responses are:
Passive and constructive responses: "That's nice" "Oh that's great. Mmmh."
Active and destructive: "Oh No! Now we have less time together." "I'm surprised."
The worst:
Passive and destructive: Ignoring the news entirely. Showing no interest: "Mmh. Did you see we got a new flower in the garden."
The only conditions for active and constructive communication are that it has to be win-win and it has to be genuine. If these are given, this way of communication can cause an upward spiral for our lovebirds.

Relationships at work

We spend most of our time at work, so let's look at the influence of relationships at the workplace. A national survey of 24,000 workers concluded that men and women with few social ties were two to three times more likely to suffer from major depression than those with strong social bonds. Another study shows that people who received emotional support during six months after a heart attack were three times more likely to survive.

Good relationships and positive interactions with our colleagues at work lower cortisol, which means we recover faster from work related stress and are better able to handle it in the future. And this is where CEOs should pay attention:

The ability to manage stress – physically and psychologically – is a significant competitive advantage. It has been found to greatly reduce a company's health care cost and rate of absenteeism. But there is more, these positive social interactions also result in employees being able to work longer hours, focus better, and perform under more difficult conditions.

A study of men over the age of 50 that had a lot of stress in their life showed that those who lacked high levels of emotional support suffered from a far higher mortality rate in the next seven years than those who had good relationships and emotional support.

When over 1,000 highly successful professionals were asked what had motivated them most during their career, they ranked friendships above financial gain and individual status, and in a study of 350 people of a financial services company, the greatest predictor of team success was how the members felt about each other.

It's a fact that the more team members are encouraged to interact face to face, the more engaged they feel, and the more energy they have. In short, the more the investments in social connections, the better the results of their work The best companies already know this and put it into practice. IBM, for example, facilitated the introduction of employees who didn't know each other. Google keeps company cafeterias open well past the hours and encourages employees to see their kids at their onsite daycare center. It's surprising that a logistic company that is all about speed encourages their drivers to have lunch together. Nevertheless, UPS does exactly that.

If employees believe and say "I have a sense of pride in my organization" a company can congratulate itself because these feelings translate into lower absenteeism and employee turnover and increased employee motivation and engagement

The most important relationship at work

The relationship between employee and the boss is the prime predictor of both daily productivity and the length of time people stay at their jobs, because "People don't change jobs, they change bosses." This is the most important relationship in a company, and it has consequences. A Gallup study found out that US Companies lose 360 billion USD each year due to lost productivity from employees who have a poor relationship with their supervisor.

If people have a difficult relationship with their bosses, it also has consequences on their health: Their blood pressure can spike all over the place, and they are 30% more likely to suffer from coronary heart disease. On the other hand, when the boss-employee relationship is strong, it's extremely beneficial for the company. And there is proof. An MIT study confirmed that employees with strong relationships with their managers bring in more money than those with only weak ties.

A Gallup study of 10 million workers came to the following conclusion:
Those who agreed to the phrase "My supervisor, or someone at work seems to care for me as a person" were more productive, contributed more profits, and were significantly more likely to stay with the company in the long term.

And although the best leaders already know all this, many of them don't put in the effort to reap the benefits of these findings. Either because they don't have the time, or because they feel a loss of authority, or because they just believe that friendship and work don't go hand in hand or as my former colleague Iñaki used to say: "If you want a friend, buy a dog".

It's really easy to create a better work environment. Once again it's common sense_ Greet colleagues, look them in the eye to create rapport and empathy, have a face-to-face meeting now and then, and talk also about things outside of work instead of talking all the time about the project or task at hand. The simple act of introducing new employees to not only to their department but also to other departments has brought tremendous benefits in the long term for companies who do it. And it's not only the new joiners. While you are at it, introduce existing employees, who don't know each other to each other.

I'm not telling you that everybody has to be BFFs at work or that everybody has to like each other all the time. What matters is mutual respect and authenticity. Team lunches and socializing after work are crucial, but relationships have to develop naturally and can't be forced.

Emotions are contagious – negative and positive ones – and they can affect a group of people almost instantly. We notice this in us as well as in others. When we feel anxious or have a real bad day, our feelings will start to creep into every interaction we have, whether we like it or not. And the results, not just our own, will suffer from this. If you ever sat close to an anxious boss who is in a bad mood for too long, you know what I'm talking about. After a while, you probably felt sad or stressed too, regardless of how you felt initially.

That's why it's so important to have a positive mindset. Science has proven over and over again that positive emotions are a tool in the quest for high performance at the workplace. The happier everyone is around you, the happier you are and vice-versa. The happier we are at work, the more positivity we transmit to our colleagues, clients, etc., which can raise the emotion of an entire team.

This was proven by an experiment at Yale:
During a group task, one member of the group was instructed to be openly positive. The experiment was video taped and tracked emotions of each individual team member before and after the session. The individual and group performances were assessed.

The results were once again spectacular: They showed that whenever the positive team member entered the room, his mood instantly infected everybody around him. His positive mood actually improved each individual team member's performance as well as their ability to accomplish the task as a group. But not only that, researchers also found that the teams with the one positive person infecting everybody with his mood had less group conflict, more cooperation, and, most importantly, greater overall performance.

The more genuinely expressive you are, the more your mindset and feelings spread. And, read this closely if you are in a leadership position, in a leadership position the power to infect you employees with positive emotions multiplies. If you, as a leader, are in a positive mood, your employees will be more likely to be happy themselves, to help each other more and to coordinate tasks more efficiently and with less effort. They'll also be more likely of being happy and describing their workplace as performance enhancing – two huge advantages in employee attraction and employee retention.

People in positive moods are also better at thinking creatively and logically, at problem-solving, and are even better negotiators.

12. The Power of the Mind-Body Connection

For a long, long time in the western society we concentrated only on what happens "neck up" but most of what happens is "neck down".

In this chapter, I'm going to talk about Tal Ben Shahar's secret wonder drug! As he says, he's not a good businessman, so he never commercialized the drug, and we can get our hands on it for free. This drug has been tested over and over again. And the best is that there are no negative side effects, on the contrary, there are tons of positive benefits:

- It's going to make you feel really, really good!
- Your self-esteem is going to rise significantly.
- Your self-confidence is going to get a boost.
- You will feel calmer and more centered.
- You'll even get smarter.
- It's also going to make you more attractive.

So here it is – the wonder drug:

- 30 minutes of physical exercise 4 times a week
- At least 15 minutes of mindful exercise 6 to 7 times a week
- 8 hours of sleep (+/-) per 24 hours
- 12 hugs a day

If you take this cocktail, you will reap many of the benefits, maybe all, and probably even much more.

One of the first people to understand the mind body connection was John Kabat Zinn.

He stated the following: "Perhaps the most fundamental development in behavioral medicine is the recognition that we can no longer think about health as being solely a characteristic of the body or the mind because body and mind are interconnected".

This was a revolution and essentially a rejection of hundreds of years of western thinking. But since then, many researchers have proven him right. They did because they were asking a new question: "How can we use the body to launch a virtuous cycle between where the mind helps the body and the body helps the mind?"

The Magic of physical exercise

We all know the advantages of physical exercise:
- It boosts our mood and enhances work performance.
- It improves our motivation and feeling of having achieved something.
- It reduces stress.
- It helps you feel better and more energetic.
- It keeps you healthy.
- It helps you to lose weight, which improves health, and also makes you look better.

Once the kilos start dropping, there is a big chance that your self-esteem will go up.

The problem is despite knowing this, most of us don't exercise. Let me show you some amazing studies that will hopefully convince you to start physical activity. The most incredible research about the positive benefits of exercise was done by Michael Babyak from Duke Medical School: He took 156 patients with major depression – people in very bad shape – showing a number of symptoms like insomnia, eating disorders, lack of desire to act, depression, and most of them were suicidal with attempts or thoughts about suicide, and divided them into three groups.

The first group did 3 x 30 minutes of exercise of moderate difficulty (jogging, swimming or brisk walking). The second group was put on medication (Zoloft), and the third group was on medication and asked to exercise. After four months, Babyak got some stunning results:

60% of the subjects were not experiencing the major symptoms of depression any more, meaning they recovered. All groups experienced similar improvements in happiness, which means that exercise proved just as helpful as antidepressants! The medication group took about 10-14 days to get over depression, while the exercise group close to a month, but later there was no difference. Amazing, isn't it? But there is more:

Six months after the study ended, when the participants were no longer given the medication or no longer pushed to exercise they had a look at a look at the relapse rate.

Out of the 60% that got better, 38 percent of the "only medication" group went back and suffered from major depression again. From the third group (medication and exercise), it was 31%. But from the exercise group, there were only 9% who fell back into depression.

This means that exercise is a powerful and lasting mood lifter. It doesn't mean that medication isn't necessary any more, but it means that we should maybe first ask whether exercise or the lack thereof is the underlying reason for the experience.

Don't get me wrong. There are and there will be people who can only be helped with medication, people who can be helped by exercise, and people who need both.

But maybe we could try exercise too. Exercise is not a fix-all. However, in most situations, it can help or prevent.

I'd say exercising is like taking an anti-depressant. Tal Ben Shahar argues that it's the other way round: Not exercising is like taking a depressant, because we just weren't made to sit through all day, we were made to run after our lunch or to run away from lions to not end up as lunch. When we don't exercise, our base level of happiness lowers. Exercise brings us back to where we are supposed to be all along.

The benefits of exercising, at least every other day, are countless:
- It increases you self-esteem and lowers stress and anxiety.
- After you go for a run, your brain is most susceptible to creating new neural pathways.
- It improves your memory, meaning that you retain material you have learnt much better.
- You become much more creative.

People who exercise are much less prone to physical diseases; significantly reducing the likelihood of diabetes; reducing by 50% or more the likelihood of heart failure; reducing the likelihood of certain kinds of cancer; and strengthening the immune system.

And if I didn't convince you by now:
You will also have better sex, both men and women. Exercise strengthens libido, and enhances the likelihood of orgasms. People who exercise more regularly have more and better sex.

Before you start your exercise program, remember: Recovery is very important and more is not always better. Funnily enough, the symptoms of overtraining are very similar to the symptoms of under training

Shahar's general recommendation is to exercise a minimum of 3 to 4 times a week, ideally 5 to 6 days for a minimum of 30 minutes at 70% of your maximum heart rate. Four times 30 minutes should be enough. Just listen to your body.

If exercise is so powerful…why do most of the people in the world not exercise?
The three most common reasons are: It's painful, not enough time, and the subconscious barrier.

1) Exercise is painful. It's not comfortable and our mind does not like pain. It tries to avoid pain.

The solution? As mostly, when you start working on a goal: Divide and Conquer. Start walking for a mile, do a 10 minutes walk, then a 20-minutes walk and gradually build it up. Your body will ask for more. If you build it up gradually, it's not about pain; it becomes positively addictive. I've seen it. My friend Marina started out walking for minutes. Five years later, she's running 10k and 20k races. Start slow and your body will ask for more.

If it gets too boring, distract yourself with TV, music, or podcasts. Whatever you can think of. Go running with other people. The number one predictor of exercise and success in the long term is to do it with other people.

2) Not enough time:
One of the first things to go when you don't have time is exercise, while it should be the last thing to go. Exercise is an investment. You might lose 45 minutes, but you gain so much more. Remember all the benefits we talked about at the beginning of the chapter.
Also remember: Don't rely on self-discipline, create rituals.

3) The subconscious barrier:

Even self-esteem or the lack thereof can come into play when we don't exercise. Part of low self-esteem is the notion that we are not worthy of happiness. Subconsciously, we often think: we are not really worthy of happiness and this can become a barrier that stops us from becoming happier. If we think we are not worthy of happiness, we will, very often, not do things that will make us happy. The solution? Like Nike said: JUST DO IT and recognize the importance of exercise on a conscious level.

Harvard Medical School Professor and Psychiatrist, John Ratey said "In a way, **exercise can be thought as a psychiatrist's dream treatment.** It works on anxiety, on panic disorder, and on stress in general, which has a lot to do with depression. And it generates the release of neurotransmitters, norephedrine, serotonin, and dopamine that are very similar to our most important psychiatric medicines. Doing a bit of exercise is like taking a little bit of Prozac, and a little bit of Ritalin right where it's supposed to go."

To finish the chapter on exercise, here is another amazing experiment:

Here's what happened when 45 minutes of some form of exercises like running, rowing, climbing, cycling etc. were implemented in schools:

Obesity levels went down from 30% to 3% in a school in Naperville, Illinois. Students became more comfortable, happier, and much less susceptible to chronic illnesses, such as cancer, heart failure, diabetes, and their grades went up significantly. Naperville scored number 16 in the world in mathematics and number 1 in the world in science. A great achievement, considering that US schools usually don't score well in international tests.

Exercise was also introduced in inner city schools in very poor areas. In Titusville, PA, grades went from way below state average to 17% above state average in one year after introducing exercise. Another advantage of introducing exercise was that violence disappeared completely as result of it. In Iowa, disciplinary problems went down from 225 to 95 in one year; in Kansas, by 67%. That's no surprise knowing that exercise calms us so we are much less likely to be aggressive.

The Power of Meditation

Meditation has gone mainstream. Maybe you've already experimented with it. If not, I highly recommend it. It's easier than you thought. And in its easiest form, you basically can't do anything wrong. There are various kinds of meditation like yoga, focusing on your breath, praying, sitting meditation, Tai Chi, and so on. All meditations have things in common like focusing on one thing, for example movement, posture, breath, or a flame and breathing deeply.

As I mentioned before, there is no good or bad meditation. It's about being present, being in the here and now, it's also about struggling with being in the here and now. When you lose you focus, simply bring it back, that's how we exercise our mind to be more focused and be more mindful.

John Kabat-Zinn and Herbert Benson studied the world's bets meditators. They directly contacted the Dalai Lama himself to send his best meditators, and the results of the studies were mind-boggling. First they looked at left to right prefrontal cortex ratio, which is important for measuring happiness. Happier people generally have more activity on the left side of the prefrontal cortex, and less happy people have more activity on the right side of the prefrontal cortex. The meditators had very high levels of well-being and happiness.

They were susceptible to positive emotions and resilient in the face of painful emotions. These were remarkable results, which have never been seen before measuring the meditators.

Another thing they looked at was the so-called startle response, something that everyone has, even military snipers. When we hear a bang, we startle. Generally the higher your level of anxiety, the easier you get startled. It's impossible to suppress the startle response. Or better said, it was impossible until Paul Ackerman brought in the meditators and asked them to maintain complete calm. He startled them. And surprise, surprise... there was no reaction at all. For the first time in recorded history, people were able to suppress the startle response.

You know that emotions are contagious. So is calmness. Calmness is as contagious as happiness. Even people who wanted to start a discussion with those people could not get angry.

Now the good news is that you don't have to meditate 8 hours a day for 30 years to get the benefits of meditation.

John Kabat Zinn conducted another experiment. He worked with two groups. The first group started meditating right away, the other group - the control group - was told they will start their meditation course in four months. The researchers wanted to make sure that the control group were people that wanted to meditate.

So group 1 started to meditate 45 minutes a day for 8 weeks. The results were once again stunning: their anxiety levels went down and they were in a happier mood. Looking at the left and right prefrontal cortex, there was a significant difference in the individuals who meditated. So Kabat-Zinn went one step further. He injected a cold virus in both groups and found out that the immune system of the meditators was significantly stronger than those who didn't meditate. Meditation strengthens both our physical as well as our psychological immune system.

And it gets even better. Herbert Benson found out that with just as little as 15 to 20 minutes of meditation a day, you can see a significant change of emotional and physical well-being over time. Did I convince you yet? If yes, here's a little help on how to start:

1. Look for a space where you won't be disturbed, and just be in silence for 15 to 20 minutes. (Start with 5 minutes if you want) Make it a ritual. It's beneficial to practice in the same spot and at the same time every day.

2. Before you start, use the power of affirmations to get yourself in a relaxed state by saying for example, "I'm now focused and calm."

3. Set your alarm clock for twenty minutes so that you are not worried about when to stop your meditation, and are fully able to concentrate.

4. Sit or lie down and shut your eyes. You can also leave your eyes open and focus on one point in the room or on nature if you are sitting facing a window.

5. While focusing, concentrate on your breath, and start relaxing.

6. When your mind wanders, let it wander. Don't resist. See your thoughts passing by like clouds in the blue sky.

Mindfulness: be here now

Everybody talks about it, a lot people do it as well. So how does it really work?

Being mindful is being fully present. Being in the now. Being aware that we are alive. Being aware of our emotions without judging them. Giving us permission to feel these emotions. Although we are always in the present moment, most of the time we are not aware of it. We walk in the woods, but our mind is in office. We eat, but we read the newspaper. Mindful walking would be to be aware of the trees, the sounds around us, the animal noises. Mindful eating would be to fully savour the taste and texture of our meal, chewing slowly, feeling how the food dissolves in our mouth, only concentrating on that, and nothing else.

Mindfulness is the awareness and acceptance of internal and external stimuli. You can feel every emotion in the body. As soon as a painful emotion starts, you can go immediately to its physical manifestation. The purpose of this is to become aware of the physical manifestation of the emotion and accept it for what it is. You connect with the present moment by concentrating on your emotions, or your breath.

Mindfulness works because it creates an alternative neural pathway. Instead of trying to fix something, accepting and observing it become the new alternative. If you feel stressed, observe what's happening to your body. What's the physical manifestation of it? Where do you feel it in your body and how do you feel it?

During the first level, you practice mindfulness by becoming aware of your body and your surroundings and as in all meditations, the practice is losing focus and coming back again. You can also practice it by reframing. Instead of feeling the stress before an important speech or presentation, you can see it as a wonderful opportunity.

Mindfulness changes our focus from DOING to BEING. The constant obsession of "How can I fix it?" very often is counterproductive when dealing with mental/psychological problems. The constant living in the future keeps you from being happy in the moment.

Here's one of the best exercises I learnt from my NLP Trainer Anna Flores. The least it will do for you – if done regularly – is sharpen your senses, but don't be surprised if it does even greater things for you. For me and some other trainees, it has done amazing things. The basics of this exercise are centred on seeing (visuals), hearing (auditive), and feeling (kinestetic). The idea is to be "in the moment" and more aware of what you see, hear, and feel.

So you start with being consciously aware of 5 things you see, 5 things you hear, and 5 things you feel. Then 4 things you see, 4 things you hear, 4 things you feel, then 3, then 2, and then finally 1.

You can do this anywhere! I did this one on a train a couple of years ago: Here we go!

5)
I see a red scarf
I see a black bike
I see a blue sweater
I see a red bag
I see a white cable
I hear voices
I hear a tone
I hear a voice
I hear something scratching
I hear a door
I feel my feet on the floor
I feel some cold air on my hands
I feel cold air on my feet
I feel somebody stepping on my toe
I feel my jeans on my skin

4)
I see a blue and white bag
I see a black bike
I see a black jacket
I see a white cable
I hear a cough
I hear voices
I hear a tone
I hear people moving
I feel my feet on the floor
I feel my jacket on the skin
I feel my feet on the floor
I feel my jeans on the skin

3)
I see a red bag
I see a red jacket
I see the sea
I hear distant voices
I hear somebody move
I hear distant voices
I feel my feet in my shoes
I feel my mobile in my hand
I feel air

2)
I see a red scarf
I see a beige jacket
I hear a beeping
I hear a distant voice
I feel my feet on the floor
I feel my jeans on my skin

1)
I see a red handle
I hear the noise of the train
I feel my back against the chair

Do this five times a day for 3 weeks and let me know what it did for you!

Breathe right and conquer

As I mentioned before, the easiest way of meditation is breathing. It's something all meditation techniques have in common and it's an easy thing to introduce in your life even if you don't meditate for 15 or 45 minutes a day.

One result of our stressed and fast-paced world is that our breathing becomes shallow. The result of shallow breathing is even more stress and anxiety. The result of even more stress and anxiety is that we go into the so-called "fight or flight" response. And that's how we live most of our days. Fortunately we can reverse this. Because our mind and body are connected and we know that calm and well-being leads to deep breathing, this means that deep breathing in turn leads to calm and well-being.

Herbert Benson found out that we can reverse the "fight and flight" response and enter what he calls the "relaxation response" with as little as three deep breaths. Three deep breaths! That's something all of us can do.

You can do a deep breath when you leave home, when you arrive at work, just before work or class starts, just after work or class ends, just when you wake up in the morning, or as the last thing you do before going to bed. I do it every time I get to a red light or when I'm in the line of the super market. Three deep breaths at strategic points through the day can transform your life.

The Importance of Sleep

Before Edison invented the light bulb, the average sleep hours were 10 hours per night. Today, the average person gets about 6.9 hours of sleep during the week, and 7.5 hours on the weekend. Who still gets a full eight hours of sleep? In the US, on average only 25% of the people between 18 and 29 years still get a full eight hours of sleep.

We have to look at sleep as an investment and make it a priority.
Sleep is so important. It strengthens the physical immune system significantly and raises energy levels. But it's a personal thing. You have to find out how many hours of sleep you need.

Some of the disadvantages of lack of sleep are putting on weight and impaired motor skills. There are 100,000 road accidents on average each year as a result of lack of sleep, which results in 40,000 injuries and 1,500 deaths on US streets. The same happens at work. Workplace accidents because of lack of sleep cost companies 100 billion USD a year.

Further, lack of sleep hurts our creativity, productivity, and memory. A big mistake I made when I used to study was to tell myself "Let me stay up two more hours to study" It's scientifically proven that I could have done a lot more studying if I went to bed early. If you sleep enough, you remember the material better, and you are far more creative.

When we don't have enough sleep, we get cranky, irritated, and anxious. Lack of sleep can lead to moodiness, and in the worst case depression
But it's not only the physiological effects of sleep. Sleep also has a psychological function. At night, our mind processes a lot of the things we have gone through throughout the day, and many times, it resolves unresolved issues. This is why when

you go to sleep with a problem you often wake up with the solution. If you don't give yourself the opportunity to "complete" your dreaming, complete your problem-solving through the night, you wake up with that problem unresolved. This happens whether you are aware of it to not. Over time, this can mount up to a lot of unresolved issues, and we are more likely to enter depression when those are suppressed.

Physical and Psychological need of sleep

Sleep more or less eight hours a day. For me, six hours plus a one and a half hour nap works best. Power naps have been proven to be very efficient. Take your internal rhythms into account. How many hours do YOU need, are you a night person or a morning person? What's right for you?

If you have problems falling a sleep because you eat too late or exercise too late, give yourself the permission to be human. You could tell yourself "Well this is an opportunity to think and reflect."

When I experience jet lag while travelling to the US from Europe, I usually wake up at 5 AM, I think "Great, 5 AM is a great time get to work any way". I get up and start working instead of rolling around not being able to sleep any more anyway.

William Dement from Stanford has studied and documented the effects of sleep deprivation on well-being. He found that cognitive skills and physical performance are impaired by sleep deprivation, but mood is affected even more. People who get less than a full night of sleep have a tendency to feel less happy, more stressed, more physically vulnerable, and subsequently, more mentally and physically exhausted. Sufficient sleep on the other hand makes us feel better, happier, and more active.

Shawn Achor talks about an incredible experiment: People who sleep 8 hours can remember 70% to 80% of positive and negative words they memorized before sleeping. People who memorized the same set of words and only slept 5 hours still remember about 70% of the negative words, but only 20% to 30% of positive words.

The Importance of Touch

Touch improves everything. It's a physical need like sleep, exercise, and relationships and has the following benefits:

- Touch strengthens our immune system significantly, while a lack thereof weakens it drastically.
- Touch helps overcome injuries.
- Children grow more when they are touched and their cognitive development is affected by touch. (On the other hand mental problems like mood disorders or eating disorders are very often associated lack of touch).
- Touch can help us overcome depression and anxiety.

William Masters & Virginia Johnson - two the most important sex therapists and researchers have shown that most sexual dysfunctions (between 70 and 95 %) can be resolved simply with the help of touch.

Tal Ben Shahar told this incredible story about a hospital ward for "Premature babies":
One of the sections in this ward had a much higher level of success compared to the other sections: The babies were getting better much more promptly, they were healthier and they showed better cognitive and physical development when they followed up with them in the long term.

So they were wondering why that happened. Everything else being identical, they thought it might be the air, or the location within the hospital.

One night, a doctor stayed in the ward, sitting somewhere out of sight when he heard a sound.

A nurse that worked in a hospital for a long time came in. She picked up a premature baby, which was against the rules of the hospital, because it was not allowed to touch the babies or take them out of the incubators. So the nurse picked up the baby and just stroked him very gently, talked to him, and then put the baby down. Walked to the next incubator, picked up the next baby, stroked him gently and put him down.

She did this to every baby in the section. She did it late at night during her shift because it was against the rules. That incident brought forward a whole line of research about the importance of touch with babies in general, especially with premature babies.

Tiffany Fields found out that premature babies who were subjected to 45 minutes of massage a day put on 47% more weight during their time in the hospital and showed better development (physically, and in their cognitive and motor skills) one year later.

Harry Hollow examined touch deprivation: He took monkeys away from their mothers. These monkeys got everything except touch. The result was that the monkeys didn't grow as much, their cognitive development was impaired and they even displayed autistic behavior.

A cruel real life example is what former Romanian dictator Ceaucescu did. He took away a lot of children from their parents, especially if their parents were dissidents. 150,000 kids were raised in homes.

These kids were around 3-10% smaller, way below IQ 100, their motor development was impaired significantly, and they showed signs of autism.

Touch is so important…and so are hugs!
Psychologist Virginia Satir states: "We need 4 hugs a day for survival, we need 8 hugs a day for maintenance, we need 12 hugs a day for growth" and Jane Clipman found out that if we give at least 5 (nonsexual) hugs a day, after 4 weeks, our happiness level goes up significantly.

Smile like your life depends on it

Smile! Even if you don't feel like it! Buddhist monk Thích Nhât Hanh knew all along what science found out recently: "Sometimes your joy is the source of your smile, but sometimes your smile can be the source of your joy".

Smiling improves the quality of your life, health, and relationships. Science has demonstrated that laughing or smiling a lot daily improves your mental state and your creativity. It tricks your brain into thinking that you are happy, so it starts producing the neurochemicals that actually do make you happy.
Some of the benefits of smiling are the following:
- It releases serotonin (makes us feel good).
- It releases endorphins (lowers pain).
- It lowers blood pressure.
- It increases clarity.
- It boosts the functioning of your immune system.
- It provides a more positive outlook on life (Try being a pessimist while you smile).

I agree: Authentic positivity is always better than a fake one, but there is significant evidence that changing your behaviour first – facial expression and posture – can dictate emotional change.

A study by Tara Kraft and Sarah Pressman at the University of Kansas demonstrated that smiling can also alter your stress response in difficult situations. The study showed that it can slow your heart rate down and decrease stress levels – even if you are not feeling happy. Smiling sends a signal to your brain that things are all right. A study by Wayne University on smiling has even found a link between smiling and longevity!

If you think you have no reason at all to smile, hold a pen or a chopstick with your teeth. It simulates a smile and might produce the same effects. When you smile, your entire body sends out the message "Life is great" to the world. Studies show that smiling people are perceived as more confident and more likely to be trusted. People just feel good around them.

To conclude this chapter, here's once again the best psychological description you'll ever get:

- At least 4 x 30 minutes a week of physical exercise
- Mindfulness meditation – if its' good for you – every day for 10-15 minutes (The very least a few deep breaths strategically placed throughout the day)
- 8 hours of sleep a night
- At least 5, ideally 12, hugs a day
- Smile a lot!   :-)

Go for it!

13. What now?

I hope I convinced you by know that YOU are in charge of your happiness. It's not easy, and you have to train a lot, but applying some of the exercises from this book, you can change your life a lot.

Remember that your life depends on the quality of the questions you ask and those questions will very often determine the direction you take. Remember to ask positive questions like "What is good about …?", "What is going well?". If you only ask negative questions, you won't see the opportunities.

Your beliefs create your reality. To great extent how you perceive reality is what actually comes true. Do you remember the two things that distinguish the extraordinary successful from the rest?
    1. They always ask questions, always want to learn.
    2. They believe in themselves.

You improve your belief by taking little risks, by putting yourself on the line, by coping instead of avoiding, and by showing yourself that you can do it by using the power of visualization.

Make failure your friend, because it's inevitable. There is no way around it, and there is no other way to learn. Learn to fail or fail to learn. Try, try, try, try, and then try once more. Remember that the most extraordinary personalities in our world are also the ones who fail most.

Accept your emotions. There are only two kinds of people that don't experience painful emotions – psychopaths and dead people. So if you are sad or angry remember the most important thing: You are alive, and you are not a psychopath.

I warned you at the beginning. After finishing this book and even doing all the exercises you'll not experience a constant high. Nobody experiences a constant high. Life will still be a rollercoaster. You'll continue having these ups and downs. Maybe not as often, and you will probably recover a lot quicker from the downs.

When you feel a painful emotion, don't fight against it. Accept it. Accept it like you would accept a rainy day or like you accept the law of gravity. Say to yourself "Ok. I'm human. This really hurts. It's not comfortable at all. I wish it were different, but I accept it".

Have a journal. Journaling works. When we share and open up, we can make sense of the experiences of our lives and enjoy higher levels of happiness.

Make gratitude a part of your life! Gratitude for me made the difference between selling 30 books a month and selling 50 a day. The more grateful you are, the more things to be grateful for will come into your life. When you appreciate the good in your life, the good grows. Unfortunately, the opposite is also true.

Simplify! Many people wonder why they are not happy although they have all the things that they want in their lives. Why? Because there can be too much of a good thing. Start cutting activities, and start saying no to people and experiences.

Take care and cultivate your relationships. They are the number one predictor of your future well-being. They matter more than anything else in the world. More than an exam and even more than how successful and admired we are. Remember that experiences can give you a spike, a high, but then you'll go back to the base level, like the professors, the lottery winners, and the highly successful individuals who thought they had made it.

Take care of your mind and your body. Remember that exercising is like taking an anti-depressant.

Take Tal Ben Shahar's wonder drug:

- Exercise 4 times a week for at least 30 minutes
- Meditation/breathe deeply
- Sleep 8 hours a day
- Touch (hug/embrace)

Remember the two types of change: The temporary high and then going back to the base level on one hand and the continuous growth on the other. The only difference between them is whether or not you introduce behavioral changes. The only and most important question will be: What you are going to do differently from now on? Produce behavioral change NOW. This is the core of all changes.

Keep studying. Keep reading. What you learned in this book is only the beginning. Remember the Carlton's study: Those who succeed the most and those who are the happiest are the ones who are lifelong learners, always asking questions, always wanting to know more.

Remember that good intentions are not enough. You have to act and apply your knowledge.

The Power of one! Happiness is contagious. If you want a happier world, start with yourself and infect everybody around you with your happiness. Take care of yourself! First, help yourself before you help others!

If you include only these five exercises in your daily routine, your life will never be the same:

- Write down three things that you are grateful for
- Write in you journal
- Exercise at least 3 x 30 minutes a week
- Meditate
- Do at least one random act of kindness every day.

I wish you all the best and would be happy to hear your feedback. You can send your e-mails or questions to marc@marcreklau.com. I love the feedback from my readers. It helps me to improve my books and find ideas for new books.

If you liked this book, please take a minute or two and leave a comment on Amazon. This will help other readers find the book and spread the message.

Thank you!
Marc

About the Author

Marc Reklau (Esslingen am Neckar, Germany, 1973) is a bestselling author, motivational speaker, and personal development expert.

Marc's mission is to empower people to create the life they want and to give them the resources and tools to make it happen. He still spends at least 20 hours every week researching, studying, and applying the principles and secrets of success and happiness. In his free time he helps his friend Jordi selling luxury Yachts.

His message is simple: A lot of people want to change things in their lives, but few are willing to do a simple set of exercises constantly over a period of time. You can plan and create success and happiness in your life by installing habits that support you on the way to your goal.

His first book "30 Days – Change your habits, change your life" became an Amazon Bestseller "over night" (after one year of hard work). After having 40,000 downloads in 72 hours, it hit Amazon's paid Bestseller lists in its category in seven Kindle stores worldwide—where it has stayed ever since.

It has a combined sale and download figure of over 180,000 copies and has been translated into Spanish, German, Korean, Japanese, Portuguese, Chinese, Russian, Afrikaans, Indonesian, Thai, and Italian.

If you want to hire Marc as trainer speaker for your event, you can directly contact him on his homepage www.goodhabitsacademy.com where you will also find more information about him and his work.

I Need Your Help

If you have been inspired by 30 DAYS, the Productivity Revolution or Destination Happiness and want to help others to reach their goals and improve their lives, here are some action steps you can take immediately to make a positive difference:

Gift *30 DAYS - change your habits change your life or one of the other books* to friends, family, colleagues and even strangers so that they can also learn that they con reach their goals and live great lives.

Please share your thoughts about these books on Twitter, Facebook and Instagram or write a book review. It helps other people to find my books.

If you own a business or if you are a manager - or even if you're not - gift some copies to your team or employees and improve the productivity of your company. Contact me at marc@marcreklau.com. **I'll give you a 30% discount on bulk orders.**

If you have a Podcast or know somebody that has one ask them to interview me. I'm always happy to spread the message of 30 DAYS and help people improve their lives. You can also ask you local newspaper, radio station, or online media outlets to interview me :)

Bring the simple steps of 30 DAYS to your Organization

Help each member of your organization to succeed. *30 DAYS - change your habits change your life* is available at a special price on bulk orders for businesses, universities, schools, governments, NGOs, and community groups.

It's the ideal gift to inspire your friends, colleagues and team members to reach their fullest potential and make real, sustainable changes.

Contact marc@marcreklau.com

To book a presentation based on 30 DAYS or my latest book Destination Happiness contact me with an e-mail to marc@marcreklau.com

Printed in Great Britain
by Amazon